ARCHITECTURAL SECURITY CODES AND GUIDELINES

BEST PRACTICES FOR TODAY'S CONSTRUCTION CHALLENGES

ABOUT THE AUTHOR

Robert C. Wible, the principal of Robert Wible and Associates and Secretary to the Alliance for Building Regulatory Reform in the Digital Age, served as the Executive Director of the National Conference of States on Building Codes and Standards, Inc. (NCSBCS) for 20 years. He has authored several studies on building regulations and economic development, and served as NCSBCS liaison to the nation's construction community. He assisted in the conceptualization and development of the Industrialized Buildings Commission, an interstate compact and was the founder (in 1979) of National Building Safety Week.

ARCHITECTURAL SECURITY CODES AND GUIDELINES

BEST PRACTICES FOR TODAY'S CONSTRUCTION CHALLENGES

Robert C. Wible

New York   Chicago   San Francisco   Lisbon   London   Madrid   Mexico City
Milan   New Delhi   San Juan   Seoul   Singapore   Sydney   Toronto

The McGraw·Hill Companies

Architectural Security Codes and Guidelines: Best Practices for Today's
Construction Challenges

1 2 3 4 5 6 7 8 9 0   DOC/DOC   0 1 9 8 7 6

ISBN-13: 978-0-07-146075-0
ISBN-10:   0-07-146075-6

*The sponsoring editor for this book was Cary Sullivan, the editorial supervisor was Patty
Mon, the production supervisor was George Anderson, the project manager was Vastavikta
Sharma, and the acquisitions coordinator was Laura Hahn. It was set in Times New Roman
PSMT by International Typesetting and Composition. The art director for the cover was
Handel Low.*

Printed and bound by R R Donnelley-Crawfordsville

McGraw-Hill books are available at special quantity discounts to use as premiums and sales
promotions or for use in corporate training programs. For more information, please write
to the Director of Special Sales, Professional Publishing, McGraw-Hill, Two Penn Plaza,
New York, NY 10121-2298. Or contact your local bookstore.

Disclaimer

While the publisher and author have used their best care in preparing this book and its reference to other resource documents, they make no representations or warranties with respect to the accuracy or completeness of the contents of this book. They specifically disclaim any implied warranties of merchantability or fitness for a particular purpose. No warranty may be created or extended by sales representatives or written sales materials. The advice and strategies, checklists and guidelines contained herein may not be suitable for your situation. You should consult with a professional where appropriate. Neither the publisher or the author shall be liable for any loss of profit or any other commercial damages, including but not limited to special, incidental, consequential or other damages.

This book is dedicated to several groups critical to its existence.

First, to the first responders, the men and women in the police, fire, emergency medical response, and building departments across the nation who on 9/11/01 and everyday, so bravely put their lives on the line for the safety of all Americans.

Second, to the members of the construction team who are responsible for the creation and maintenance of a safe built environment in this nation.

Third, to my wife, Kim, our daughters Lisa and Cristin, my parents David and Dorothy, and to family and friends who encouraged me to undertake this work.

Last, to all of our partners in the Alliance for Building Regulatory Reform in the Digital Age and our new National Partnership to Streamline Government, who are joining us in the ongoing campaign to make our nation's building regulatory and construction processes more effective and efficient and our nation more resilient to the challenges that lie ahead.

Contents

6 Existing Buildings: Inspections and Retrofitting 187

Part III Addressing New Issues: Viewing the Building as a Complete Life-Cycle System 239

7 Homeland Security and the Issues of Energy, Sustainability, Environment, Accessibility and New Products, Materials and Techniques. . . . 241

8 A World Transformed: A Vision of One Possible Future for the Construction Industry and Construction Team 281

Appendix: Resources, Web sites, and Chapter Notes 303

Foreword

If our nation and its construction community learned just one lesson from 9/11, the subsequent anthrax attacks, and the 2004 to 2005 hurricanes, it is how critical man-made structures are to sheltering and protecting the precious and fragile lives of our citizens. As Katrina proved, this is not only true in terms of being able to keep people alive, but in the ability of buildings to be readily repaired and put back into use after a major disaster. To better meet that challenge we must design, build, and operate our buildings with greater attention to their performance under stress.

I am writing the opening of this book sitting in my hotel room on the twenty-first floor overlooking a nearly deserted and very dark and quiet New Orleans, just two months after Hurricanes Katrina and then Rita hit the Gulf States. The anger over the inability of a man-made structure to withstand a disaster is still palpable here just as it was in New York City in the months immediately following 9/11 and in Washington, D.C., after the spread of anthrax through two federal facilities.

Here, the structures involved were levees as opposed to the World Trade Center's Twin Towers, a federal postal facility, and the Senate Hart Building. Here the investigations regarding the levee's failures have only just begun. In New York City, however, the final report of the National Institute of Standards and Technology on the World Trade Center Twin Towers has been issued, removing from the Towers the taint of improper design. The lessons learned from that tragedy are beginning to make their way into our nation's codes and standards. In Washington, D.C., studies of the spread of anthrax spores already have resulted in recommended changes in the design and operation of air handling and filtration systems.

The purpose of this book is to share with the building design and construction community technical information on the actions taken in the wake of 9/11 to make changes in the design, construction, and operation of new and retrofit of existing buildings to better protect them from man-made and natural disasters. This work also looks at those changes in the context of other forces impacting building design and construction, including the growing demand for sustainable and environmentally friendly construction.

More than just providing the reader with access to enhancements in construction codes and standards, design checklists, and operation guidelines, this book looks at changes that are occurring in the roles, relationships, and responsibilities of the construction team. Comprised of building owners, architects, engineers, contractors, product manufacturers and suppliers, codes and standards community, building officials, and building managers, in that aftermath of 9/11, the construction team bears greater individual and collective accountability for the public's safety in the built environment. The chapters of this book look at what is being done now, and what can be done in the immediate future to meet that challenge.

Acknowledgments

In writing this book numerous people and organizations provided valuable information and suggestions concerning its content as well as encouragement for undertaking this project.

I especially want to thank the following individuals and organizations who either took the time to review and comment on chapter content for both accuracy and readability, or provided contacts and information needed to complete this work. Their time, expertise, and support have been greatly valued.

First, I want to acknowledge the encouragement, chapter review, and support from several of my former colleagues at the National Conference of States on Building Codes and Standards, particularly NCSBCS past presidents and state governor appointed delegates, James Hanna (Maryland), Richard Conrad (California), and Charles Dinezio (Massachusetts). Throughout this project their wisdom and guidance have been invaluable.

Second, I want to thank the following organizations and individuals who have been members of the Alliance for Building Regulatory Reform in the Digital Age and/or the new National Partnership to Streamline Government for their input and support:

NIST Building and Fire Research Laboratory: James Hill, Director BFRL, for his support and access to NIST staff and research reports and publications; Shyam Sunder, Deputy Director BFRL, for his review of World Trade Center portions of Chapter 3; Paul Domich, BFRL Associate Director, for his contacts and support; James St Pierre, Acting Chief Materials and Construction and Stephen Cauffman, Research Engineer, for their contacts and for their review of portions of Chapter 5; and Robert Chapman for clarifications on his NIST report on "Cost Effective Responses to Terrorist Risks in Constructed Facilities."

I especially want to thank Hill for permission to quote and use charts from several NIST publications including the September, 2005, "Final Report on the Collapse of the World Trade Center Towers."

FIATECH: Ric Jackson for his encouragement and support and permission to reprint FIATECH materials in Chapter 8.

Building Diagnostics Research Institute: James Woods, PhD, PE, Executive Director, for his technical input and chapter review on risk-threat assessment and HVAC systems in Chapters 5 and 6, and also for his recommendations concerning ASHRAE resources and for his analogy of building diagnostics and medical diagnostics.

American Society of Civil Engineers and colleagues at The Infrastructure Security Partnership: At ASCE: Larry Roth, PE, Assistant Executive Director ASCE; Marla Dalton, PE,

Executive Director TISP and TISP colleagues Paula Scalangi, Second Vice Chair TISP and Edward J. Hecker, Chief Homeland Security Officer, U. S. Army Corps of Engineers and First Vice Chair TISP, for materials on ASCE research on Pentagon disaster, the TISP Regional Disaster Resilience Guide.

American Institute of Architects: Paul Mendelsohn, State Government Affairs and Andrew Goldberg, Manager Federal Regulatory Activities, for their contacts in architectural community and recommendations concerning resources.

Department of Homeland Security: Patricia Malak, Chief, Policy Analysis Branch Office of State and Local Government Coordination and Preparedness and Todd Sharpe, Program Coordinator, for recommendations concerning DHS information, policy, and programs.

Federal Emergency Management Agency: Ted Litty, Program Specialist, Recovery Division and John Ingargiola, Civil Engineer, Building Sciences and Technology Section, for their recommendation of FEMA resources and materials available for use in this book; and to the FEMA staff who produced and maintains these invaluable guides.

General Services Administration: Stephen Hagan, FAIA, Project Knowledge Center, GSA Public Building Service, for contacts and direction to GSA materials and invitation to participate in the Virtual Builders Roundtable Workshop cited in Chapter 8.

International Code Council: James Lee Witt, President, for the quote at opening of Chapter 6; Richard Kuchnicki, for access to ICC codes and publications; and Mark Johnson, Senior Vice President, Business Product Development, for permission to reprint proposed code changes based upon the work of the ICC's code committee in response to the NIST WTC report and the ICC codes and standards process information provided in the Appendix.

National Fire Protection Association: John Biechman, Vice President, Government Affairs, and Nancy McNabb, Director, Government Relations, for access to NFPA Codes and Standards described in this publication and permission to reprint in the Appendix NFPA's text on its codes and standards generating process.

U.S. Department of Housing and Urban Development, Office of Policy Development and Research: David Engel, Division Director, and Dana Bres, Deputy Director, for information from HUD user on Smart Codes, the PATH project and access to the contents of the about to be released "Guide to More Effective and Efficient Building Regulatory Processes Through Information Technology," contained in the Appendix.

U.S. Department of Energy: Jean Boulin, Senior Architect, Building Technologies Program, for his support and access to information on DOE Energy programs including those on Energy Efficiency and Renewable Energy.

Stanford University, Center for Integrated Facility Engineering: Martin Fisher, for his input on Building Information Management and review and comment on Chapters 7 and 8.

National Association of Home Builders: Ken Ford, Program Manager, Civil Engineering, for access to housing data and information on the NAHB Model Green Home Program.

National Institute of Building Sciences: David Harris, President and Sandy Shaw, for information on numerous NIBS programs including the "Whole Building Design Guide," HAZUS, the NIBS National BIM Standards Project, and Multi-Hazard Mitigation Council.

Building Owners and Managers Association International: Ron Burton, Executive Director, Advocacy and Research Advancement, for input on perspective of their members to events of 9/11 and copy of their input to the NIST World Trade Center Report.

American Planning Association: Peter Hawley, Assistant Policy Director for Outreach, for sharing information on Smart growth and urban security.

Association of Major City Building Officials: Claude Cooper, Chairman and Richmond Building Official, for his comments and insights of major city building officials to man-made and natural disasters and to his colleagues at AMCBO who provided input on their city building codes and regulatory practices as regards architectural security, and building codes administration and enforcement:

- New Orleans, Michael Centineo, Director Department of Safety and Permits and Curtis Mann, Chief Building Official.
- Patricia Lancaster, Commissioner New York City Building and James Colgate, Executive Architect, for copies of New York City ordinances passed in aftermath of 9/11.
- City of Los Angeles: Andrew Adelman, Director Department of Building Safety, and Steve Ikkanda, Code Development Engineer, for background and copy of relevant city of Los Angeles ordinance and opportunity to photograph building department in action.
- City of Pittsburgh: Ron Graziano, Chief Bureau of Building Inspection for access.
- City of Philadelphia: David Perri, Chief Code Official.
- Stephen Garnier, Code Enforcement Coordinator, Fairfax County, Virginia.

National Science Foundation: Vilas Mujumdar, Project Director Earthquake Engineering Research Centers, for access to update on NSF research relative to building codes and public safety and building response to man-made and natural disasters (especially seismic events).

State of Oregon: Mark Long, Administrator, Oregon Building Codes Division.

State of Florida: Rick Dixon, Code Director, and Ila Jones, Program Administrator Codes and Standards Department of Community Affairs.

State of Rhode Island Department of Health Office of Occupational and Radiological Health Indoor Air Quality Program for right to quote sections of the "HVAC Building Vulnerability Assessment Tool" that appear in Chapter 6.

Third, I also want to thank the following individuals for their invaluable assistance in this project:

John Voeller, PE, ASME Fellow, White House Office of Science and Technology Policy.

Michael Chipley, Vice President, Strategic Development and Geospatial Solutions, Technology Associates, for quote in Chapter 6 and comments on disaster resiliency.

Matt Morrison, Executive Director, Pacific NorthWest Economic Region for invitation to participate in the Blue Cascades III exercise.

Marsha Maaz, Technical Assistance Coordinator, U.S. Architectural and Transportation Barriers Compliance Board (ATBCB), input on outcome of 2004 Conference on "Emergency Evacuation of People with Disabilities," which is covered in Chapter 5.

Judith Kunoff, AIA; Douglas Eberhard, Chief Technology Officer; and Tim Case, Deputy Chief Technology Officer at Parsons Brinkerhoff, for information on and access to a computer-assisted virtual environment.

Ron Klemencic, PE, Council on Tall Buildings, and Urban Habitat's report on "The Future" and comments on World Trade Center disaster and its impact on high-rise structure.

Authors of several invaluable works referenced throughout this publication: Barbara Nadel, *Building Security: Handbook for Architectural Planning and Design*; Joseph Demkin, AIA, *Security Planning and Design: A Guide for Architects and Building Design Professionals*.

Engineering News Record: Jan Tuchman, Editor-in-Chief, Nadine Post, Editor-at-Large, Building, Design, and Construction, Tom Sawyer, Associate Editor, Information Technology.

McGraw-Hill Professional Publications: Cary Sullivan, Editor, and her assistant and Editorial Coordinator, Laura Hahn, whose guidance and support were critical to this project. I would also like to thank the editorial supervisor, Mon Patty and the production supervisor, George Anderson at McGraw-Hill, and Vastavikta Sharma at International Typesetting and Composition.

Last, I want to thank family and friends for their encouragement and support throughout this endeavor. I especially want to thank my daughters, Cristin Corcoran and Lisa Wible, and their husbands, Andrew Corcoran and Justin Huggins, for their steady supply of Stumptown Coffee (which fueled much of my work). I also want to thank Lisa for her closing 2006 World Trade Center Ground Zero photograph; son-in law Andrew Corcoran for his original artwork and schematic diagrams used in Chapters 5 and 6; and finally my wife, Kim, for her constant encouragement and support (moral and logistical) during the writing of this book.

Part I Overview

The man-made and natural disasters of 2001 to 2006 brought increased national attention to the critical role that the built environment plays in keeping people safe and the American economy strong. The first three chapters of this book provide an overview of the construction system and roles, relationships and responsibilities of each of the parties in that system. In addition, these chapters look at the actions taken since September 11, 2001, and the lessons that have been learned regarding our construction process and building codes, standards and guidelines that are used to design new buildings and renovate existing structures.

Part II (Chapters 4 to 6) reviews the construction codes, standards, and guidelines that currently are available to provide a safer built environment. The third and final part (Chapters 7 to 8) of this publication looks at other forces that are reshaping our built environment and actions that are being taken to not only enhance public safety but help our nation remain economically competitive in the global economy.

1

Codes and Regulations and the Construction Team

In the construction world today, there seems to be more pressure to pull apart teams rather than build them. Owners often want landmark structures to enhance their prestige or business interests but only offer baloney budgets. They restlessly are driving costs down and shifting risks to close that gap and satisfy the short-term attention of shareholders.

—*Engineering News Record*, February 21, 2005, editorial referring to the May 23, 2005, partial collapse of the concourse at Charles de Gaulle Airport in Paris.

The building construction industry in the United States is a $3.1 trillion industry that together with real estate accounts for 20% of our gross domestic product. Our buildings shelter and provide recreation and work space to 290 million Americans and are the site of over 80% of our economic activity.

Today Americans work in over 5 million commercial buildings with another 2 to 4% more commercial buildings being built each year. It is estimated that 85% of the buildings that will be standing 25 years from now have already been built.

New York City, for example, lists a total of over 900,000 buildings in five boroughs and, at any given time, has between 25 and 50 high-rise commercial buildings under construction. In 2006, Los Angeles had 56 mid-to-high-rise structures under design or construction, and Clark County, Nevada, which includes Las Vegas, has added over 30 mid-to-high-rise structures to their skyline in the past 5 years.

It has always been a daunting task to design, build, and operate new buildings and renovate existing building stock in a manner that assures that they meet the structural loads that have been designed to perform under the stress of natural hazards typical in their region. That our nation has few structural collapses, high-rise fires, or other life-threatening conditions is testament to the quality, integrity, and skills of our building design, construction, codes and standards, and regulatory, building owner, and operator communities.

Figure 1-1
New York City
skyline

Figure 1-2
Atlanta skyline

Figure 1-3
Westin
Bonaventure Hotel,
Los Angeles

The events of 9/11, together with the bombing of the Murrah Building in 1995, the 2001 anthrax attacks in Washington, D.C., and the recent large scale regional devastation of Hurricanes Katrina, Rita, and Wilma have heightened the public's awareness, as well as that of the construction industry's, concerning security and safety in the planning, design, construction and operation of our buildings to make certain we adequately address both the threats of terrorism (domestic and foreign) and natural disasters.

In the wake of these large scale disasters our nation is undertaking recovery projects of previously unimagined scales and making changes in the security of our buildings.

- After Katrina, Rita, and Wilma in the Gulf Region, over one million displaced citizens are in need of housing.
- After 9/11 in New York City, the Lower Manhattan Development Corporation was charged with working with the State and City in helping to coordinate recovery; now the first buildings are coming online.

Figure 1-4

Informal memorial
at World Trade
Center site

- In New York, Chicago and several other cities, emergency amendments were made to their building codes, and new high-rise safety ordinances have been adopted with some jurisdictions considering mandating that building owners annually conduct full scale evacuation drills of their buildings.
- The Federal Government's General Services Administration completed the development and application of a sophisticated risk-threat evaluation of all of its structures that house over 10 employees and shared that evaluation system and criteria with the private sector.
- Owners and architectural firms now are regularly bringing in building security specialists to assist them in their designs in cities and locations where future terrorist events might be expected to occur.
- The nation's model building and fire code organizations and other groups concerned with standards are working on special code provisions to address a number of the findings from the Federal investigation of the World Trade Center collapse.

In response to the events of 9/11 and the devastation caused in the Gulf Region by the 2005 hurricanes, new information, technologies and roles, relationships, and responsibilities are occurring within our country's building design, construction, regulation, and operation community to help us better prepare for, respond to, and recover from the "next" attack by nature or man.

Figure 1-5
High-rise damage
in New Orleans
after Hurricane
Katrina

To better understand these changes and the framework within which new codes and standards provisions are being developed and applied to increase building security, this chapter looks at the pre-9/11 roles and relationships within the construction community, including those relationships lamented in the opening *Engineering News Record* editorial. While this review may be elementary for many readers, it nonetheless sets the stage for appreciating the changes which 9/11 and other recent disasters are making upon the construction industry.

TRADITIONAL ROLES

There has been little change since the early 1900s in the roles, relationships and responsibilities of each of the parties concerned with the conception, design, construction, regulation, operation, and maintenance of buildings in our nation.

Traditionally, construction of large commercial and other structures has been handled under the design, bid and build process where each occupation has fairly straightforward responsibilities over the quality and cost of the work they provide. The following summarizes those traditional roles.

- Working together with building owners, architects have had the role of taking the functional needs of the building and giving them life in design and form.

- Engineers have provided their expertise to assure the stresses and other forces applied against the building are met by the building when it is completed and occupied.

- Construction managers and/or primary contractors have worked with owners and architects to assemble and manage all of the specialty contractors that may be engaged in erecting the structure.

- Manufacturers of building components and structural materials have made certain that their products meet the specifications and codes mandated by the architect and the jurisdiction in which the building is being built.

- A diverse and fragmented building codes and standards community has developed model construction requirements regarding minimum life safety and health of building occupants that have been adopted into law by elected officials in state and local governments.

- Building officials in over 40,000 jurisdictions who adopt and or enforce building codes have checked that the designs, materials, and construction meet the requirements for health, welfare, and life safety in the nation's model building, fire, electrical, mechanical, plumbing, and energy and architectural accessibility codes.

- Building owners and operators have been responsible for assuring that once commissioned, the buildings are operated and maintained in the manner for which they were designed.

Each of the preceding parties have traditionally operated in their own realm, with their own contracts, liability insurance policies, training or certifications and with each group connected to the party before it and after it in the design, construction and operation life cycle of the building. Unfortunately, far too often these parties do not function as a cohesive and well-coordinated team.

TRADITIONAL ROLE OF BUILDING OWNERS, ARCHITECTS, ENGINEERS, AND CONTRACTORS

More than anything else, the roles and relationships between building owners, architects, engineers, and contractors have been governed by Contract Law as defined by the evolution of both English Common Law and by changes in construction materials, practices, and technology. Common Law, as defined in the U.S. Commercial Code holds that anyone who is party to a contract and has been injured by a breach of that contract by one or more of the other signatories is entitled to recover only those damages as were reasonably foreseen under the circumstances known at the time the contract was executed.

Contract law itself has evolved through court cases that have helped interpret and at times redefine the legal responsibilities between the building owner and the architects, engineers, and contractors he or she ultimately pays to design and build the building. These relationships are also governed by a series of legal relationships where interrelated services are defined and provided within a specified time frame and within the design and construction codes, standards and specifications adopted by the jurisdiction in which the building is built.

The actual terms of these contracts are rarely prescribed by law leaving parties free, based upon their relative strengths and interests, to define the nature of and terms of the services that they are to provide in the design and construction of a new building or in the renovation of an existing building.

As they evolved during the second half of the twentieth century, construction contracts generally lay out in great detail the economic relationships of all parties in accordance with the adopted licensing requirements, zoning, land use, and building codes and standards of the governing state and/or locality.

Figure 1-6

Mid-rise construction, Reston, Virginia

Figure 1-7

Flow Chart
showing design
bid build process

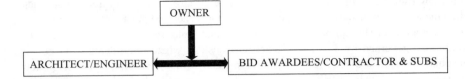

DESIGN–BID–BUILD PROCESS

Most construction follows the design–bid–build model where an owner contracts with an architect to design a building and lay out its construction specifications. When the design warrants, the owner may on his or her own or through the architect also contract with an engineering firm to assure that the structure meets applicable load and stress requirements of the building codes and standards of the jurisdiction where the building is being constructed.

Preliminary construction documents are then drawn up and sent out to contractors for competitive bidding. Owners through the architect then review the bids that are received from primary contractors and their team of subcontractors and select the lowest bid that addresses the design and specifications requirements and work time frame that has been established by the client.

The selected contractor and his or her subcontractors then begin construction working with the architect to apply for and receive the appropriate building permits.

Under this system, the basic obligation of the prime contractor is to build the building in accordance with the approved plans and architect's (and engineer's) specifications while maintaining the owner's schedule and adopted budget.

The owner is responsible for paying the architect, engineer, and prime contractor the contract price in a phased manner based upon the completion of various stages of construction—excavation, foundation, erection of the building frame, completion of electrical, mechanical, and plumbing installation through to the completion of the building itself and its commissioning before turning it over to the owner.

Figure 1-8

Chart of the
phasing of the
design bid build
process

1. Owner Engages Architect for
    Concept Phase of Project
    Schematic Phase
    Design Development
    Construction Documents

2. Bid Documents Prepared and Issued Based on
    Construction Documents

3. Bids Received, Reviewed and Awarded
    Generally to the Lowest Bidder

4. Contractor and Subs Awarded Contract
    Start Work on Construction with Oversight
    by Architect / Engineer Retained by Owner

The advantage of the traditional approach (see Figures 1-1 through 1-8) has been that the owner generally attains construction cost savings by contracting with the lowest qualified bidder. The disadvantage is that the estimates made prior to issuing the bid and the actual cost of construction when completed tend to be out of alignment and there tends to be less control over the quality and work of the primary and subcontractors.

DESIGN–BUILD PROCESS

Of increasing popularity in the Federal government from the 1980s to the present is the design–build process of construction. In design–build, the owner selects the complete team that will build the building and can involve the engineering firm and contractors more directly in determining the cost of constructing the building that is being designed. Input from the specialty contractors, especially in regard to security matters, can be brought in up front while the building is still in the design stage when it is less costly to make changes or add security design features to address the specific risks that the owner believes the building must be prepared to withstand during its lifetime.

In either case (design–bid–build or design–build), the contractors and their subcontractors are held responsible for providing workmanlike construction in accordance with the approved plans, and they warrant their work and usually indemnify the owner (and occasionally the architect as well) against claims and liability for the work they perform on the building. In 34 states, contractors and subcontractors must hold current state licenses for the specific trade in which they are engaged (building, electrical, mechanical, plumbing, and so on).

For their part, owners must provide building plans that indeed are buildable and not misleading (the Spearin Doctrine) and pay the contractor (and through the contractor the subcontractors) for the work completed against a project construction schedule.

All parties—owner, architect, engineer, primary contractor, and subcontractors—also must carry valid insurance for liability and worker's compensation, and under the law of Torts meet all obligations that are imposed upon them by the law regardless of whether the parties agree or not. This includes the issues of negligence in their work, worker's compensation, attractive nuisance (protecting construction sites from outsiders), economic loss, fraud, and negligent misrepresentation.

The growing litigious nature of American society has caused insurance premiums for all parties—owners, architects, engineers, primary contractors, and subcontractors—to escalate, often doubling over a 10-year period. The net effect in many cases has been to cause each of these parties to take steps wherever possible in the construction process to limit their responsibilities and function less as a member of a cohesive "construction team."

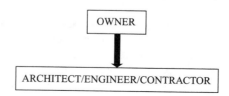

Figure 1-9

Chart of the design build structure

Figure 1-10

Chart of the phasing of design bid build process

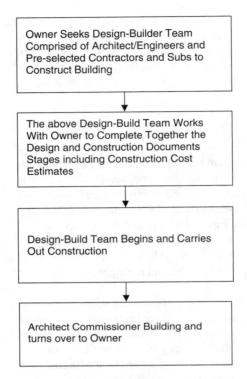

Owner Seeks Design-Builder Team Comprised of Architect/Engineers and Pre-selected Contractors and Subs to Construct Building

The above Design-Build Team Works With Owner to Complete Together the Design and Construction Documents Stages including Construction Cost Estimates

Design-Build Team Begins and Carries Out Construction

Architect Commissioner Building and turns over to Owner

TRADITIONAL ROLE OF BUILDING PRODUCT MANUFACTURERS AND SUPPLIERS

Building product manufacturers and suppliers provide products specified by the architect in their plans for the building being constructed or renovated. Contracts and contract law equally govern their responsibilities to provide on-time products that meet the specifications called for by the building plans and, where appropriate, listed or certified as meeting professional industry standards for such issues as energy conservation, durability, and resistances to the elements.

Depending on the nature of the project, the specifications list may be one or two pages or several thousand pages in length. The documents supporting those specifications frequently include drawings and, where appropriate, reference building codes and professional product standards which themselves can be several thousand pages long.

These specifications may be descriptive or performance based. A descriptive specification tells exactly what product is to be used and its location in the building, while a performance-based specification does not name the product but rather describes how the product that is to be supplied must perform. The latter provides the contractor greater flexibility in selecting products to be included in the building.

Figure 1-11
Construction materials on site

TRADITIONAL ROLE OF BUILDING CODES AND STANDARDS

Throughout history, building codes and later construction standards, have evolved in response to catastrophes such as fires, structural collapses, earthquakes, storms and other disasters involving substantial losses of life or property.

—*Introduction to Building Codes:A Guide to Understanding Building Codes and How They Work,* National Conference of States on Building Codes and Standards, Inc., 2004

Basic laws governing the construction of buildings date back to the Code of Hammurabi in 1780 BC, which included provisions putting the builder to death if the structure they built collapsed and killed anyone. The Romans added building laws of their own which became basic requirements for classical construction from their era onward.

The forerunner of modern building codes was written in England in 1189 by Henry Fitz-Elwyne. The ordinance, called the "Assize of Buildings," governed the basics of structural and fire safety.

Figure 1-12
Colonial
Williamsburg,
Virginia

In response to the Great Fire of London in 1666, fire codes were adopted in England. These statutes subsequently found their way to the American colonies along with similar laws from the Dutch who founded New Amsterdam/New York City. Such regulations, incorporated into municipal laws, covered fireplace construction and maintenance, spaces between housing, roofing materials, basic sanitation, and building demolition requirements.

When the American Constitution was written, state governments retained their "policy power," over the adoption and enforcement of regulations assuring the health and life safety of their citizens. This included the basic building and fire safety laws brought to the New World from Europe. Initially, every state delegated the authority for such laws to their local governments.

Modern building codes began to emerge in 1905 in response to fires and large losses of life and property.

As the United States grew, larger percentage of the population began to live in urban areas and additional health and life safety requirements were incorporated into municipal laws. As in the past, major disasters, especially those involving fires in Chicago, New York, Baltimore, Boston, and Philadelphia and the 1906 earthquake and fire in San Francisco, stimulated the expansion of such safety provisions. Leading that effort was a number of major insurance companies that sought to reduce the losses of life and property caused by such disasters.

Technical construction standards regarding structural design, fire safety, and new technologies (elevators) also began to emerge at the beginning of the twentieth century. In 1896, the National Fire Protection Association was founded, and in 1897 they published their first technical standards regarding automatic sprinklers. Founded in 1919, the National Board of Boiler and Pressure Vessel Inspectors published the first technical standards governing boilers and pressure vessels in the early 1920s. In 1921, the American Society of Mechanical Engineers published the first technical standards governing elevators and in 1911, the National Fire Protection Association (NFPA) published the first electrical code in the United States.

Modern building codes governing the basic design and construction of commercial, assembly, industrial, hotel, and government buildings began to emerge in 1905 with the National Board of Fire Underwriters (the forerunner of the American Insurance Association) model building code.

Major jurisdictions compiled these codes and standards and wrote their own building codes in the early 1900s. The need to pool professional expertise and write model building code documents that were applicable to climatic and geologic conditions within different parts of the nationz emerged in the period between 1915 and 1940. In the Midwest and Northeast region in 1915, Building Officials and Code Administrators (BOCA) was established to coordinate code enforcement issues resulting in the publication of their first building code in 1930. In 1922, the International Conference of Building Officials (ICBO) was founded on the West Coast. This organization wrote a building code in 1927 that recognized some of the first seismic safety requirements of that region.

The Southern Building Code Congress (SBCCI) was established in 1940, reflecting the needs of its region, and in 1941, they published their first building code.

Supported by the architectural, engineering, construction contractors, and building product manufacturers and suppliers, the model building and fire codes produced by BOCA, ICBO, SBCCI and NFPA expanded across the nation. Code adoption also was stimulated by jurisdictions responding to man-made and natural disasters that impacted their own or neighboring communities.

By the 1960s, most jurisdictions that adopted building codes did so using as a basis one of the model codes provided by these organizations to which local (and several state) governments added other construction provisions which they felt were unique or otherwise important to their jurisdiction. Stimulated in part by Federal programs that supported urban development and the need for greater code uniformity within states to help stimulate both economic development and public safety, in the late 1960s and early 1970s, the number of states adopting building codes and standards on a uniform statewide basis grew from just two states (Wisconsin and North Carolina which adopted statewide codes in the early 1900s) to 28 states.

Figure 1-13

Rhode Island State capitol building, Providence, Rhode Island

Figure 1-14

City Hall, San Jose, California, the heart of Silicon Valley

Meanwhile advances in construction technology, including the wide and rapid growth in the use of air-conditioning in the immediate post World War II era, brought about further growth in the number of technical standards governing various aspects of building design and construction. In 1959, the American Society of Heating and Ventilating Engineers merged with the American Society of Refrigerating Engineers and founded the American Society of Heating Refrigerating and Air Conditioning Engineers (ASHRAE), and issued new joint national standards governing the production, installation, and use of those products.

In 1963, the nation's first architectural accessibility standards were produced and issued by the American National Standards Institute (ANSI). Model energy conservation codes for new buildings emerged in response to the energy crisis of the mid-1970s and to the joint work of ASHRAE, the National Bureau of Standards (now the National Institute of Standards and Technology [NIST]), and the National Conference of States on Building Codes and Standards (NCSBCS) and the nation's three model building code organizations.

Faced with the need for even greater uniformity in construction codes more major cities in the 1990s adopted and enforced a model building code as opposed to one written by that city. In the mid-1990s, the nation's three model building code organizations (BOCA, ICBO, and SBCCI) came together to form the International Code Council (ICC) and produced a consolidated single family of building codes including codes governing structural, mechanical, plumbing, residential, energy, and building property maintenance and rehabilitation.

Revisions to these codes and standards, including those of the NFPA, addressed not only changes in construction technology, but like their predecessors, included new or revised provisions for structural, wind and fire safety based upon natural and man-made disasters that struck the nation from 1950 through 2001.

Among such provisions were those governing the following:

- Fire hazards of materials in buildings, electrical computer equipment, equipment for fire fighters and explosion protection systems in the wake of the fires during that time frame.

- Increased building seismic safety provisions following the earthquakes in California including Kern County (1952), Loma Prieta (1989), and Northridge (1994).
- Wind and water damage provisions have been modified based upon Hurricanes Camille (1969), Hugo (1989), and Andrew (1992).

During this same period, construction provisions regarding Federal buildings, including embassies and consulates and military facilities abroad, were modified to incorporate blast-proofing and security and other related requirements based upon the terrorist bombings of the Embassy and Marine barracks in Beirut, Lebanon (1983), the Murrah Building in Oklahoma City (1995), and the Khobar Towers (1999) in Saudi Arabia.

Building codes focus more on occupant life safety than they do on minimizing damage to buildings.

In general, building codes and standards and Federal construction requirements regarding man-made and natural disasters contain provisions that focus more on occupant life safety than on minimizing the damage to the buildings themselves so that the buildings could remain operational following an event. While there were some discussions in the 1980s and 1990s concerning the possible need to develop a separate building security code, no such document was produced.

Last, the traditional procedures under which building codes and the supportive construction industry standards are developed is through a deliberative process involving committees of subject matter experts, administrative processes and procedures, hearings and committee votes under the American National Standards Institute's approved standards development processes. These processes generate new standards and building codes in cycles that range from as little as three years to as many as 10. (Descriptions of the ICC and NFPA codes and standards generating processes are provided in the Appendix.)

Once these model codes and standards are issued, however, they do not become enforceable under law until they are adopted by the appropriate level of government (Federal, state and/or local). The code adoption process varies from state to state and in many cases from jurisdiction to jurisdiction. This generally involves either a one-year cycle of public hearings to adopt a code administratively or a two- to five-year process to adopt an updated code (and supporting standards) legislatively. Over 40,000 jurisdictions in the United States today adopt and/or enforce building codes. (See the Appendix for charts on the codes' adoption process.)

TRADITIONAL ROLE OF BUILDING OFFICIALS

The building official is responsible for helping the construction community ensure that the buildings which are being built or renovated indeed are safe for the building's stated use by meeting the provisions of the adopted building codes and standards in that jurisdiction. This covers 85% of all buildings built in the United States, with the remaining 15% either being built in areas that do not have a building code or being built by the Federal or state government with construction being overseen under their own regulatory

Figure 1-15

Milpitas, California, building department permit counter

oversight provisions and agencies (Department of Defense, General Services Administration for the Federal government, State government Departments of Administration, General Services or Public Works for states).

As public officials, building department permit processors, plan reviewers and inspectors are governed by civil service statutes and in the performance of their duties carry the sovereign immunity of the jurisdiction provided they do not engage in any illegal activities or gross incompetence in their work. In an increasing number of states, building officials must obtain and maintain professional certifications in their areas of expertise. Such states generally also have annual training requirements that each building official must meet to retain their certification.

In plan review, the architect's drawings and accompanying support documentation are checked against the current electrical, mechanical, plumbing, building, fire, architectural access, and energy conservation codes and standards. These codes include provisions for wind and snow loads, fire, seismic safety, and building egress. Depending on the complexity and type of structure, these reviews may be of the entire document or checks of key portions of the building design.

Field inspectors then visit the construction site during various phases of construction to help assure that the builder and his or her contractors and subcontractors indeed are building to the approved plans. This includes checking to see that some of the products such as heating, ventilation, and air conditioning (HVAC) units meet the provisions of the jurisdictions energy and mechanical codes. (See Appendix for charts on the building regulatory process.)

TRADITIONAL ROLE OF OWNERS AND BUILDING MANAGERS

Building maintenance and operations personnel have rarely been thought of as members of the "construction team," but after the events of 9/11 their role is being seen differently. How well these individuals are able to perform their duties plays a critical role in helping to ensure that the various safety and security features built into a structure operate properly when a building is put under the stress of a man-made or natural disaster.

Last, once the building has been built and commissioned by the architect to assure the owner that the building meets the performance requirements contained in the contract documents, the final relationship is that of the owners and their employees to oversee the operation and maintenance of the facility.

Traditionally building managers have focused their work on maintaining HVAC systems, addressing tenant issues on building access and egress, and on any leaks that may occur throughout the structure and, in some cases, monitoring fire safety and security systems. In the 1990s, increasingly building managers for more complex structures have become licensed as a part of their professional qualifications.

HOW THE CONSTRUCTION TEAM FUNCTIONED IN THE PRE-9/11 WORLD

The traditional approach toward the construction team limited liability, but at the cost of restricting the ability to see and treat the building as a whole.

Figure 1-16

Buildings in downtown Los Angeles, California

Figure 1-17

Midtown
Manhattan near
Penn Station

In 2001, the construction team for non-Federal owned construction all too often generally functioned less as a team and more as a collection of individual professions brought
together for a unique event—the design, construction, commissioning, operation, and
maintenance of a "one of a kind," building, be it residential, commercial, industrial, place
of assembly, governmental, school, factory, warehouse, or chemical or power plant.

In general, each of the component members of the construction team saw themselves
just as that—an individual player with a role in some portion of the life of that structure.

• The building owner and the architect hold the vision of the building and its functional
  design.

• The engineers (structural, electrical, mechanical, plumbing) hold the details that
  made the building safe to function for its stated purpose.

• The product manufacturers and suppliers provide the components of the building
  against the specifications of the architect and engineers.

- The contractors and subcontractors are responsible for the assembly of all of these pieces.
- The individual codes and standards generating bodies produce virtually thousands of codes and standards (including product standards) that are used in the construction of a high-rise building, and update their documents largely concerned with their own codes and standards. Far too often this work has been done without studying the cumulative impact of all the adopted codes and standards on the building when it is under duress from a man-made or natural disaster.
- The building official spot-checks the designs and construction to make sure the components all come together as per the appropriate provisions of the relevant minimum codes and standards that were adopted in that community.
- The owner and its management staff are then responsible for the buildings operation over its life but are also concerned about the cost of operating the building.

As noted earlier, contract law and building codes and standards support this uncoordinated view by dividing and parceling out liability among the aforementioned participants in the conception, design, construction, and operating life of a building. Each member of the construction team in this litigious society therefore all too often ends up seeking through his or her attorney and contract provisions to limit his or her liability to just those pieces of the design, construction, and building operation process that they directly controlled.

While this traditional piecemeal approach indeed has limited liability, it also has tended to limit the ability to look at the building in its totality and effectively address issues that may arise out of the interface between the jobs and responsibilities of the preceding professions. The approach, especially under the design–bid–build process, also has restricted the ability to more cost-effectively include building security requirements into the building during the early design stage. Such divisions also have limited the ability to head off and address the "unintended" consequences that can occur when someone is not looking at the building as a whole and how all of these components and systems interact and perform when the building is under the extreme stresses of a man-made or natural disaster. (This is being changed somewhat by the advent of four-dimensional computer design and is addressed in Chapter 8, " A World Transformed: A Vision of One Possible Future for the Construction Industry and Construction Team.")

The events of 9/11 and the anthrax attacks in Washington, D.C. slowly have begun to change all of the issues for the private sector. Parties in the design, construction, and regulatory and building operations processes are beginning to look at buildings under extreme stress of a terrorist attack or natural disaster in a more holistic fashion rather than just as an assembly of different systems put together by separate groups of professionals.

As reconstructed by the NIST within their "Final Report on the Collapse of the World Trade Center Towers," the Towers on that September morning demonstrated the interaction between all of these elements. On 9/11, building design, codes and standards, structural integrity, fire proofing, elevators, emergency communications and egress, HVAC systems, building access and controls, and how people (both occupants and first responders) actually responded to emergencies all came together in the 56 to 100 minutes plus between the impact of the planes and the collapse of the two Towers.

Figure 1-18

Cover of reports
on World Trade
Center disaster:
FEMA report and
NIST report

September 11, 2001, also accelerated changes that already were underway in the Federal government based upon terrorist events of the 1980s and 1990s and at the state and local level in the wake of Hurricane Andrew (1992) and the Loma Prieta (1989) and Northridge (1994) earthquakes.

Chapter 2 summarizes a number of those changes and the challenges that are driving our construction team to further reassess their roles, relationships, and responsibilities to better apply the new codes, standards, and construction guidelines that are being developed to better secure the built environment.

Chapter 3 takes a more detailed look at the lessons that have been learned regarding building design, construction, and operation from the events of 9/11 and the 2004-2005 hurricane season.

2 Challenges Facing the Construction Team: Revising Codes and Standards, Redefining Roles and Responsibilities

What level of safety should the industry design for? What level do owners and tenants want? What level should public officials demand?

—*Engineering News Record*, Editorial in the October 31, 2005, issue

A WORLD TRANSFORMED: THE IMPACT OF 9/11 AND LARGE-SCALE NATURAL DISASTERS ON THE CONSTRUCTION TEAM AND CONSTRUCTION CODES AND STANDARDS

It is part of human nature after every major disaster involving large losses of life or of property damage to seek culpability and vow to make changes so that this event "never happens again."

Every event—from the 1906 San Francisco earthquake and fire through the fire at the Coconut Grove in 1942, Hurricanes Camille, Hugo, and Andrew of the last half of the twentieth century—has resulted in trying to find out if human beings themselves were totally or partially responsible for large losses of life due to improper codes and standards, design, construction, building materials, construction oversight, or building operation and maintenance.

In the weeks immediately following the loss of 2,830 people on September 11, 2001 in New York City, the airwaves and print media were filled with questions regarding the possible inadequacy of or failure to comply with adopted codes and standards governing the design, construction, or materials used in the World Trade Center (WTC) towers and in the eight neighboring structures that either collapsed or received major damage in the terrorist event. Were there such problems? Were they to blame for large losses of life when the Twin Towers ultimately collapsed? Concerns also were voiced by some that the uniqueness of the Twin Towers design, the fire protection, and emergency egress and communications systems and perhaps the use of substandard steel and other materials may have contributed to the Towers' collapse.

23

Figure 2-1

World Trade Center complex prior to 9/11 from National Institute of Standards and Technology Report, Figure 1-2, Source: NASA

In talk shows and editorials the news media asked the questions:

- Was the WTC inherently unsafe?
- Are other high-rise structures inherently unsafe?
- Is it unrealistic to believe that the nation could and should afford to design and operate its high-rise buildings to withstand attacks by large fuel-laden aircraft?

The initial study to "determine the probable failure mechanisms" performed within eight months of 9/11 for the Federal Emergency Management Agency (FEMA) by the

Figure 2-2

Media coverage of 9/11 World Trade Center disaster

American Society of Civil Engineers (ASCE) began to address these questions. Issued in May 2002, that report pointed to the magnitude and uniqueness of the deliberate crashing of large fuel-laden jets into the upper stories of these high-rise structures as the overarching cause of the Towers' collapse and not the work of the construction team that originally built the WTC: the owner (the Port Authority of New York and New Jersey), the architects, engineers, contractors, and subcontractors.

The subsequent and much more arduous three-year study conducted under the National Construction Safety Team Act by the National Institute of Standards and Technology (NIST) corroborated in detail many of those initial findings. From their much more detailed research, NIST painstakingly reconstructed the disaster, related it to the design, construction and maintenance of the Twin Towers and offered for national consideration a series of technical recommendations regarding building design, codes and standards, and the construction process which the study team believed would reduce future losses of life in high-rise structures subjected to such events.

Figure 2-3

Cover of the Federal Emergency Management Agency World Trade Center Report, May 2002

This chapter looks at ways in which the partners in the construction team, as well as the building codes and standards that are adopted and enforced by state and local governments and Federal agencies, are being transformed by the events of 9/11 and by other recent large-scale disasters. This chapter also offers an initial perspective regarding the questions raised by *Engineering News Record* in the above quote from their October 31, 2005 editorial.

Chapter 3, " Findings from the World Trade Center Tower Collapse and Other Post 9/11 Disasters," offers a detailed look at the outcome of the NIST Report on the WTC Collapse, including the list of 30 recommendations for needed improvements in the construction process, building operations, and the nation's codes and standards. Also included is a summary of similar technical findings from the 9/11 attack on the Pentagon, the anthrax attack on the nation, and the 2004 to 2005 hurricanes.

Chapter 4, "Beginning with the End in Mind—Assessing Risk, Threats and Mitigation Strategies," Chapter 5, "Existing Construction Standards, Codes, Practices and Guidelines that Promote Security and Disaster Resilience in New Construction," and Chapter 6, "Existing Buildings: Inspections and Retrofitting," provide details on and access to the updated guidelines, codes, standards, and construction and building operations practices that the construction team have put in place since 9/11 to enhance building security.

Chapter 7, "Homeland Security and the Issues of Energy, Sustainability, Environment, Accessibility and New Products, Materials and Techniques," describes those actions to update codes, standards, and construction practices and materials that remain under development and looks at other important issues impacting construction and the construction team.

The Construction Team's National Response to 9/11 and Actions to Meet the Challenges of Future Large-Scale Disasters

Within hours of the collapse of the WTC Towers, construction industry associations were in communication with their members regarding assistance to New York City and beginning discussions on the scope of the disaster and potential impact on their industry.

The immediate reaction by all segments of the construction industry in the wake of the terrorist attacks on 9/11 on the WTC and on the Pentagon in Arlington, Virginia, was a rush to offer to New York City, the Department of Defense (DoD) and Arlington County whatever manpower and professional expertise that might be of assistance to the massive disaster-response effort that was then underway. Contractors in the tri-State area around lower Manhattan offered heavy debris removal equipment; structural engineers and architects offered their services; and building officials offered their support along with their jurisdiction's police and fire and EMS personnel.

In addition to trying to mount a major coordinated federal, state and local disaster response, in the first hours after the collapse of the WTC's Twin Towers, construction industry professional and standards writing societies, Federal agencies, model code bodies, and trade associations were in communication with their members and staff regarding the scope of that disaster and its potential impact on their area in the construction process. Within a matter of days, several of these bodies formed work groups to look into the impact of the events of 9/11 on their industry and the construction practices and materials they use and/or their codes and standards.

Among early issues that were discussed were:

- The adequacy of existing egress requirements in the building and fire codes
- The frequency and adequacy of egress drills in the buildings
- The fire suppression systems
- Storage of fuel in upper stories of buildings to support back-up power generators
- Fire-proofing of steel frames
- Emergency communications systems in buildings
- Emergency egress for the disabled
- Operation of elevators in emergency situations
- Causes of and means to reduce the collateral damage to neighboring structures
- How you go about conducting an assessment of risk to both new and existing buildings given this new chapter in the war on terrorism

The fear that the events of 9/11 were only the opening salvo in a wider range of terrorist attacks on the United States also placed growing attention on security aspects of building access and use. The anthrax that was found within the Brentwood postal facility in Washington, D.C., and shut down the Senate Hart Building in October 2001 added concern over air intake locations and heating, ventilation and air conditioning (HVAC) systems among other construction and building operation areas.

The 9/11 attacks in New York City and at the Pentagon in Arlington, Virginia, spurred segments of the Federal government into an intensive reassessment of Federal construction guidelines and practices. Dating back to terrorist attacks on U.S. overseas diplomatic and military facilities in the 1970s and 1980s, the Department of State

Figure 2-4

U.S. Capitol Complex from top of Washington Monument

and the DoD already had in place new building design and retrofit security requirements that included protection of building access and blast mitigation.

The massive performance test on 9/11 that took 200 lives when American Airlines Flight 77 crashed into a portion of the Pentagon that had just been retrofitted with more blast-resistant window and structural features, gave the Federal government data on the efficacy of their building security retrofit program and new impetus to its rapid application to other potentially vulnerable Federal facilities, including the Eisenhower Executive Office Building in Washington, D.C.

While the 1993 bombing of the WTC and the 1995 domestic terrorist attack on the Murrah Building in Oklahoma City demonstrated to the American public and the construction community that our buildings indeed were vulnerable to terrorism, the sheer magnitude of the events of 9/11 coupled with the spread of anthrax through federal facilities in Washington, D.C., began a huge change in the construction community—rushing some initial building security programs to completion and stimulating new projects and approaches.

Figure 2-5

Eisenhower
Executive Office
Building,
Washington, D.C.,
undergoing security
retrofit, 2005

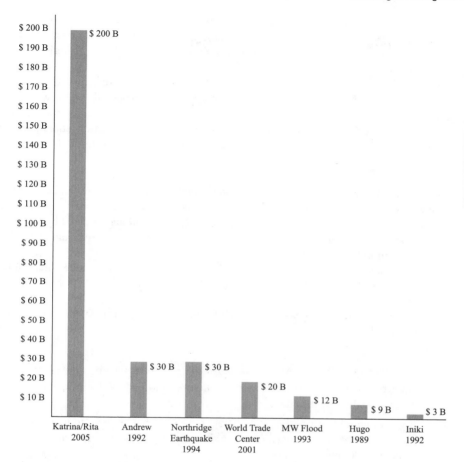

Figure 2-6

Financial losses from major U.S. disasters from1989 to 2005.

Source: American Geophysical Union, Federal Emergency Management Agency, U.S. Department of Commerce

Source: FEMA, American Geophysical Union

Adding additional impetus to the events of 9/11, Hurricane Katrina followed by Rita and Wilma provided the nation in 2005 with its first weapons of mass destruction (WMD) scaled disaster event. While the weapons of those hurricanes were water and wind and not biological, chemical, or radiological, these hurricanes met nearly every other WMD definition when they forced the long-term evacuation of over one million Americans and deprived a portion of our county for what will be a considerable period of the use of land, infrastructure, jobs, and housing. As shown in Figure 2-6, financial losses from Hurricane Katrina have proved to be six times larger than the losses from the nation's next largest disasters (Hurricane Andrew in1992 and the Northridge Earthquake in 1994).

Private Sector Response and Actions

The Work of Professional Societies and Codes and Standards Development Bodies

The private sector in the wake of 9/11 immediately looked at the need for risk assessment tools and cost-effective modifications that could be made in building design, operations and mainte-nance to readily enhance public safety.

Construction industry related professional societies (American Institute of Architects [AIA], American Institute of Steel Construction [AISC], ASCE, American Society of Heating Refrigerating and Air Conditioning Engineers [ASHRAE], American Society for Industrial Security [ASIS], Building Owners and Managers Association [BOMA], Construction Industry Institute [University of Texas, CII], International Code Council [ICC] and National Fire Protection Association [NFPA], especially those which write and issue construction standards, have a long history of reviewing man-made and natural disasters and of making modifications to existing construction standards when needed in order to make buildings more resistant to life-injuring failure or major damage.

That research (much of which has been conducted by Federal agencies and colleges and universities) and the processes by which standards are developed are of necessity deliberative processes. Standards are generally regularly reviewed and updated by the professional societies that write them on a five- to ten-year cycle. Where warranted, however, emergency modifications are issued for some standards under a shorter cycle based upon the emergence of new scientific data or changes in construction practices, materials, or technology.

One of the most disturbing aspects of 9/11 and the anthrax attacks was that it raised in the United States a series of questions around the issue of just what is safe anymore.

- What kind of attack with what kind of weapons will the terrorists use next?
- Will terrorists continue to strike iconic structures and Federal facilities in our largest cities or will they shift targets?
- Can you or should you design and operate buildings that are near to iconic structures in big cities to be equally blast proof or able to minimize collateral damage resulting from attacks on their neighbors?
- How do you adequately seal a building to protect occupants against an outside biological, chemical or radiological attack?
- How do you ventilate a building and provide adequate emergency egress to protect the building occupants against an internal biological, chemical, or radiological attack?
- How do you effectively evacuate disabled individuals from the upper stories of high-rise buildings?
- What are the potential liabilities to owners if a disaster does occur taking lives and property after they conducted a risk assessment, engaged outside firms for suggestions to strengthen the ability of the building to resist damage from a future man-made or natural disaster, and then rejected the recommendations?
- If you develop designs and technology to address all these issues, should they be put into the building codes and be mandated for some buildings? For all buildings? Can the nation afford to build, retrofit, and operate buildings to withstand such attacks?
- Do we understand how all the diverse construction codes and standards and the ways in which the construction team members (owner, architect, engineer, contractors, product suppliers, building codes and standards bodies, code enforcement officials, and building managers) interact help buildings better perform under stress?

- Will modifying our buildings to more effectively address one kind of disaster inter-fere with the normal performance of the building in its intended daily use or the build-ing's ability to provide safety to its occupants in another type of disaster?

Between 9/11 and the present, often in coordination with each other and with agencies of the Federal, state and local government, the private sector took the following actions to begin to address a number of these questions.

"Beginning with the End in Mind," The Need for Risk Assessment Tools

Following the preceding oft quoted management guideline by Stephen Covey ("Begin with the end in mind"), several trade associations and standards bodies began work after 9/11 and the anthrax attacks in Washington, D.C., to develop various types of risk assessment tools for their members. Tools were developed for building owners and managers, architects, and contractors. These tools generally were built upon risk assessment expertise already available within the construction industry and upon early risk assessment criteria for natural and man-made hazards developed by the FEMA and the DoD.

One of the earliest such tools was developed and released in January 2003 by ASHRAE. That document, "Risk Management Guidance for Health, Safety, and Environmental Security under Extraordinary Incidents," was assembled by the association's "Presidential Ad Hoc Committee for Building Health and Safety under Extraordinary Events," which began work on that document in October 2001. The objective of the document, "is to provide guidance for new and existing buildings regarding protection of air, water and food systems within buildings," and covered public use and occupancy buildings, commercial and institutional and educational facilities and other areas of assembly including stadiums, coliseums, vehicle tunnels, and subways.

Described in greater detail in Chapter 4, "Beginning with the End in Mind: Assessing Risk, Threat and Mitigation Strategies," the ASHRAE report defined risk as "the vul-nerability of a given building to extraordinary physical injury or attack," and looked specifically at the issue of biochemical hazards. One of the immediate areas at risk in existing buildings described in the report was "outdoor air intakes that are not protected from external sources of contamination, away from publicly accessible areas."

In addition to the preceding report, ASIS issued several risk assessment documents, "General Security Risk Assessment Guideline" and a "Business Continuity Guideline," for businesses and the public sector.

Building Security: Best Practices, Guides and Standards

With funding from NIST under their Dissemination and Technical Assistance Program (DTAP), the Construction Industry Institute in 2002 began work on a "Security Best Practices Guide," which provides guidance for implementing security-related practices, "during the delivery process (planning through start up) of chemical manufacturing and energy production and distribution projects."

The Guide which has applicability for other types of structures is designed "to increase the likelihood that cost-effective protective measures will be implemented," and provides a "Security Rating Index (SRI)" to give building owners and managers "a quantitative means to determine the level of use of security-related practices and for assessing their impacts on key project outcomes specifically—cost, schedule, and safety." Chapter 6, "Existing Buildings: Inspections and Retrofitting," describes the SRI in greater detail.

The AIA in 2004 issued several documents for their members regarding building security design. A reference book on "Security Planning and Design, A Guide for Architects and Building Design Professionals," published for AIA by John Wiley and Sons, shares with AIA members and readers "fundamental up-to-date information for security planning in both new and existing facilities." The book bases much of its content on the evolution of early security work of Oscar Newman, who in 1971 issued his book, "Defensible Space," and the early 1990's work in the same field of Tim Crowe who together helped shaped the concept of "crime prevention through environmental design (CPTED)." (CPTED and other aspects of building security design are covered in Chapter 6, "Existing Buildings: Inspections and Retrofitting").

Figure 2-7

Summary from the July, 2004 Symposium by American Society of Landscape Architects, "Designing for Security and Civic Values"

In July 2004, the American Society of Landscape Architects (ASLA) joined together with the AIA, the American Planning Association (APA), the General Services Administration (GSA), the National Institute of Building Sciences (NIBS), and The Infrastructure Security Partnership (TISP) and hosted a security design symposium entitled, "Safe Spaces: Designing for Security and Civic Values." The symposium highlighted technical standards and practices in the design of spaces that were available to the design and construction community to better protect the community from terrorism and crime. The program included presentations on CPTED and on the Federal Emergency Management Agency's Risk Management Series including:

- FEMA 430, "Primer for Incorporating Building Security Components in Architectural Design." (being issued in Fall 2006)
- FEMA 452, "Methodology for Preparing Threat Assessments for Commercial Buildings."
- Pending FEMA document 455, "Rapid Visual Screening for Building Security."
- Pending FEMA document 459, "Incremental Rehabilitation to Improve Security Buildings."

In addition, a number of technical guides were put out by other construction industry associations and several text books were produced. The latter included Barbara Nadel's "Building Security—Handbook for Architectural Planning and Design," McGraw-Hill, 2004.

In December 2005, the ASCE announced the creation of a Building Security Council to oversee a voluntary, fee-based rating system that enables building owners to evaluate and improve the security for their facilities.

Building Operations Manuals to Enhance Security

Several associations representing the owners of different types of buildings assembled best practices and offered training courses to their members on ways to enhance building security through better attention to building maintenance and day-to-day operations. These included guides and courses offered by the BOMA, the National Association of State Building Facility Administrators, the National Multi-Family Housing Council and ASIS International.

Among the best practices and other materials offered to their members by the aforementioned associations were recommendations and guidelines on conducting evacuation drills for building occupants. Several groups felt that the attack on the WTC would for sometime (if not forever) change the psychology of the occupants of high-rise structures, making more people want to totally evacuate the structure under any future disaster situation rather than follow the traditional fire department provisions that occupants evacuate two floors above and two floors below the floor in which a disaster, such as a fire, had occurred.

Standards to Minimize Blast Damage

The AISC in 2004 issued a detailed guide for its members, "Facts for Steel Buildings— Blast and Progressive Collapse," which was developed to "provide the latest information and guidance available for commercial and industrial buildings subjected to these (blast) extraordinary loads and responses." Looking back at lessons learned from the Murrah Building bombing, Khobar Towers and other bombings in Europe and America, the document provides a "primer for engineers, architects, developers and owners." AISC is developing a follow-up companion, "Design Guide for Blast and Progressive Collapse," that will be published in late 2006.

Standards to Minimize Wind and Seismic Damage

In response to further insights into wind destruction from hurricanes in the early 1990s and from seismic events during that same time frame in 2005, the ASCE updated "Minimum Design Loads for Buildings and Other Structures" contained in ASCE/SEI 7-02. The new ASCE/SEI 7-05 contains significantly revised provisions of seismic design of structures, as well as revisions on the previous provisions for determining live, flood, wind, snow, and atmospheric ice loads. The 2005 edition is compatible with the 2006 edition of the International Building Code which adopts most of the provisions of ASCE/SEI 7-05 by reference.

In addition to the preceding changes, the 2004 and 2005 hurricane season in Florida and along the Gulf Coast also brought together some of the nation's window and roofing products manufacturers with the state of Florida's Department of Community Affairs that adopts the statewide building code, to look at and assess existing product and installation standards for residential and other types of construction. Proposed changes to the Florida building code based in part on their research are currently out for public comment and are scheduled for final action in late 2006.

The ongoing research and testing, including storm damage assessment reports that will come about after the 2006 hurricane season, will undoubtedly lead to further upgrades in these provisions as well as adoption by communities in other hurricane regions of our nation.

Building and Fire Codes and Standards

As noted in Chapter 1, "Construction Codes, Guidelines and the Construction Team: Security in the Built Environment," the nation's model building and fire code writing bodies have code change and adoption processes that continually look at new products, building designs, and construction practices and the outcome of man-made and natural disaster events on buildings. Both the ICC and the NFPA have three-year code change cycles for the codes and standards listed in the Table 2-1, whereby new code provisions are considered for incorporation into these documents.

In the immediate wake of 9/11, the ICC and NFPA considered and made changes to several of their codes and standards. The ICC made a change to the 2003 edition of the high-rise construction section of the International Building Code that eliminated any trade-offs for not including sprinkler systems above the 420 ft level in such construction.

The NFPA modified the 2003 edition of their building code (NFPA 5000) to increase fire resistance rates used on certain tall buildings to 3 and 4 hours. The 2006 NFPA "101 Life Safety Code" and "5000 Building Code" include provisions for an increase in stair width from a 44-inch minimum to a 56-inch minimum width of stairs for buildings

Table 2-1

List of Codes and Standards Produced by the International Code Council (ICC) and National Fire Protection Association (NFPA)

List of ICC Codes	
IBC	International Building Code
IEBC	International Existing Building Code
IECC	International Energy Conservation Code
IFC	International Fire Code
IFGS	International Fuel Gas Code
IMC	International Mechanical Code
IPC	International Plumbing Code
IPMC/ZC	International Property Maintenance Code/Zoning Code
IRC	International Residential Code

Partial Listing of NFPA Codes and Standards	
NFPA 1	Uniform Fire Code
NFPA 13 & 13D	Standards on Installation of Sprinkler Systems
NFPA 70	National Electrical Code
NFPA 92	National Fire Alarm Code
NFPA 80	Standards for Fire Doors and Fire Windows
NFPA 85	Boiler and Combustion Systems Hazard Code
NFPA 90	Standards for HVAC Systems
NFPA 92	Standards for Smoke Management Systems in Mall, Atria, and Large Spaces
NFPA 99	Standard for Health Care Facilities
NFPA 101	Life Safety Code
NFPA 101B	Code for Means of Egress from Building Structures
NFPA 110	Standards for Emergency Standby Power Supplies
NFPA 251	Standard Methods for Tests of Fire Resistance of Building Construction and Materials
NFPA 730	Guide to Premises Security
NFPA 731	Standard for the Installation of Electronic Premises Security Systems
NFPA 900	Building Energy Code
NFPA 1600	Standard on Disaster/Emergency Management and Business Continuity Programs
NFPA 5000	Building Construction and Safety Code

with 2000 or more occupants and mandate the installation of stair ascent devices for persons with mobility impairments under certain conditions. Last, NFPA incorporated into the 2006 edition of its building code the adoption of the structural frame approach for fire resistance ratings. (Additional details on these are found in Chapter 5.)

Figure 2-8

National Fire
Protection
Association
Building Code,
NFPA 5000 and
the International
Code Council's
International
Building Code

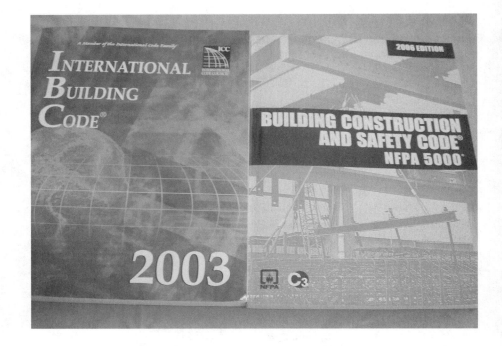

Both the ICC and the NFPA also formed work groups to look at the lessons being learned from research into the WTC collapse and the anthrax attack in Washington, D.C., and to consider possible changes to relevant sections of the codes and standards that they issue in 2006 and beyond.

The ICC formed two work groups—the ICC Ad Hoc Committee on Terrorism Resistant Buildings (AHC-TRB) and a group working on the development of an ICC Hazard Abatement in Existing Buildings Code.

In addition, the ICC assigned to its Code Technology Committee the task of studying the possible need for changes in the use of elevators for occupant evaluation and balanced fire-resistive design. The Code Technology Committee is coordinating its work with the American Society of Mechanical Engineers (ASME) and ASCE as they consider appropriate changes to ASME's 17 elevator standard and ASCE's 7 load standard based upon the events of 9/11.

In response to new data gathered from recent hurricanes, the ICC has two projects to enhance safety and building performance: the ICC Consensus Committee on Hurricane Resistant Residential Construction, which is in the process of updating the 1999 Southern Building Code Standard for Hurricane Resistant Residential Construction (ICC-SSTD-1099) and the joint ICC/National Storm Shelter Association (NSSA) Consensus Committee on Storm Shelters.

Figure 2-9
The International Code Council's code change hearing

In 2003, the NFPA formed a High-Rise Building Safety Advisory Committee (HBSAC). In addition to making the previously mentioned post 9/11 changes in NFPA codes and standards, this body is studying other potentially needed changes to various NFPA documents.

The ICC and the NFPA also are participating on a special committee established by the NIBS under funding from NIST to study the recommendations made by NIST in their "Final Report on the Collapse of the WTC Towers" to translate them into proposed code changes for the nation's model building codes. The work of that committee and the changes being made to the previously referenced ICC and NFPA codes are described in greater detail in Chapter 5, "Existing Construction Standards, Codes, Practices, and Guidelines that Promote Security and Disaster Resilience in New Construction," and Chapter 6, "Existing Buildings: Inspections and Retrofitting."

Industry-Wide Discussions on Roles, Relationships, Responsibilities: Building Design, Construction, Operation and Disaster Preparedness, Response and Recovery

Last, within the private sector there have been numerous conferences and symposia discussing ways in which terrorist attacks of 9/11, the anthrax events, and large-scale natural disasters such as Katrina are reshaping the way all parties in the building design, construction, regulation, and operation industry do their jobs.

These discussions have included debates on whether or not

- specific provisions to protect against blast, and progressive collapse and biochemical attacks on buildings should be mandated in some form within the nation's existing model building and fire codes that are adopted by state and local governments.
- there should be a separate building code for high-rise structures.
- the preceding issues should instead become design guidelines that building owners and their architects and engineers would put into their buildings on a case-by-case basis based upon a risk-threat analysis against that building and its occupants.

- there should be better understanding of and coordination of the roles, relationships and responsibilities of the construction team to enable our new and existing buildings to better respond to man-made and natural disasters.

The annual meetings of the major private and public sector construction industry associations also have featured speakers from other professional areas and from federal, state and local governments calling for closer coordination between building owners, architects, engineers, contractors, subcontractors, government officials, and building managers in helping our nation's buildings (new and existing) better meet the twin challenges of terrorism and major natural disasters.

One important outgrowth from 9/11 was the creation of a public private sector coordination group called The Infrastructure Security Partnership (TISP). Over 120 national associations, governmental agencies, colleges, and universities came together in 2002–2003 to share information on what they were doing and to identify areas of collaboration to improve "the resilience of the nation's critical infrastructure against the adverse impacts of natural and man-made disasters."

Figure 2-10

Cover of The Infrastructure Security Partnership's Regional Disaster Resilience Guide

Figure 2-11

From 2002–2005 conference's like McGraw-Hill's annual Homeland Security Summit brought together parties to discuss needed improvements in construction to protect buildings from disasters

Among TISP's objectives are the following:

- Raising awareness of the importance of achieving national and regional disaster resilience for critical infrastructure.
- Creating effective, task-forced, multidisciplinary work groups to improve regional disaster resilience for critical infrastructure.
- Fostering the creation and development of regional public-private partnerships to address infrastructure interdependence and interoperability.
- Disseminating knowledge on infrastructure security and disaster preparedness.
- Promoting the improvement and application of risk assessment and management methodologies.

In carrying out those objectives, in February 2006, the TISP Regional Disaster Resilience Task Force released a guide that enables public and private sector groups in different regions of the nation to come together to develop and implement a collaborative approach toward working together to develop a well-coordinated plan for disaster preparedness, response and recovery. That guide and other TISP actions are covered in greater detail in Chapter 7 "Homeland Security and the Issues of Energy, Sustainability, Environment, Accessibility and New Products, Materials, and Techniques."

In addition to the preceding forums, the events of 9/11 and Katrina are forcing a dialogue to occur between previously relatively unrelated groups—parties who have not been at the table together before—economic development officials, and building design professionals, building officials and bankers, contractors, and neighborhood organizations.

PUBLIC SECTOR ACTIONS TO 9/11

Work of the Federal Government: White House, Congress, and Federal Agencies

As noted earlier, the events of 9/11 expedited the completion of a number of then existing Federal government activities in the area of assessing and reducing federal building vulnerabilities to terrorist attacks and natural disasters.

Figure 2-12

The White House,
Washington, D.C.

Figure 2-13

U.S. Capitol
Building,
Washington, D.C.

Figure 2-14

National Institute of Standards and Technology, Gaithersburg, Maryland

Since its establishment in 1979, the FEMA has joined, along with other federal agencies including the National Science Foundation and Federal national laboratories (including NIST), to sponsor and conduct research into the impact of man-made and natural disasters on buildings. Spurred by the 1995 Oklahoma City bombing, the White House established the Interagency Security Committee to assess Federal building vulnerability to acts of terrorism and establish minimum security guidelines for such buildings.

These efforts resulted in many changes to the Federal construction requirements and the building codes and standards adopted by state and local governments throughout this nation. Funding for that research has come from the U.S. Congress, often at the encouragement and with the support of the White House.

September 11 also gave birth to new programs and projects including the "standing up" of the largest single agency in the Federal government outside of the DoD, the Department of Homeland Security (DHS), and the conducting by NIST, under the National Construction Safety Team Act, 2002, of one of the most extensive disaster assessment studies ever done—the "Building and Fire Safety Investigation into the World Trade Center Collapse."

The following are some of the changes to the building design, construction and operations processes, and the nation's code and standards that have developed from 9/11, the anthrax attack and the hurricanes of 2004-2005. Details on a number of these changes, including the findings of the NIST's WTC Collapse Report are provided in Chapter 3.

Expansion of Existing Projects

Expanding Risk Assessment Tools

The events of 9/11 brought the DoD, the Interagency Security Committee, the GSA, and FEMA to accelerate work they had underway in either developing or finalizing risk assessment tools for public and private facilities.

Figure 2-15

Jersey Walls
as security
barricades at a
Federal building,
Washington, D.C.

The GSA in 2004 completed their security risk assessments for their facilities nationwide that hold more than ten government employees and substantially completed security enhancements in those buildings as well. The GSA included within its "Protective Design and Security Implementation Guidelines," released to the general public, information on the components of conducting a risk assessment for public buildings. The GSA guidelines include provisions for physical security and protection against blasts and biochemical agents.

FEMA continued to refine and release its previous risk assessment tools, which included FEMA publication 386-2, "Understanding Your Risks: Identifying Hazards and Estimating Losses." The DoD and the State Department continued between 2001 and the present to either refine or develop additional risk assessment tools for military and diplomatic facilities.

Based upon an industry consensus standard for life-cycle cost analysis (ASTM's E- 917) NIST developed software that is now available for building owners and managers to identify and guard against terrorist threats—Version 1.1 "Cost Effectiveness Tool for Capital Asset Protection (CET)." Version 2.0 will be available in the fall of 2006. Described in greater detail in Chapter 4, this tool can be downloaded from the NIST Web site: www.2.bfrl.nist.gov/software/CET/

Upgrading Security and Blast and Biochemical Protection of Federal Facilities

The U.S. State Department, the DoD and GSA during the 1980s and 1990s each initiated and conducted programs to prioritize and undertake renovations to their existing facilities and design new facilities that were better able to protect their occupants from terrorist blasts and biochemical and radiological attacks.

To assist the public and private sector in addressing terrorism issues in building design and operation, the DoD in July 2002 released an unclassified version of "Minimum Antiterrorism Standards for Buildings."

The Defense Advanced Research Projects Agency (DARPA) in May 2005 conducted a classified one-day workshop with leaders from the construction industry and academia to share and discuss further advances in making buildings more immune and more rapidly recoverable from biochemical and radiological attacks. The program included a look at developing cost-benefit analysis for building owners to apply in considering what renovations to make in existing buildings and what technologies and designs to use in new buildings to make them "immune" to such threats. Among projects under consideration, including materials for use by private sector, is a Building Protection Tool Kit that provides resources to conduct an analysis of a building to protect its occupants from various types of contaminates.

FEMA provided the public and private sector with their recommendations concerning ways of improving building performance from blast events—FEMA Disaster Action Report 277, "Oklahoma City Bombing: Improving Building Performance."

Other useful FEMA disaster mitigation design documents (not previously mentioned) include the following:

- FEMA 426, "Reference Manual to Mitigate Potential Terrorist Attacks Against Buildings"
- FEMA 427, "Primer for Design of Commercial Buildings to Mitigate Terrorist Attacks"
- FEMA 428, "Primer for Design of Safe School Projects in Case of Terrorist Attacks"
- FEMA 429, "Insurance, Finance, and Regulation Primer for Terrorism Risk Management in Buildings"
- FEMA 155, "Building Design for Homeland Security"

Looking at Other Large-Scale Disasters: Seismic, Wind and Flood

FEMA published similar disaster action reports following the Florida Hurricanes of 2004 and, in early 2006, issued their findings from Hurricane Katrina. In addition to these reports, FEMA has published several guideline documents concerning actions

Figure 2-16

Katrina aftermath in a New Orleans neighborhood

that building owners and homeowners can and should take to better prepare their property to survive other natural disasters. These include the following:

- FEMA 55, "Coastal Construction Manual"
- FEMA 424, "Design Guide for Improving School Safety in Earthquakes, Floods and Wind"
- FEMA "How To Series"—a series of two pagers for consumers and the building community on how to reduce risks from various natural disasters

New Federal Initiatives

The Federal Building and Fire Safety Investigation of the World Trade Center Disaster

In response to 9/11, with support of the White House, the U.S. Congress enacted the National Construction Safety Team Act establishing within the U.S. Department of Commerce's NIST a program to investigate and report on significant accidents involving buildings. Under that authority, in 2002, NIST announced that it was undertaking a detailed multiyear investigation of the WTC disaster to accomplish the following:

- Investigate the building construction, materials used, and technical conditions that contributed to the outcome of the WTC disaster after terrorists flew large jet-fuel-laden commercial airliners into the WTC Towers.
- Use that investigation as the basis for:
  - Improvements in the way buildings are designed, constructed, maintained and used
  - Improving tools and guidance for industry and safety officials
  - Recommending revisions to current codes, standards and practices
  - Improving public safety

The specific objectives of the investigation were to determine the following:

- Why and how WTC buildings One and Two collapsed following the initial impact of the aircraft and why and how building Seven collapsed?
- Why the injuries and fatalities were so high or low depending on location, including all technical aspects of fire protection, occupant behavior, evacuation, and emergency response?
- What procedures and practices were used in the design, construction and operation, and maintenance of WTC buildings One, Two, and Seven?
- Identify, as specifically as possible, areas in current building and fire codes, standards, and practices that warrant revision based on the technical finds of the investigation.

As detailed in the Chapter 3, over the next three years following 9/11, NIST and a group of specialists in a number of technical areas conducted interviews, reviewed photographs, videos, and construction documents, and designed and carried out investigations and research to complete the preceding project.

Figure 2-17

Photo of damage to structural steel from one of the World Trade Center Towers, National Institute of Standards and Technology Report, September 2005

September 13 to 15, 2005, NIST hosted a national conference to share with the public and the nation's construction community the findings and recommendations in their "Final Report on the Collapse of the World Trade Center Towers."

In their findings, NIST determined that the towers collapsed as a result of the combination of the damage caused by the impact of the two jets, the extensive and intensive fires that then raged from the combination of the aviation fuel and the contents of the affected floors of the two towers. NIST noted that, "The World Trade Center towers likely would not have collapsed under the combined effects of aircraft impact damage and the extensive, multifloor fires that were encountered on 9/11 if the thermal insulation had not been widely dislodged or had been only minimally dislodged by aircraft impact."

The final report contained 30 recommendations that fell into 8 major groupings:

- Increased structural integrity
- Enhanced fire endurance of structures
- New methods for fire resistant design of structures
- Improved active fire protection
- Improved building evacuation
- Improved emergency response
- Improved procedures and practices
- Education and training

Within the 30 recommendations were recommendations for additional areas of research and for possible changes or improvements to 37 specific national standards, building and fire codes, and practices, guidelines, or recommendations governing construction and operation practices for high-rise construction and other structures. Those documents include a number that are maintained by the NFPA, ICC, ASCE, ASTM, ASME, AISC, ACI, AIA and BOMA.

As noted earlier in this chapter, following through on its WTC study charge, NIST awarded a contract in the fall of 2005 to the NIBS to convene a panel of building code experts, representing the diverse technical areas covered by the WTC recommendations to do the following:

1. Develop a strategy to implement relevant recommendations into model building and fire codes
2. Develop awareness of activities of other groups already focusing on implementing the final report's recommendations (e.g., NFPA, ICC, ASCE, ASTM, ASME, AISC, AIA, ACI and BOMA)
3. Develop initial proposals for changes to the model building and fire codes
4. Shepherd proposed changes through the code-change processes
5. Identify additional steps to be taken with respect to relevant standards
6. Identify any needed training and education tools

NIST and the NIBS Model Code Committee (MCC) are currently in the process of finalizing several proposed recommended changes to the International Building Code and NFPA codes. The ICC's International Building Code will issue a supplement in 2007 based upon proposed changes submitted to the ICC by the NIBS committee in March 2006. NFPA, which as previously noted, has already incorporated some changes based on the WTC experience into their codes and standards, will make other changes that emerged from the NIBS MCC committee in the 2009 edition of their building code.

Chapter 3 includes a detailed review of the 30 recommendations contained in the NIST "Final Report on the World Trade Center Disaster." Chapter 5 looks at a number of the draft proposed code changes that members of the two ICC committees and the NIBS work group submitted to the ICC in March 2006. Several recommendations to NFPA for consideration in NFPA's family of codes and standards also will be reviewed.

Creation of the Department of Homeland Security and NIMS, NRC and NIPP

In 2002, the Homeland Security Act established the U.S. DHS out of an assemblage of 21 different government agencies and programs including those familiar to the construction industry from FEMA, the Office of Domestic Preparedness at the Justice Department and the Federal Bureau of Investigation's National Infrastructure Protection Center.

While the DHS was originally established as a coordinated national response to terrorism, with the incorporation of FEMA into DHS, the Department's programs and policies quickly took on an "All Hazards Approach" (natural as well as man-made disasters) toward public safety for all Americans. The strategic goals for the department are awareness, prevention, protection, response, recovery, and service.

DHS reaches out to over 87,000 different governmental jurisdictions at the federal, state, local and tribal government levels that have varying degrees of homeland security responsibility. Guiding DHS activities are a number of documents including Presidential Directives, the National Response Plan, the National Incident Management System, and the National Infrastructure Protection Plan.

The construction industry, including building officials and building owners are integral parts of various DHS programs. These programs and their impact on building codes and standards and building design and operation will be covered in greater detail in Chapter 7 of this book.

State and Local Government Actions

Work of State and Local Governments and Their Elected Officials

State and local governments were not idle in the months after 9/11 while their counterparts in the Federal government and in the private sector were updating existing codes and standards and risk assessment guidelines. Legislatures and governors and mayors and county officials mandated upgrades in building security within their communities including reviews of the security, construction, and building operation requirements for public buildings.

Major city building and fire departments with high-rise structures also took action in the wake of 9/11. New York City began immediate work with its construction community to address modifications on certain provisions within the city's building and fire codes that govern high-rise structures. In 2004, the city amended several sections of the city's construction codes to require retrofit of high-rise structures over a multiyear period to upgrade provisions for elevator vestibules, exit lighting, exit signs, signs in sleeping rooms, ventilation in buildings, sprinklers, fire alarm systems, fire command

Figure 2-18

Upper house of the Rhode Island legislature

Figure 2-19

Skyline of the city of Providence, Rhode Island

and communications systems, elevators in readiness, locks on hoist way doors, firemen's service, and oil storage and pumping for generators on upper floors of buildings.

The city of Chicago in 2004 enacted "Life Safety and High Rise Sprinkler Ordinances" that focused on improving over a multiyear period the life safety attributes of the 1,700 existing high-rise buildings in the city, 1,300 of which were built prior to 1975 when the city put its first high-rise fire ordinance in place for new construction. Among the requirements of the new Chicago statute are the phased installation of sprinklers in high-rise structures not containing them, mandatory life safety evaluations of all high rises, improved voice communication systems, upgraded fire-rated stairway doors and frames in residential high rises, and a life safety data sheet for each building.

In response to hurricanes that swept their state in 2004, Florida's Department of Community Affairs in coordination with the public and private sector funded research into areas where the new statewide building code's wind and water resistance provisions could be upgraded. As noted earlier, those provisions currently are out for public consideration as amendments to the existing statewide code.

Last, through the associations of the National Conference of States on Building Codes and Standards, the Association of Major City and County Building Officials from 2001 through the present, state and local building officials have shared copies of ordinances, proposed code changes and building codes administration and regulatory best practices that help improve the ability of building officials to strengthen the disaster resistance of the buildings being designed, constructed or retrofit in their communities. These associations also helped share information from FEMA, the DHS, the codes and standards community and TISP with state and local building officials.

COLLABORATIVE PUBLIC-PRIVATE SECTOR INITIATIVES: THE ALL HAZARDS APPROACH AND CALL FOR REGIONAL PREPAREDNESS, RESPONSE, AND RECOVERY

This chapter has outlined the actions taken by both the public and private sector in the wake of the events of 9/11, the anthrax attacks in Washington, D.C, and the nation's

Figure 2-20
Empire State
Building,
Manhattan,
New York City

Figure 2-21
The Chicago
skyline

Figure 2-22

Session on
streamlining at
an annual meeting
of the National
Conference of
States on Building
Codes and
Standards

large-scale natural disasters of 2004 and 2005 to enhance the ability of our buildings to protect the public from natural and man-made disasters.

One important factor in our nation's response to 9/11 has been the coming together of both the public and private sector members of the construction team (building owners, architects, engineers, contractors, product manufacturers, codes and standards bodies, building officials, and building operators) in multiple forums to share their expertise and their concerns and begin to take cooperative actions to improve our built environment.

The nearly simultaneous decisions by the private and public sectors to address the issues of better protection of the public in buildings through a multihazard approach dealing with both the diverse range of natural and man-made disasters has been an important step. Katrina and Rita have shown the wisdom of that approach and also documented to the construction team the need to look at disaster preparedness, response, and recovery including building reconstruction and continuity of business operations on a regional and not just on a local or single state scale.

Thus far all of these efforts have not produced definitive answers to the questions raised by the *Engineering News Record* in its October 31, 2005, editorial: "What level of safety should the industry design for? What level do owners and tenants want? What level should public officials demand?" This chapter's summary of actions that have been taken after 9/11, however, show that our nation's construction team is taking a deliberative approach toward addressing these issues.

The following chapters of this book will move from this general overview of what is being done into a detailed look at both the lessons learned from disasters since 9/11 (Chapter 3) and at specific provisions in the codes, standards, and guidelines that are now currently available to building owners, architects, engineers, contractors, building officials, and building operators to improve the performance of their structures (Chapters 4 to 6).

3 Findings from the World Trade Center Towers Collapse and Other Post-9/11 Disasters: What Is It That We Want Buildings to Do?

- What is it that we want buildings to do?
  - Be functional and cost-effective?
  - Disaster resistant?
  - Immune from terrorism?
  - All of the above?

Key components of all of our nation's construction codes, standards and guidelines are the principles of functionality, affordability, constructability and, more importantly, the protection of the public from natural hazards and the man-made hazards of fire and panic.

As noted in Chapter 1, "Codes, Regulations and the Construction Team," our modern building codes, standards, and construction guidelines evolved over the past 100 years out of changes in technology, practices, and materials and also in response to lessons that we learned from disasters—fire, flood, earthquake, wind, as well as the stampeding of the public during a panic situation.

Drawing upon those lessons learned, the goal of modern codes and standards has not necessarily been the protection of the structure per se except within the context that in the face of predictable natural and man-made disasters the building must stand long enough to protect the lives of the people who occupy or use that building. For the average commercial, governmental building throughout the past 100 years such general principles have been more than adequate to protect the health, welfare, and lives of our citizens.

The exceptions to this rule have been buildings built and/or used by our military and diplomatic service. These are buildings that are not subject to normal use, but unfortunately are buildings that increasingly since the 1960s have been the targets of military and terrorist attacks.

In the wake of the bombing of the Murrah Building in Oklahoma City, the U.S. General Services Administration began applying the construction guidelines developed by our Department of Defense (DoD) and the State Department to selected Federal facilities across the United States to reduce their vulnerability to such future attacks.

A structural engineer recently noted that designing and constructing a building that is virtually immune from known terrorist methods of attack is relatively easy to do. What is impossible is designing and constructing a building that is not only immune from known terrorist methods of attack but at the same time is affordable, functional and relatively comfortable to work in. Technically we know how to build such secure facilities, but at what cost and for what real purpose do we mandate such construction through changes in our construction codes, standards, guidelines, and practices for all construction in this nation?

This point is a basic one for every building owner, and subsequently to all of the members of the construction team. What is it that I want my building to do, to be used for? From what realistic, risks, threats, and hazards am I trying to protect my building occupants and visitors?

The events of 9/11, and not the previous attacks on American embassies and military bases overseas or the bombing of the Murrah building, have been the catalyst of public concern over our buildings safety from terrorism. To address the preceding questions and how existing codes, standards, checklists, and practices can help us better protect

Figure 3-1

Ground Zero,
World Trade
Center, New York
Informal Memorial

Figure 3-2

"Falling Glass," sign below New Orleans High-rise after Katrina, November 2005

the public, we therefore must look at the attack on the World Trade Center's (WTC's) Twin Towers. What really are the lessons about our construction codes, standards, and processes, including the roles of the members of the construction team, that have been learned from the attack on the WTC and the Pentagon that day?

WHAT IS IT THAT 9/11 TAUGHT US? A LOOK AT THE NIST WORLD TRADE CENTER REPORT

Findings and Recommendations as a Reflection on What Is Currently Available

In total, 2,803 people including 403 emergency responders lost their lives that day; 10 major buildings experienced partial or total collapse and 30 million square feet of commercial office space was removed from service, of which 12 million belonged to the WTC complex.

—Federal Emergency Management Agency's Executive Summary, "World Trade Performance Study" May 2002

Chapter 2 provided a very brief overview of the origin, purpose and findings of the causes of the ultimate collapses of the Twin Towers based on the extensive study done under the provisions of the National Construction Safety Team Act by the National Institute of Standards and Technology (NIST).

Released in September 2005, the NIST "Final Report on the Collapse of the World Trade Center Towers" ultimately laid the collapse of the towers not on improper design and faulty steel as some had speculated. With extensive research and great detail, including the analysis of 150 hours of video tapes, about 7,000 photographs, and analysis of steel, NIST determined that the collapse were a result of a combination of damage. That damage was caused by the immediate impact of the two jets, the extensive and intensive fires that then raged from both the fuel from the aircraft and the contents of the affected floors of the two buildings. (For a copy of the complete NIST report, visit the NIST WTC website at http://wtc.nist.gov.)

As important as it was to determine the cause of the collapses, the NIST report went further:

- Why were injuries and fatalities so high or low depending upon the location within the towers?
- What were the procedures and practices used in the design, construction, and operation and maintenance of the towers?
- What current building and fire codes, standards, and practices warrant revision based upon technical findings of the investigation?

Heading the National Construction Safety Team for that project, Shyam Sunder, Deputy Director of NIST's Building and Fire Research Laboratory, oversaw an extensive two-year project that involved over 200 of NIST staff, 28 private sector contractors and the cooperation of 21 other organizations, agencies, and companies. Among the latter group were Boeing aircraft, American and United Airlines, the City of New York, the Port Authority of New York and New Jersey, and the National Commission on Terrorist Attacks Upon the United States.

With the hard work of this extensive collection of experts, NIST produced a report that offered the construction community, building regulators, and public important recommendations for making buildings safer, not only from large fuel-laden aircraft but from far more likely disaster scenarios including fires of other origin or even earthquakes.

THE CODES AND STANDARDS PROVISIONS IN PLACE IN THE WORLD TRADE CENTER TOWERS ON 9/11 AND UNIQUE CONSTRUCTION ELEMENTS

The firm of architect Minoru Yamasaki was commissioned in 1962 by the Port Authority of New York and New Jersey to construct twin towers to replace the Empire State Building as the signature buildings of New York City, as well as to build the world's two tallest buildings.

Figure 3-3
World Trade Center Complex, 1984, from the National Institute of Standards and Technology Report, Figure 1.2

As an interstate compact, the Port Authority was exempt from having to comply with the then in place provisions of the 1938 New York City Building Code. Because of the unique nature of the WTC, the Port Authority chose instead to follow the provisions, then in the final steps of adoption, of the 1965 New York City Building Code—a code that recognized changes in building materials and design and life-safety improvements over the previous decades.

Unique Construction Elements

Given the requirements of the owner that the tower's maximize the availability of use-able floor space, Yamasaki went beyond conventional design, which would have made the building heavier and with much less useable space per floor. Yamasaki based his design on the framed-tube technique and rather than use spandrel beams or girders to connect the columns, he used a band of deep plates as spandrel members tieing the perimeter columns together.

He thus created the first high-rise steel structure using the framed-tube design to pro-vide resistance to wind loads. In his design, the exterior frame system resists the force of the wind. The exterior columns carry a portion of the building gravity loads and, when the winds are not present, all of the columns are in compression.

Wind tunnel tests were performed at the University of Western Ontario on the stiffness of the wall panels used in the WTC construction prior to the final design. In addition to these tests, wind tunnel tests were run at both Colorado State University and Britain's National Physical Laboratory (NPL) to estimate how the towers would perform during and after construction. Input from these tests went into the building's final design. The latter test resulted in adding the first application of damping units to reduce oscillations in the buildings, assuring that occupants on the higher floors would not become uncomfortable in high winds.

Other unique design considerations included the use of long-span composite floor assemblies including the use of open-web, lightweight steel trusses topped with a lightweight concrete slab and composite action of steel and concrete through the truss diagonals extending above the top chord and into the poured concrete.

When completed and opened, approximately 40,000 people worked or visited the two WTC towers every day. Because of those large numbers and their great height, both towers used a three-tier elevator system, involving a series of express and local elevators. Twenty-four local elevators took people to floors 9 through 40. For those going to floors 44 to 76, an express elevator took them to the 44th floor where they got off at the "Skylobby" and transferred to another block of 24 local elevators that served floors in that range. Those heading above the 78th floor (78 to 107) took another set of express elevators to the Skylobby on the 78th floor, then they transferred to one of 24 local elevators taking them to their final destination. The stacking of these three sets of 24 elevators within the same elevator shafts reduced the amount of total space used within the two towers for elevator shafts.

In addition to the aforementioned elevators, each tower had one express elevator that went from the lobby all the way to the top of the building. In WTC One, there was one that went to the "Windows on the World" restaurant and in WTC Two, there was one that took you to the Observation Deck. Eight freight elevators also served the two buildings and these were equipped to incorporate firefighter emergency operation requirements.

Compartmentation within the structure included the use of vertical shaft wall panels (for elevators, stairs, utilities, and ventilation) that alleviated the need for framing and instead used gypsum planks placed into metal channels at the floor and ceiling slabs. The assembled walls within the building were then covered with gypsum wallboard. The unique design also called for an extremely broad number of different grades of steel (14, 12 of which were actually used) ordered from multiple steel fabricators and suppliers.

The WTC was a class 1 (fire-resistive) structure. Under the 1968 version of the New York City Building Code, the Port Authority called for class IB protection, which specified a three-hour rating for columns and girders that supported more than one floor and a two-hour rating for floors including beams.

Two different methods were used to protect steel from fire. In certain locations, steel was enclosed in gypsum wallboard. In other locations the building used sprayed fire-resistive material (SFRM). SFRM used for protecting floor trusses was new in high-rise construction and the requirements for application and thickness "evolved" during the construction of the Twin Towers.

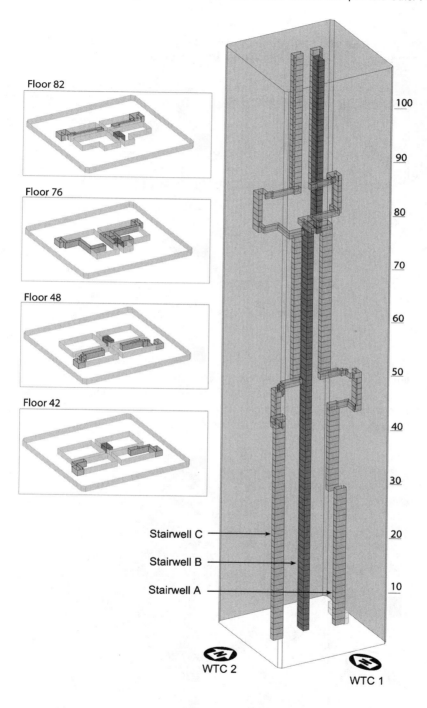

Floor 82

Floor 76

Floor 48

Floor 42

100

90

80

70

60

50

40

30

20

10

Stairwell C

Stairwell B

Stairwell A

WTC 2

WTC 1

Figure 3-4

Configuration of Elevators, World Trade Center from the National Institute of Standards and Technology World Trade Center Report, Figure 1.9

Figure 3-5

Diagram of steel trusses and sprayed fire-resistive material from the National Institute of Standards and Technology, World Trade Center Report

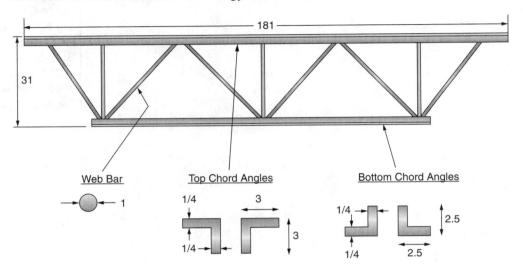

Walls separating tenant spaces were required to achieve a one-hour fire rating. When tenant spaces were later altered, the Port Authority mandated that partitions separating tenant spaces within the building from exit access corridors have a two-hour rating. Firestopping was required and applied where ever gaps in walls and floors existed through which smoke and flames might pass.

Figure 3-6

Photos of steel trusses and sprayed fire-resistive material from the National Institute of Standards and Technology World Trade Center Report

Egress Requirements

The standard evacuation plans for most high-rise structures in case of a fire incident is generally for occupants at the site of the fire not to evacuate the entire building but to evacuate either two floors above or two floors below the fire. This was the standard procedure within the WTC on 9/11.

While the WTC had a number of high-speed elevators, these were never designed or used as the means of egress during a fire event or other emergency. Three stairways located in the Towers' cores were the primary egress system. Under the provisions of the 1968 New York City Building Code there was no enclosed staircase accessible through a naturally ventilated vestibule—a fire tower (which the 1938 code provided for). Moreover under the 1968 code, the number of required stairwells had been reduced from the 1938 code's mandatory six to three.

The widths of the WTC stairwells varied. Two were 44 inches wide and one was 56 inches wide. None of the building codes in place in 1968 required the widths of stairwells be conditioned by the number of stories in a building. The 1968 New York City Building Code required that stairwells be "as far apart as practicable."

In the fire and airplane impact zones in WTC Building One, the stairwells were closer together than in the fire and impact zones in WTC Two. This issue became a factor when the planes slammed into both towers. In WTC One (the North Tower), in the area of impact and above, all of the stairwells were destroyed. In WTC Two (the South Tower), one of the three stairwells, though damaged, was at least partially accessible to those above the point of impact.

Late 1960s technology and a fire safety plan were the two systems for providing fire safety within the Towers. The fire safety plan involved each Tower having a fire safety director, who oversaw emergency response until the New York City Fire Department arrived; fire safety directors who manned each building's Fire Command Desk (FCD) located in the lobby of each building and at the Skylobbies (the transfer floors to connect between the high-speed elevators for the lower and the upper floors); and fire wardens and deputy fire wardens on every floor. These were tied together with communications systems.

The fire safety technology in the Towers included an alarm system to alert occupants to a fire, an automatic sprinkler system and standpipe system for putting water on the fire, and a smoke purge system to be used after an incident to enable occupants to see well enough to move to the exits.

In the wake of the 1993 terrorist bombing of WTC One, vulnerabilities of this system were rectified. A new communications system was put into the buildings; more pull stations and monitors were added, along with over 10,000 fire detectors and 30,000 notification speakers and strobe lights (for the hearing impaired); and the fire sprinkler system acquired a water-flow indicator that showed the water pressure and also if it was working.

The retrofit of the Two Towers to include all of these features was over 80% completed by 9/11. An analysis of these systems completed in 2002, estimated that on 9/11 about 25% of the old systems elements were still in use.

Impact of Aircraft, Resultant Fires, Evacuations, and Collapse

So how did all of these structures and systems function and the occupants of the WTC Twin Towers respond on 9/11?

On the morning of 9/11, the number of occupants of the Twin Towers were significantly less than was normal. People were late going into work that day—instead of 20,000 people being in WTC One as was typical by 9:00 a.m., there were only approximately 8,900 people at 8:45 a.m.

At 8:46 a.m. on 9/11 WTC One (the North Tower) was struck between the 93d and 99th floor by a 767-200 ER American Airlines Flight 11 moving at 440 mph, having banked at a 25° angle with its 76 passengers and crew of 11. The Tower absorbed the planes strike and remained standing.

Figure 3-7

South face damage of World Trade Center One with key aircraft component locations marked; National Institute of Standards and Technology World Trade Center Report, Figure 2.3

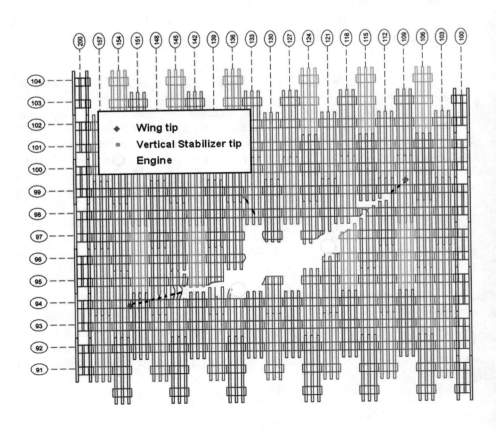

The impact of the plane destroyed perimeter columns and severed and heavily damaged core columns, taking out elevators, fire suppression systems, and three exit stairways, dislodging thermal fireproofing from the trusses and columns and spreading fire from the fuel and 13 tons of aircraft to office furnishings and combustibles. While the initial fireball from the plane's impact had died down within minutes, fresh air entering the building from the damaged façade coupled with the remaining jet fuel and building furnishings to cause the fires to grow and spread deeper into the building. This water from the ruptured piping, that normally would have provided water to sprinklers that would have suppressed any fire, flowed down the building's damaged stairwells. At that time, the manually activated smoke purging system that was supposed to be used for smoke removal after the fire was not turned on and, even if it had been, damage to the vent shafts on upper floors was so severe that in NIST's view in all likelihood it would not have worked at all.

As the fires continued to spread, the heat began to affect and soften the steel of the floor joists and columns that had their fire-proofing knocked from them by the airplane's impact. This ultimately caused WTC One to collapse within 102 minutes of the plane's impact, killing those first responders and other personnel still in the tower at the time, as well as those people trapped above the impact area (455 people, of which over 110 ended their lives by jumping from the building before its collapse).

Even though the building-wide emergency broadcast from the Fire Command Desk in the lobby was destroyed by the plane's impact, within minutes of the airplanes striking the Tower most of the 7,545 people located below the 92nd floor began exiting the building via the three stairwells that now held water, debris, the smell, of aviation fuel, and a haze of pulverized thermal insulation, gypsum, and concrete.

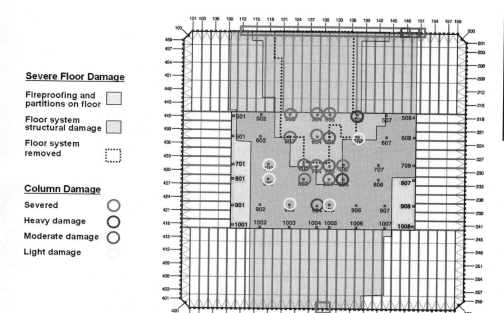

Severe Floor Damage

Fireproofing and partitions on floor

Floor system structural damage

Floor system removed

Column Damage

Severed

Heavy damage

Moderate damage

Light damage

Figure 3-8

National Institute of Standards and Technology World Trade Center Report, floor damage World Trade Center One

Approximately 25% of the occupants of the North Tower working in the building since before the 1993 WTC bombing, together with the evacuation training provided to all employees after the 1993 bombing, helped people conduct their evacuation in a orderly fashion. By the time the tower collapsed, 7,450 people had successfully evacuated the building from all floors below the 91st.

By 8:50 a.m., the first of the fire trucks arrived at the WTC One and the Fire Command Center was established in that building's lobby. By 8:55 a.m., with the objective of aiding evacuation and then cutting their way through to the fire to rescue those above the 92d floor, the first firefighters entered the stairwells each carrying as much as 100 lb of firefighting gear.

By 9:00 a.m., 66 New York City Fire Department units had been dispatched to the WTC and a senior Port Authority Police Department official had called for the evacuation of all of the seven buildings in the WTC complex. Based upon interviews and other research, NIST concluded that the call was not heard and not heeded.

WTC Two (the South Tower), which also would have normally had up to 20,000 people at work within it, also had a light occupancy with only approximately 8,600 persons.

At approximately 9:03 a.m., 767-200 ER United Airlines Flight 175 with 51 passengers aboard and 9 crew members struck at 540 mph between the 78th and the 86th floors of the east side of the south face of the South Tower. In addition to its passengers and crew, this Extend Range 767 with its heavy fuel load, mail, luggage, electrical equipment, and food carried 14 tons of solid combustibles.

As with the impact of American Flight 11 into the North Tower, there was light damage where the wing tips entered the building, but major damage from where the engines and fuselage struck the building to floor joists, perimeter and core columns, and fire suppression system. The plane also dislodged the SFRM from the steel trusses and columns. Gypsum fire protection likewise was stripped away by the airplane's impact.

As with WTC One, WTC Two absorbed the plane's impact and remained standing. Unlike the strike at WTC One, United Airlines 175 did not destroy all the stairways at the impact floors—one of the three remained marginally passable at least for some time.

Also unlike WTC One, by 9:03 a.m., approximately 40% of the occupants of WTC Two, despite conflicting public announcements, already had begun evacuation. Of those, 90% survived the disaster. The availability of one stairwell to the occupants above the impacted floor enabled 18 persons to evacuate the building from those levels prior to the building's collapse; 619 people on or above the impacted floors, however, did not survive.

The intense fires that raged in WTC Two were caused by the massive amount of jet fuel, the aircraft and the impact's piling up of the combustibles and furniture into the north-eastern corner of the impacted floors. These intense fires quickly began to weaken the structural integrity of the South Tower. At approximately 9:59 a.m., 56 minutes after

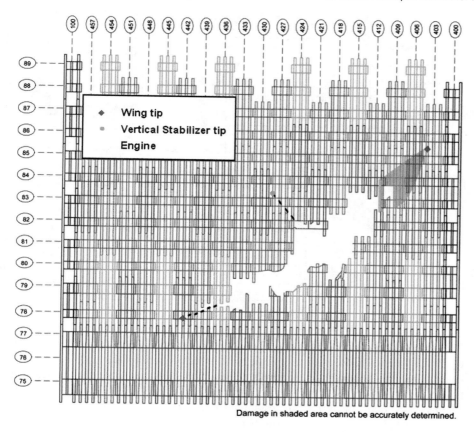

Figure 3-9

National Institute of Standards and Technology World Trade Center Report, Figure 3.2, South face damage of World Trade Center Two with key aircraft component locations marked

Damage in shaded area cannot be accurately determined.

being struck, the South Tower began to collapse taking the lives of those who remained at or above the floors of impact and those firefighters and others who were aiding in the building's evacuation.

Twenty-eight minutes later the North Tower collapsed. The collapse of these two towers caused collateral destruction or damage to WTC buildings Seven, Three (destruction), and Four, Five and Six, a number of neighboring buildings, and the subway stations located beneath the towers.

While both towers collapsed in slightly different manners, the NIST report documented that ultimately the towers collapsed for the following reasons: Struck from the north, the North Tower was hit by a plane flying at a lower speed than the plane that struck the South Tower. Fires started on the north side of the building and took a much longer time (one hour or so versus 40 minutes) than they did in the South Tower to move around to the rest of the building.

Inward bowing was observed on the buildings' south face as the result of the fires and the plane's impact, and because of this the columns on the south face tipped up and took on an additional axial load. Sagging under the heat to which they were subjected, the long span floors to which these columns were connected pulled the columns inward.

Figure 3-10

National Institute of Standards and Technology World Trade Center Report, floor damage World Trade Center Two

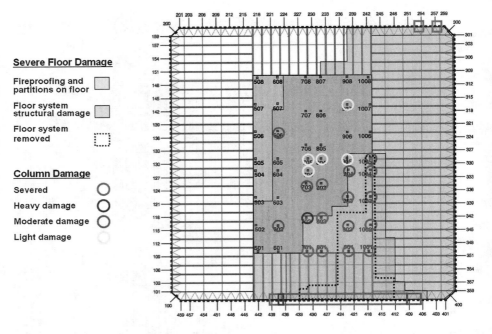

Severe Floor Damage

Fireproofing and partitions on floor

Floor system structural damage

Floor system removed

Column Damage

Severed

Heavy damage

Moderate damage

Light damage

Then as the fires burned, the North Tower reached a point where the building became unstable on the south side. At that time the building tried to redistribute the load through the hat truss cap on the building (a feature applied to both buildings to support the television antennas). The instability of the south face then spread its load to all of the building's adjacent faces, including the places where columns were missing due to the plane's impact. As a result at 10:28 a.m., the North Tower then tilted toward the south and started to collapse.

Struck from the south, the South Tower was hit by a plane flying at a higher speed than that of the North Tower. Because of the greater velocity with which the plane struck and because of the location and intensity of its fires, there was an inward bowing of the east face of that building. The fire on the east face affected the columns, and there was an inward pull on the east face because the long span floors began to sag under the fires.

The plane wreckage and internal building contents were pushed to the northeastern corner on the building's 80th and 81st floors so the fires persisted on the east side of the building from the beginning of the event. NIST found photos showing that this inward bowing occurred within 18 minutes of impact as columns with dislodged thermal insulation elongated due to thermal expansion and the forces pulling inward from the sagging floors. As those temperatures continued to rise, the columns thermally weakened and shortened.

NIST found, "The south exterior wall displaced downward by the aircraft impact, but did not displace further until the east wall became unstable 43 minutes later." The inward bowing of the east wall ultimately caused the failure of the exterior column splices and spandrels making the east wall columns unstable. As that instability progressed horizontally across the east face of the building, the east wall was unable to bear its gravity load and tried to redistribute them to the thermally weakened core through the hat truss and through the spandrels to the east and west walls.

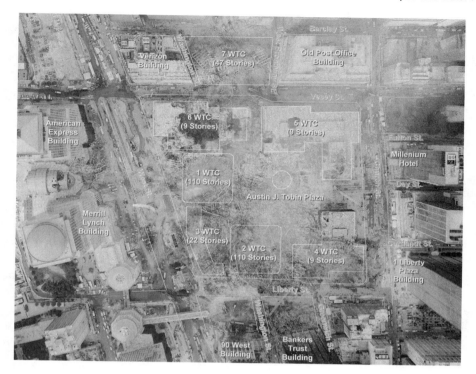

Figure 3-11
World Trade Center site on September 17, 2001, Figure 4.1 from the National Institute of Standards and Technology World Trade Center Report, Source National Oceanographic and Atmospheric Administration

This instability then caused the building sections above the 93d floor to begin tilting to the east and south, which had been weakened and could not carry the increased gravity loads. With the remaining core and perimeter columns no longer able to support the gravity loads from the above floors, the upper section of the building began moving downward and that energy could not be absorbed by the rest of the structure and "global collapse ensued."

The terrorist attacks took a total of 2,749 lives of WTC One and Two occupants, Port Authority, fire, police, and other emergency responders, passengers and crew of the two aircraft and bystanders and nearby building occupants.

NIST Findings Concerning Structural and Fire Safety

Following through on its extensive research, modeling, analysis of video and photographs, interviews with survivors, and discussions, and review of documents regarding the buildings' construction, operation, and maintenance, the NIST study and report of its National Construction Safety Team had two major findings and 30 some recommendations for the nation's construction, codes, standards, enforcement, and research communities.

The two major findings were the following:

1. Overall the collapse of the two towers occurred from a combination of the following factors:
   - The airplanes and their impact
   - Fires and their fuel

- The resultant weakening of the buildings' cores and their floors sagging
- The resultant inward bowing of the exterior walls

No one item caused the collapse by itself—it was a combination of the preceding factors and *not* the light frame construction of the building or core itself that were the problems.

2. If the fire-proofing had not been dislodged by the impact of the planes, then NIST could not predict that the buildings would have collapsed just on the basis of the impact of the planes or the fuel and fires that were encountered on 9/11. NIST noted that we do not design buildings for such airplane impacts, nor should the nation do so for commercial structures. As one NIST official noted in a conference call with state and local building officials in the late spring of 2005, "We therefore must keep terrorists away from airplanes and airplanes away from buildings."

NIST and the National Construction Safety Team were not only charged with determining the procedures and practices used in the design, construction, and operation of the WTC and the exact causes of its collapse, but they were charged to do the following as well:

- Determine why the injuries and fatalities were so high or low depending upon the locations in the buildings and all technical aspects of fire protection including occupant behavior, evacuation, and emergency response
- Identify, as specifically as possible, areas in current building and fire codes, standards, and practices that warrant revision based on the technical findings of the investigation

NIST in their report and in public briefing sessions, including those for state and local building officials, noted that the Twin Towers were unique buildings and therefore the issues and recommendations that they formulated based upon their research were not broadly applicable to all buildings, especially to all high-rise buildings. Because the procedures and practices used to design buildings and carry out evacuation and egress response are common practices, NIST offered within its 30 overall recommendations a number pertaining to evacuation and stairway design.

Egress Issues

NIST conducted over 1000 interviews for their report—900 with occupants and 115 with first responders, firefighters, Port Authority, and New York City police. On the morning of 9/11 there were over 17,000 people in the two Towers instead of the usual 40,000 occupants and visitors. Of those, some 6% had mobility impairments including those who had recent surgery, heart conditions, and asthma, or were pregnant, on medications, or in wheelchairs.

NIST calculated that had the towers been fully occupied that morning, the full evacuation of those buildings would have taken 3 hours. "Under those circumstances about 14,000 occupants might have perished in the buildings' collapses." Of the 1,462 to 1,533 occupants who died in the North Tower, only 107 were below the area where American Airlines Flight 11 struck the building and no one above the 91st floor survived due to the airplane's impact and inability to evacuate the building by the destroyed stairwells or the locked roof.

Figure 3-12

"Thank You America," from Port Authority of New York And New Jersey Police at Ground Zero, 2002

In the South Tower, somewhere between 630 and 701 occupants died, only 11 of whom died on floors below the area where United Airlines Flight 175 struck the building. Because of their quick thinking, some 75% of those occupants above the 78th floor survived. These individuals were aided in their prompt evacuation prior to 9:03 a.m. by the availability of all of the building's elevators. This pre-strike self-evacuation occurred despite conflicting announcements through the buildings safety warning system: first the occupants were told to return to their offices at 9:00 a.m. and then at 9:02 a.m. they were told to evacuate if the situation warranted.

NIST found that two-thirds of the occupants of both the North and South Towers had participated in a fire drill in the building within the past year prior to 9/11 and nearly all (93%) had been instructed where the stairwells were, but only one half of the survivors had ever used a stairwell before. Indeed, NIST noted that prior to 9/11 New York City Local Law 5 forbade building occupants from using stairwells during evacuation drills.

NIST also found that occupants at the higher levels were slower to leave their spaces, were physically challenged by the full building evacuation, and were not prepared for the horizontal transfers within certain floors. In addition, no one interviewed in the North Tower recalled ever hearing any public address system announcements that the Fire Command Station made; evacuation rates slowed considerably in the final 20 minutes before each tower collapsed, and mobility-impaired persons were generally assisted by others in evacuating the building. Of those who perished in the towers there did not appear to be a disproportionate number of disabled individuals among them.

NIST Findings on Operational Codes, Standards, and Practices

Within their September 2005 report NIST offered six pages on "Findings on Operational Codes, Standards, and Practices which include the areas of: General, Structural Safety, Fire Safety, and Future Factors that Could have Improved Life Safety." Among the general findings NIST found the following:

- The Architect of Record was responsible for the specifications for fire protection and designing the system for building evacuation, but was not required (and still is not required) to engage a fire protection engineer in the process.
- "The current state-of-practice for engineers does not include engineers routinely analyzing the performance of an entire structural system for a prescribed design-basis fire scenario."

Among the Structural Safety Findings were:

- When the towers were designed, there were no "explicit structural integrity provisions to mitigate progressive collapse."
- When the towers were designed, there were no "explicit minimum structural integrity requirements for the means of egress (stairwells and elevators)."

Included in the findings for fire safety were the following:

- No technical basis was found for selecting SFRM and the degree of its thickness.
- There were no code provisions that specifically required the conduction of a fire resistance test if no adequate data existed from other building components and assemblies to qualify as an untested building element.
- Structural design did not (and still does not) consider fire as a design condition as it does dead, live, wind and earthquake loads.

Among the factors that could have improved life safety, NIST found the following:

- Thermal insulation that bonds more firmly to structural steel
- Improved compartmentation and stairwell enclosures
- Fire-protected and structurally hardened elevators for use in evacuation and fire responder access
- More accurate and reliable communications among emergency responders and building occupants
- Better evacuation training

NIST 30 Recommendations

Chapter 9 of NIST's "Final Report on the WTC Collapse" details each of the 30 recommendations that emerged from NIST's study of the Twin Towers. On page 202 of their report, NIST notes that they

- "Believe that these recommendations are both realistic and achievable within a reasonable period of time and that their implementation would make buildings safer for occupants and emergency responders in future emergencies."
- "Strongly urge that immediate and serious consideration be given to these recommendations by the building and fire safety communities—especially designers, owners, developers, codes and standards development organizations, regulators, fire safety professionals, and emergency responders."

- "Strongly urge building owners and public officials to (1) evaluate the safety implications of these recommendations to their existing inventory of buildings, and (2) take the steps necessary to mitigate any unwarranted risks without waiting for changes to occur in codes, standards, and practices."

As shown in Table 3-1, each of the 30 recommendations in their report was cross-walked with other recommendations and was listed as to which community was primarily responsible for that recommendation's area. The responsible communities included education and training, and further research and development/study; adoption and enforcement; standards, codes, and regulations, and one of eight recommendation areas. Those eight areas included:

1. Increased structural integrity
2. Enhance fire endurance of structures
3. New methods for fire resistant design of structures
4. Improved active fire protection
5. Improved building evacuation
6. Improved emergency response
7. Improved procedures and practices
8. Education and training

Briefly summarized below are each of the 30 recommendations divided into the eight subject area categories:

Group 1: Increased Structural Integrity

The standards for estimating the load effects of potential hazards (e.g., progressive collapse, wind) and the design of structural systems to mitigate the effects of those hazards should be improved to enhance structural integrity.

Recommendation #1 - NIST recommends that (1) progressive collapse be prevented in buildings through the development and nationwide adoption of consensus standards and code provisions, along with the tools and guidelines needed for their use in practices and (2) a standard methodology be developed—supported by analytical design tools and practical design guidance—to reliably predict the potential for complex failures in structural systems subjected to multiple hazards.

Recommendation # 2 - NIST recommends that nationally accepted performance standards be developed for (1) conducting wind tunnel testing of prototype structures based on sound technical methods that result in repeatable and reproducible results among testing laboratories, and (2) estimating wind loads and their effects on tall buildings for use in design, based on wind tunnel testing and directional wind speed data.

Recommendation #3 - NIST recommends that an appropriate criterion be developed and implemented to enhance the performance of tall buildings by limiting how much they sway under lateral load design considerations (e.g., winds and earthquakes).

Table 3-1

Recommendations for improved public safety in tall and high-rise buildings, Table E-1 from the National Institute of Standards and Technology World Trade Center Report

Recommendation Area	Recommendation Group	Recommendation Number	Practices	Standards, Codes, Regulations	Adoption & Enforcement	R&D/Further Study	Education & Training	All Tall Buildings	Selected Other Buildings	Related	Unrelated
Increased Structural Integrity	1	1	✓	✓	✓	✓	✓	✓	✓	✓	
		2	✓	✓		✓		✓	✓		✓
		3	✓	✓		✓		✓			✓
Enhanced Fire Endurance of Structures	2	4	✓	✓		✓		✓			✓
		5		✓		✓		✓			✓
		6	✓	✓	✓	✓		✓			✓
		7		✓	✓			✓	✓		✓
New Methods for Fire Resistant Design of Structures	3	8	✓	✓	✓	✓		✓	✓	✓	
		9	✓	✓		✓	✓	✓	✓		✓
		10	✓	✓	✓		✓	✓	✓	✓	
		11	✓			✓	✓	✓	✓		✓
Improved Active Fire Protection	4	12	✓	✓		✓		✓		✓	
		13	✓	✓		✓		✓		✓	
		14	✓	✓		✓		✓	✓	✓	
		15	✓	✓		✓		✓	✓	✓	

Category	#									
Improved Building Evacuation	16	✓		✓	✓		✓	✓		✓
	17	✓		✓	✓	✓	✓	✓		✓
	18				✓		✓	✓	✓	✓
	19			✓	✓	✓	✓	✓	✓	✓
	20				✓	✓	✓	✓	✓	✓
Improved Emergency Response	21	✓			✓	✓	✓	✓	✓	✓
	22	✓			✓	✓	✓	✓	✓	✓
	23			✓	✓	✓	✓	✓	✓	✓
	24			✓	✓	✓	✓		✓	✓
Improved Procedures and Practices	25	✓	✓			✓	✓	✓	✓	✓
	26	✓	✓		✓	✓	✓	✓	✓	✓
	27		✓	✓	✓	✓	✓		✓	✓
	28		✓	✓	✓	✓		✓	✓	✓
Education and Training	29		✓	✓	✓	✓		✓	✓	✓
	30	✓		✓	✓	✓		✓	✓	✓

Group 2: Enhanced Fire Endurance of Structures

The procedures and practices used to ensure the fire endurance of structures be enhanced by improving the technical basis for construction classifications and fire resistance ratings, and the technical basis for standard fire resistance testing methods, use of the "structural frame" approach to fire resistance ratings, and developing in-service performance requirements and conformance criteria for sprayed fire-resistive materials.

Recommendation # 4 - NIST recommends evaluating, and where needed improving, the technical basis for determining appropriate construction classification and fire rating requirements (especially for tall buildings)—and making related code changes as much as possible—by explicitly considering factors including:

- Timely access by emergency responders and full evacuation of occupants, or the time required to burnout without partial collapse;
- The extent to which redundancy in active fire protection (sprinkler and standpipe, fire alarm, and smoke management) systems should be credited for occupant life safety;
- The need for redundancy in fire protection systems that are critical to structural integrity;
- The ability of the structure and local floor systems to withstand a maximum credible fire scenario without collapse, recognizing that sprinklers could be compromised not operational or non-existent;
- Compartmentation requirements (e.g., 12,0000 square feet) to protect the structure, including fire rated doors, and automatic enclosures and limiting air supply (e.g., thermally resistant window assemblies) to retard fire spread in buildings with large, open floor plans.
- The effect of spaces containing unusually large fuel concentrations for expected occupancy of the building; and,
- The extent to which fire control systems, including suppression by automatic or manual means, should be credited as part of the prevention of fire spread.

Recommendation # 5 - NIST recommends that the technical basis for the century-old standard for fire resistance testing of components, assemblies, and systems be improved through a national effort. Necessary guidance also should be developed for extrapolating the results of tested assemblies to prototypical building systems. A key step in fulfilling this recommendation is to establish a capability for studying and testing the components, assemblies, and systems under realistic fire and load conditions.

Recommendation # 6 - NIST recommends the development of criteria, test methods, and standards (1) for the in-service performance of sprayed fire-resistive materials (SFRM, also commonly referred to as fireproofing or insulation used to protect structural components; and (2) to ensure that these materials, as installed, conform to conditions in tests used to establish the fire resistance rating of components, assemblies, and systems.

Recommendation # 7 - NIST recommends the adoption and use of the "structural frame" approach to fire resistance ratings.

Group 3: New Methods for Fire-Resistant Design of Structures

The procedures and practices used in fire resistant design of structures should be enhanced by requiring an objective that uncontrolled fires result in burnout without partial or global (total) collapse. Performance-based methods are an alternative to prescriptive design methods. This effort should include the development and evaluation of new fire-resistive coating materials and technologies and evaluation of the fire performance of conventional and high-performance structural materials.

Recommendation # 8 - NIST recommends that the fire resistance of structures be enhanced by requiring a performance objective that uncontrolled building fires result in burnout without partial or global (total) collapse.

Recommendation # 9 - NIST recommends the development of (1) performance-based standards and code provisions, as an alternative to current prescriptive design methods, to enable the design and retrofit of structures to resist real building fire conditions, including the ability to achieve the performance objective of burnout without structural or floor collapse; and (2) tools, guidelines, and test methods necessary to evaluate the fire performance of the structure as a whole system.

Recommendation # 10 - NIST recommends the development and evaluation of new fire-resistive coating materials, systems, and technologies with significantly enhanced performance and durability to provide protection following major events.

Recommendation # 11 - NIST recommends that the performance and suitability of advanced structural steel, reinforced and pre-stressed concrete, and other high-performance material systems be evaluated for use under conditions expected in building fires.

Group 4: Improved Active Fire Protection

Active fire protection systems (i.e. sprinklers, standpipes/hoses, fire alarms, and smoke management systems) should be enhanced through improvements to design, performance, reliability, and redundancy of such systems.

Recommendation # 12 - NIST recommends that the performance and possibly the redundancy of active fire protection systems (sprinklers, standpipes/hoses, fire alarms, and smoke management systems) in buildings be enhanced to accommodate greater risks associated with increasing building height and population, increased use of open spaces, high-risk building activities, fire department response limits, transient fuel loads, and higher threat profile.

Recommendation # 13 - NIST recommends that fire alarm and communication systems in buildings be developed to provide continuous, reliable, and accurate information on the status of life safety conditions at a level of detail sufficient to manage the evacuation process in building fire emergencies; all communication and control paths in buildings need to be designed and installed to have the same resistance to failure and increased survivability above that specified in the present codes.

Recommendation # 14 - NIST recommends that control panels at fire/emergency command sections in buildings be adapted to accept and interpret a large quantity of more reliable information from the active fire protection systems that provide tactical decision aids to fireground commanders, including water flow rates from pressure and flow measurement devices, and that standards for their performance be developed.

Recommendation # 15 - NIST recommends that systems be developed and implemented for: (1) real-time off-site secure transmission of valuable information from fire alarm and other monitored building systems for use by emergency responders, at any location, to enhance situational awareness and response decisions and maintain safe and efficient operations; and (2) preservation of that information either off-site or in a black box that will survive a fire or other building failure for purposes of subsequent investigations and analysis. Standards for the performance of such systems should be developed, and their use should be required.

Group 5: Improved Building Evacuation

Building evacuation should be improved to include system designs that facilitate safe and rapid egress, methods for ensuring clear and timely emergency communications to occupants, better occupant preparedness regarding their roles and duties for evacuation during emergencies, and incorporation of appropriate egress technologies.

Recommendation # 16 - NIST recommends that public agencies, non-profit organizations concerned with building and fire safety and building owners and managers develop and carry out public education and training campaigns, jointly and on a nationwide scale, to improve building occupants' preparedness for evacuation in case of building emergencies.

Recommendation # 17 - NIST recommends that tall buildings be designed to accommodate timely full building evacuation of occupants when required in building-specific or large-scale emergencies such as widespread power outages, major earthquakes, tornadoes, hurricanes, without sufficient advanced warning, fires, explosions, and terrorist attacks. Building size, population, function, and iconic status should be taken into account in designing the egress system. Stairwell capacity and stair discharge door width should be adequate to accommodate counterflow due to emergency access by responders.

Recommendation # 18 - NIST recommends that egress systems be designed: (1) to maximize remoteness of egress components (i.e., stairs, elevators, exits) without negatively impacting the average travel distance; (2) to maintain their functional integrity and survivability under foreseeable building-specific or large-scale emergencies; and (3) with consistent layouts, standard signage, and guidance so that systems become intuitive and obvious to building occupants during evacuations.

Recommendation # 19 - NIST recommends that building owners, managers, and emergency responders develop a joint plan and take steps to ensure that accurate emergency information is communicated in a timely manner to enhance the situational awareness of building occupants and emergency responders affected by an event. This should be accomplished through better coordination of information among different emergency responder groups, efficient sharing of that information among building occupants and emergency responders, more robust design of emergency public address systems, improved emergency responder communications systems, and use of the Emergency Broadcast System (now known as the Integrated Public Alert and Warning System) and Community Emergency Alert Network.

Recommendation # 20 - NIST recommends that the full range of current and next generation evacuation technologies should be evaluated for future use, including protected/hardened elevators, exterior escape devices, and stairwell descent devices, which may allow all occupants an equal opportunity for evacuation and facilitate emergency response access.

Group 6: Improved Emergency Response

Technologies and procedures for emergency response should be improved to enable better access to buildings, response operations, emergency communications, and command and control in large scale emergencies.

Recommendation # 21 - NIST recommends the installation of fire-protected and structurally hardened elevators to improve emergency response activities in tall buildings by providing timely emergency access to responders and allowing evacuation of mobility-impaired building occupants.

Recommendation # 22 - NIST recommends the installation, inspection, and testing of emergency communications systems, radio communications, and associated operating protocols to ensure that the systems and protocols: (1) are effective for large-scale emergencies in buildings with challenging radio frequency propagation environments; and (2) can be used to identify, locate, and track emergency responders within indoor building environments and in the field.

Recommendation # 23 - NIST recommends the establishment and implementation of detailed procedure and methods for gathering, processing, and delivering critical information through integration of relevant voice, video, graphical, and written data to enhance the situational awareness of all emergency responders. An information intelligence sector should be established to coordinate the effort for each incident.

Recommendation # 24 - NIST recommends the establishment and implementation of codes and protocols for ensuring effective and uninterrupted operation of the command and control system for large-scale building emergencies.

Group 7: Improved Procedures and Practices

The procedures and practices used in the design, construction, maintenance, and operation of buildings should be improved to include encouraging code compliance by nongovernmental and quasi-governmental entities, adoption and application of egress and sprinkler requirements in codes for existing buildings, and retention and availability of building documents over the life of a building.

Recommendation # 25 - Nongovernmental and quasi-governmental entities own or lease buildings and are not subject to building and fire safety code requirements of any governmental jurisdiction are nevertheless concerned about the safety of the building occupants and the responding emergency personnel. NIST recommends that such entities be encouraged to provide a level of safety that equals or exceeds that would be provided by strict compliance with the code requirements of an appropriate governmental jurisdiction.

Recommendation # 26 - NIST recommends that state and local jurisdictions adopt and aggressively enforce available provisions in building codes to ensure that egress and sprinkler requirements are met by existing buildings. Further, occupancy requirements should be modified where needed (such as when there are assembly use spaces within an office building) to meet the requirements in model building codes.

Recommendation # 27 - NIST recommends that building codes incorporate a provision that requires building owners to retain documents, including supporting calculations and test data, related to building design, construction, maintenance and modifications over the entire life of the building. Means should be developed for offsite storage and maintenance of the documents. In addition, NIST recommends that relevant building information be made available in suitably designed hard copy or electronic format for use by emergency responders.

Recommendation # 28 - NIST recommends that the role of the "Design Professional in Responsible Charge" be clarified to ensure that: (1) all appropriate design professionals (including e.g., the fire protection engineer) are part of the design team providing the standard of care when designing buildings employing innovative or unusual fire safety systems; and (2) all appropriate design professionals (including, e.g. the structural engineer) are part of the design team providing the standard of care when designing the structure to resist fires, in buildings that employ innovative or unusual structural and fire safety systems.

Group 8: Education and Training

The professional skills of building and fire safety professionals should be upgraded through a national education and training efforts for fire protection engineers, structural engineers, and architects. The skills of the building regulatory and fire service personnel should also be upgraded to provide sufficient understanding and the necessary skills to conduct the review, inspection, and approval tasks for which they are responsible.

Recommendation # 29 - NIST recommends that the continuing education curricula be developed and programs be implemented for (1) training fire protection engineers and architects in structural engineering principles and design; and (2) training structural engineers, architects, fire protection engineers, and code enforcement officials in modern fire protection principles and technologies, including fire-resistive design of structures, and (3) training building regulatory and fire service personnel to upgrade their understanding and skills to conduct the review, inspection, and approval tasks for which they are responsible.

Recommendation # 30 - NIST recommends that academic, professional short-course, and web-based training materials in the use of computational fire dynamics and thermostructural analysis tools be developed and delivered to strengthen the base of available technical capabilities and human resources.

NIST also documented at the close of its report a list of standards that are affected by its 30 recommendations (see Table 3-2).

Relevance of the NIST Findings and Recommendations to an All Hazards Approach toward Construction

The NIST findings and subsequent recommendations make an assumption that the lessons from the WTC are relevant to multiple hazards and not just to helping buildings stand longer so that the people safely evacuate the next high-rise structure that a terrorist group strikes with a large fuel-laden commercial aircraft.

Within their report, NIST noted that most of the 30 recommendations have relevance to buildings that are subjected to blast, earthquakes, fire, and even wind and water events. The report also describes the importance of each member of the construction team knowing and fulfilling their respective roles in the design, construction, inspection, and operation of a building.

It is for these reasons that the NIST report on the WTC warrants serious review and consideration by all segments of the building construction team: owner, architect, engineer, contractors, building product manufacturer and suppliers, building codes and standards generating community, code enforcement personnel, and building operations and maintenance staff.

Affected Standard	Group Number	Recommendation
American Concrete Institute, ACI 318 -Building Code Requirements for Structural Concrete	1. Increased Structural Integrity 3. New Methods for Fire Resistant Design of Structures	1, 3, 8, 9, 11
American Institute of Architects, AIA MASTERSPEC – Master Specification System for Design Professionals and the Building/Construction Industry	2. Enhanced Fire Endurance of Structures 3. New Methods for Fire Resistant Design of Structures	6, 10
American Institute of Architects Practice Guidelines	7. Improved Procedures and Practices	28
American Institute of Steel Construction Specification for Structural Steel Buildings	1. Increased Structural Integrity 3. New Methods for Fire Resistant Design of Structures	1, 3, 8, 9, 11
American Society of Civil Engineers, ASCE 7 – Minimum Design Loads for Buildings and Other Structures	1. Increased Structural Integrity 3. New Methods for Fire Resistant Design of Structures	1, 2, 3, 8, 9
American Society of Civil Engineers, ASCE 29 – Standard Calculation Methods for Structural Fire Protection	1. Increased Structural Integrity 3. New Methods for Fire Resistant Design of Structures	1, 8, 9
American Society of Mechanical Engineers, ASME A 17 – Elevators and Escalators, and A 17.1 – Safety Code for Elevators and Escalators	5. Improved Building Evacuation 6. Improved Emergency Response	17, 20, 21
American Society of Mechanical Engineers, ASME A 17.3 – Safety Code for Existing Elevators and Escalators	7. Improved Procedures and Practices	26
Association of the Wall and Ceiling Industry AWCI 12 – Design Selection Utilizing Sprayed Fire-Resistive Materials AWCI 12-A – Standard Practice for the Testing and Inspection of Field Applied Fire-Resistive Materials AWCI 12-B – Standard Practice for the Testing and Inspection of Field Applied Intumescent Fire-Resistive Materials	2. Enhanced Fire Endurance of Structures 3. New Methods for Fire Resistant Design of Structures	6, 10
ASTM International Committee E 06, Performance of Buildings; Subcommittee E 06.77, High-Rise Building External Evacuation Devices	5. Improved Building Evacuation	20
ASTM International, ASTM E 119 – Standard Test Methods for Fire Tests of Building Construction and Materials	2. Enhanced Fire Endurance of Structures 3. New Methods for Fire Resistant Design of Structures	5, 11
Department of Homeland Security, National Incident Management System (NIMS)	6. Improved Emergency Response	23, 24
Department of Homeland Security, National Response Plan (NRP)	6. Improved Emergency Response	23, 24
Department of Homeland Security, SAFECOM	6. Improved Emergency Response	22, 23, 24
Federal Communications Commission, Emergency Responder Radio Communications Regulations	6. Improved Emergency Response	22, 23, 24
International Code Commission/American National Standards Institute, ICC/ANSI A117.1 – Accessible and Usable Buildings and Facilities	5. Improved Building Evacuation 6. Improved Emergency Response	16, 20, 21

Table 3-2a & b

National Institute of Standards and Technology World Trade Center Report, Table 9-2a "Standards Affected by Recommendations," and Table 9-2b "Model Codes Affected by the Recommendations"

Table 3-2a & b
(*Continued*)

Affected Standard	Group Number	Recommendation
International Organization for Standardization, ISO 834 – Fire Resistance Tests	2. Enhanced Fire Endurance of Structures 3. New Methods for Fire Resistant Design of Structures	5, 11
National Fire Protection Association, NFPA 1 – Fire Prevention Code	4. Enhanced Active Fire Protection 7. Improved Procedures and Practices	12, 13, 14, 15, 26
National Fire Protection Association, NFPA 13 – Installation of Sprinkler Systems	4. Enhanced Active Fire Protection	12
National Fire Protection Association, NFPA 14 – Installation of Standpipe and Hose Systems	4. Enhanced Active Fire Protection	12
National Fire Protection Association, NFPA 20 – Installation of Stationary Pumps for Fire Protection	4. Enhanced Active Fire Protection	12
National Fire Protection Association, NFPA 70 – National Electrical Code	6. Improved Emergency Response	21, 22
National Fire Protection Association, NFPA 72 – National Fire Alarm Code	4. Enhanced Active Fire Protection	12, 13, 14, 15
National Fire Protection Association, NFPA 90A – Standard for Installation of Air-Conditioning and Ventilating Systems	4. Enhanced Active Fire Protection	12
National Fire Protection Association, NFPA 101 – Life Safety Code	4. Enhanced Active Fire Protection 5. Improved Building Evacuation 7. Improved Procedures and Practices	12, 13, 14, 15, 16, 17, 18, 19, 20, 21, 26
National Fire Protection Association, NFPA 251 – Standard Methods of Tests of Fire Endurance of Building Construction and Materials	2. Enhanced Fire Endurance of Structures 3. New Methods for Fire Resistant Design of Structures	5, 11
National Fire Protection Association, NFPA 297 – Guide on Principles and Practices for Communications Systems	6. Improved Emergency Response	22
National Fire Protection Association, NFPA 1221 – Standard for the Installation, Maintenance, and Use of Emergency Service Communications Systems	6. Improved Emergency Response	21, 22, 23, 24
National Fire Protection Association, NFPA 1500 – Standard on Fire Department Occupational Safety and Health	6. Improved Emergency Response	21, 23, 24
National Fire Protection Association, NFPA 1561 – Standard on Emergency Services Incident Management System	6. Improved Emergency Response	21, 23, 24
National Fire Protection Association, NFPA 1620 – Recommended Practice for Pre-Incident Planning	6. Improved Emergency Response	21, 23, 24
National Fire Protection Association, NFPA 1710 – Standard for the Organization and Deployment of Fire Suppression Operations, Emergency Medical Operations, and Special Operations to the Public by Career Fire Departments	6. Improved Emergency Response	21, 23, 24
Underwriters Laboratories, UL 263 – Fire Tests of Building Construction and Materials	2. Enhanced Fire Endurance of Structures 3. New Methods for Fire Resistant Design of Structures	5, 9, 11

Table 3-2a & b
(Continued)

Affected Model Code	Group	Recommendation
International Building Code	1. Increased structural integrity 2. Enhanced fire endurance of structures 3. New methods for fire-resistant design of structures 4. Improved active fire protection 5. Improved building evacuation 6. Improved emergency response 7. Improved procedures and practices 8. Education and training	1–24, 26–29
International Existing Building Code	7. Improved procedures and practices	26
International Fire Code	7. Improved procedures and practices	26
National Fire Protection Association, NFPA 5000: Building Construction and Safety Code	1. Increased structural integrity 2. Enhanced fire endurance of structures 3. New methods for fire resistant design of structures 4. Improved active fire protection 5. Improved building evacuation 6. Improved emergency response 7. Improved procedures and practices 8. Education and training	1–24, 26–29

In the over 650 formal written comments that NIST received in the summer and early fall of 2005 when a first draft of their final report including these 30 recommendations was released, many commentators offered basic endorsement of approximately half of the recommendations and suggested further study of the other half. Of those calling for further study, the majority noted that they believed that further data or research was needed to document or better explain how a specific recommendation would actually improve public safety in buildings under stress conditions or, specifically, would have made any changes in the number of people who would have survived the WTC collapse.

Examples of the latter were comments on how any of the proposed changes to building codes in the area of progressive collapse would have changed the events on 9/11 (or for that matter the Oklahoma City bombing in 1995). Several others asked NIST to substantiate with data from past events that there indeed was any "increased risk" in taller buildings to warrant some of the additional fire protection requirements recommended by NIST in their report.

Most notably, NIST was asked to look at the cost of developing and/or applying many of these recommendations to the construction community and to the general public at large. A number of others suggested that NIST look at working with the construction community to make some of these recommended actions voluntary guidelines that the owner of either a new high-rise under design or an existing building undergoing renovation could pick and choose which features were cost-appropriate given the nature of the building, its occupancy use and its location to other buildings, which might have a high level of risk from either a man-made or natural disaster.

The response to the NIST report thus far has been fairly universal in recommending that not all buildings, indeed not all high-rise buildings should include all of the features called for in the NIST recommendations. Existing high-rise buildings (see Chapter 6, "Existing Buildings: Inspections and Retrofitting") need to remain commercially viable within their communities and therefore any amendments to existing state and/or local building rehabilitation requirements to include a number of the 30 recommendations should be carefully considered on the basis not only of cost but on the likelihood that the building indeed will be subjected to multiple events over its lifetime that may exceed the building's existing structural integrity, egress, and other life-safety elements.

This clearly has been the case in preliminary feedback received not only from design and construction firms, building owners, and operators but also from the membership of the nation's model building and fire code organizations who have committees that are now actually considering adding new provisions based upon several of the WTC report recommendations in the next editions of their codes and standards (see Chapter 2, page 34–37). NIST has actively participated in those committee meetings. On March 24, 2006, the ICC received the first 19 proposed changes to the model codes as submitted by code experts associated with the two International Code Council (ICC) committees, the National Institute of Building Sciences, and the General Services Administration.

In addition to the ongoing code update effort, NIST itself is continuing to conduct research based upon its findings. As will be covered in Chapter 5, NIST continues work on a multiyear research project to develop criteria for the prevention of progressive collapse.

Figure 3-13

High-rise under construction in New York City, 2002

Among the best practices and documents being reviewed by NIST is a 1968 standard from the United Kingdom to avoid progressive collapse in "large panel construction."

LESSONS FROM THE ATTACK ON THE PENTAGON

On September 11, 2001, 190 people died at the Pentagon in Arlington, Virginia; 126 were employees at their stations inside the Pentagon and 64 were passengers and crew on the hijacked American Airlines Flight 77. At approximately 350 mph, the aircraft slammed into the outer three rings of the five-ringed structure. The strike occurred at 9:40 a.m. By 10:10 a.m., a walled section of the west side of the Pentagon that was penetrated by the plane collapsed. Because of the Pentagon's original design and recent retrofitting with more blastproof windows and structural features, emergency personnel were able to evacuate all of the injured prior to that collapse.

The fires from the plane, its fuel and the office furniture and papers were so intense that it wasn't until 1:00 p.m., however, that the fires had subsided enough for rescuers to enter the impact area.

The American Society of Civil Engineers (ASCE), in coordination with the DoD, assembled a team of structural and other experts to undertake a seven-month study of the attack on the Pentagon and offer findings and recommendations concerning that event and the design, construction, and retrofit of DoD structures and other structures that might be subjected to such disasters. On January 23, 2003, the Pentagon Building Performance Study, headed by Paul F. Mlakar, PE, of the U.S. Army Corps of Engineers, issued their report with the following findings.

Original Construction of Pentagon

Constructed during World War II, the Pentagon was designed to support heavier loads than normal office construction at that time. It was envisioned prior to the beginning of its construction in September 1941, that following United States participation in World War II (the designers anticipated ultimate entry into that conflict), the Pentagon would continue its life as a major storage facility for government records and files. That construction, plus a blastproofing retrofit upgrade that had been completed for major portions of the west side of the Pentagon prior to 9/11, put the building in good stead to minimize the amount of destruction and losses of life from the impact of the American Airlines plane.

In their study, the engineers noted that the plane's impact destroyed approximately 50 support columns on the first floor and six columns on the second in the exterior wall. The fire that erupted from aviation fuel, airplane, and building contents caused "moderate damage to the Pentagon's reinforced concrete frame in relatively small areas on the first and second floors which later collapsed."

The original structural design helped arrest the progression of collapse and resultant to structural design elements include short spans between structural supports; redundant and alternate paths of the floor system, allowing for one support system to redistribute the load should another fail, providing substantial continuity of the steel floor reinforcement through the supports. Many columns withstood extreme lateral loads, from the impact of the plane;

and the floor system from its original design was capable of significant load redistribution without collapse when several adjacent supporting columns were removed.

Pentagon Retrofit

The Pentagon Building Performance Study went on to note that a large number of lives indeed were saved because the plane struck the one portion of the Pentagon where the Pentagon renovation program had completed its work installing blast-resistant windows and mullions. Indeed losses of life were also reduced because sections of the Pentagon immediately adjacent to the point of impact had recently been unoccupied in preparation for renovation work. In particular, the report noted that "windows installed as a part of the Pentagon Renovation Program performed well in resisting the aircraft impact and pressure from the massive ignition of fuel."

Areas for Future Research

The report recommended that the Federal government undertake further research and "development in the prevention of progressive collapse and structural response to improbable events."

Other research for the Federal DoD consideration included:

- "The load carrying capacity of columns and other structural elements after they have been severely deformed."
- "The vertical load on floor systems resulting from a horizontally deformed column, and"
- "The energy-absorbing capacity of concrete elements when they are subjected to impact loads that result in large deformation."

In addition to the preceding findings, the Pentagon disaster demonstrated the importance of having a close working relationship between the architect, engineers, building product manufacturers, and construction contractors to assure that the updated windows mandated by the Pentagon renovation program were indeed manufactured and installed properly.

In Chapters 5 and 6, we will look at existing code provisions and construction guidelines that are now available to address some of the lessons learned from the attack on the Pentagon.

LESSONS FROM THE ANTHRAX ATTACKS

Letters containing anthrax spores were mailed to news agencies in New York and Florida within one week of 9/11. By mid-October 2001, an anthrax-laden letter was received and opened at the Senate Hart Building in Washington., D.C., after having been processed through (and contaminated) the nearby Brentwood postal facility in the Nation's Capital.

All these events caused five deaths and 23 illnesses and set off a wave of concern over the security of the U.S. mail, with many businesses setting up special provisions and locations for handling and opening their daily mail.

Figure 3-14
Post-anthrax attack, checking the mail

Unlike the WTC and Pentagon disasters, no major Federal or private sector studies were commissioned with public findings released that addressed the impact of the anthrax attacks on the structure, design, or operation of the Federal postal facilities or the private sector or government office buildings in which the anthrax-laden letters were either processed or opened.

The U.S. Postal Service, General Services Administration, and Office of the Architect of the U.S. Capitol, all conducted internal reviews of their mail-processing procedures and of the air handling systems for their buildings and have taken steps to modify those systems to reduce potential future losses of life or damage from any future anthrax threats.

In general, lessons learned from the anthrax attacks as applied by both the public and private sector, beyond those that are mail-process oriented, have been in three areas:

1. The hardening of the building envelope
2. The design and use of enhanced filtration and air-cleaning systems
3. Design and use of emergency stop-start, pressurization, and other control strategies

These areas also will be looked at in greater detail in Chapters 5 and 6

LESSONS FROM NATURAL DISASTERS: 2004 AND 2005 HURRICANE SEASONS

In addition to the 2001 man-made disasters, the issue of public safety in the built environment and the adequacy of the provisions of our current codes and standards also have been challenged by the magnitude of destruction caused by the 2004 and 2005 hurricane season in the United States. With the United States currently predicted to be in only year 5 of a 15- to 20-year cycle of more intense hurricanes, lessons learned from the events of 2004 and 2005 are of major importance to those owning or living in buildings along the Atlantic and Gulf Coasts.

Even though the 2006 season has been much less severe than the record-breaking 2005 season with its 27 named storms, the multiyear projection of more severe storms has remained unchanged.

While Hurricane Katrina with its over 1,836 deaths stands out as the most catastrophic of U.S. hurricanes, its impact on building codes and standards was not as significant as were the hurricanes that struck the United States during the 2004 season—the largest of which were Charley, Ivan, Frances, and Jeanne with a loss of over 44 lives in the United States and combined damage totalling $45 billion.

The 2004 hurricanes that struck Florida provided some significant lessons learned regarding the upgraded statewide Florida building code. Research conducted by the State of Florida (in conjunction with its universities) and by the U.S. Department of Housing and Urban Development (HUD) documented how much better homes built to the 2002 Florida Statewide building code performed over those built prior to the implementation of that code.

Many of these findings were shared with the public and private sectors at a February 2005 hurricane symposium held in Tampa, Florida, and hosted by the state of Florida, the ICC, Federal Emergency Management Agency (FEMA), the Institute for Business and Home Safety and the Building Officials Association of Florida.

Additionally, the 2004 hurricane events exposed several areas in residential construction design and construction, especially as regarded wind-driven water penetration around windows and soffits that have caused the state of Florida to currently consider amending these sections of their construction code (see Chapters 5 and 6).

The 2005 hurricane season with its devastating storms in the Gulf Coast documented the importance of the effective adoption and enforcement of the most recent editions of building codes with hurricane provisions by states and localities that previously did not have such codes or enforcement mechanisms in place. For example, as follow-up to the 2005 storms, in April 2006, Louisiana's legislature adopted a uniform statewide building code

Figure 3-15

James Lee Witt, Executive Director, International Code Council at 2005 hurricane symposium, Tampa, Florida

and Mississippi adopted a mandatory building code for its three Gulf coast counties . The June, 2006, NIST publication, "Performance of Physical Structures in Hurricane Katrina and Hurricane Rita: A Reconnaissance Report" applauded those actions and encouraged stricter code enforcement throughout hurricane prone regions of the nation.

Application of Lessons Learned

On all fronts lessons are learned from the man-made and natural disasters of 2001 to 2005. As noted in Chapter 2, the ICC, National Fire Protection Association, and some major jurisdictions, including New York City, have already fast tracked a few findings and lessons from the WTC disaster into their codes and standards.

Lessons learned from the Pentagon attack are being used to speed up DoD retrofits of their buildings and are shaping a research agenda for the Pentagon and its Federal partners including the NIST. Lessons learned from the anthrax events while slow to develop are being applied to building design and retrofit considerations regarding raising the level of air intakes for buildings and research into new air filtration systems.

As noted earlier, in the Southeastern United States building codes are being adopted and/or upgraded and design, products, and installation processes are being reviewed to make buildings more resistant to water penetration from hurricanes. It will take a considerable amount of time (five years or more) for the majority of the recommendations from these disaster reports to generate new provisions in the nation's existing model building codes and standards and for elected officials to adopt and begin to enforce those provisions in their building codes.

While building owners and their colleagues on the construction team await the outcome of such efforts, there are, however, actions that the construction community can take now within existing codes, standards, and guidelines that can add additional protection and security to the American public from some terrorist events as well as from natural disasters.

WHAT PROVISIONS ARE CURRENTLY AVAILABLE IN OUR CODES, STANDARDS, AND OTHER DOCUMENTS TO PROTECT THE PUBLIC?

Looking beyond the areas within the NIST and ASCE reports for further study or action as the result of the 9/11 disasters, and the natural disasters of 2004 and 2005, there are already in place in the United States a wide range of building code provisions and construction practices and guidelines that owners, architects, engineers, contractors, building product manufacturers, and other members of the construction team can use to enhance public safety if they are either applied voluntarily or mandated under state or local statutes and ordinances.

At this time, recommendations for new construction and renovation from NIST and others fall more into the category of advisory information to owners, architects, engineers, and building operations and maintenance personnel. That being the case, what tools, codes, and standards are already out there that can be used by the construction team to enhance the safety of their occupants from multihazards—both man-made and natural events?

Figure 3-16
Federal Building,
Portland, Oregon

Figure 3-17
City Hall,
Philadelphia,
Pennsylvania

Figure 3-18
Mid-rise building in Washington, D.C., undergoing renovation

These resources fall into one of the following four groupings, which will be discussed in Part II of this book:

- Risk assessment tools
- Construction standards and guidelines
- Building and fire codes
- Recent changes to statutes and ordinances

Part II   Existing Guidelines, Codes and Standards, and How They Protect Buildings and the Public from Disasters

Building codes and standards have evolved to address new technologies, construction materials, processes, and natural hazards, and not to protect buildings or people from terrorist acts. Nevertheless, there are provisions in modern building codes and standards and Federal guidelines that can provide greater public protection where the owner finds the situation warrants their application.

OVERVIEW

While the professional societies, government agencies and model codes and standards bodies noted in the previous chapters are considering making further modifications to their codes and standards to address a number of lessons that have been learned from the World Trade Center, the anthrax attacks, and recent hurricanes, effectively following the provisions of existing codes, updated standards, construction guidelines, and risk assessment tools and applying basic security procedures can provide greater public safety in new and retrofit construction.

Designed to afford the public a minimum level of health and life safety in all types of structures, building codes and standards have evolved to address new technologies, construction materials, processes, and natural disaster hazards. Codes and standards have not, however, evolved to address the kinds of hazards now presented by modern terrorists; people who have an infinite amount of time and patience to plan and carry out attacks on our people and our nation's infrastructure.

In preparing Part II of this book, a small survey was sent out to public safety departments and architectural and engineering firms across the nation regarding what they were doing differently since 9/11 to address lessons that were emerging from those events.

In general, the private sector noted that while few if any changes had been made to the codes and standards they followed, a number of them did spend more time than before with their clients conducting risk-threat analysis of the buildings that were being designed and, where necessary, were bringing in security experts to provide recommendations as to cost-effective approaches to address any risks that were identified.

Several survey respondents noted that many of these risks did not necessarily call for new provisions in our building codes and standards but could be readily addressed by following guidelines provided by some segments of the construction community or, in the case of risk from blast, looking at following some of the new Federal building setback provisions and the seismic safety provisions that exist in current model codes that make the buildings more resistant to structural collapse.

The public sector respondents likewise noted they did not think the events of 9/11 warranted significant changes to our existing codes and standards. Four major jurisdictions responding to the survey noted that they made a few such changes and several more building departments reported that together with their fire-safety services they had adopted new or modified existing ordinances governing evacuation provisions for high-rise structures.

The following three chapters address those provisions and offer guidance and some best practices for more disaster resistant construction. Chapter 4, "Beginning with the End in Mind: Assessing Risk, Threat, and Mitigation Strategies," addresses the basic philosophy of our codes and standards and how to assess risk and threats to determine strategies to protect our buildings and their occupants. Chapters 5 and 6 build upon that background by looking at what existing codes, standards, and guidelines make sense for us to consider in new and renovated structures. This includes a review of what construction guidelines can be drawn upon from Federal agencies that further enhance security.

bomb throwing anarchists of the 1890s and early 1900s, or Timothy McVey, is to make a political statement, cause panic among the public and especially now do as much damage to the American economy, infrastructure, and psyche as possible. Clearly their objective is twofold, make Americans afraid of their daily routines: (1) boarding an airplane, riding the subway or working in the upper stories of a modern high-rise building; and (2) do damage to our economy by adding additional costs to our nation to try and mitigate those fears. This is exactly what the terrorists are after wherever they strike, here in the United States or overseas in Great Britain, Spain, or the Middle East.

Al Qaeda would like to see our codes and standards modified to require all high-rises to become fortresses or have us ban high-rises altogether and thus have to expend our resources to promoting urban sprawl, thereby forcing us to purchase and use more oil.

And just exactly what would we accomplish by making such changes besides making all buildings or at least a certain class of buildings uneconomical to build, own, and operate?

No sooner would we pass such laws, emptying and pulling down our existing high-rises than the terrorists will find some totally different part of our infrastructure to attack using some totally different delivery mechanism or weapon: agriculture, transportation nodes, or healthcare system. The list is endless and so are the patience and resources of terrorists—both domestic and foreign.

While the preceding is true, it is equally true that without giving in to the objectives of terrorism, there are things that we have already done and can do in the future with our construction codes, standards, guidelines, and practices and the roles of members of the construction team that do make economic sense in the long as well as in the short term. The All Hazards Approach addresses realistic levels of the added threat of terrorism but also addresses the extreme stress put on buildings by natural disasters.

To take such actions, however, first we need to understand our new levels of risk and what guidelines, codes, and standards we can use now to mitigate those risks.

Figure 4-2

Aerial photo of suburban sprawl outside Baltimore, Maryland

RISK ASSESSMENT TOOLS

> Risk management is a systematic approach to the discovery and treatment of risks facing an organization or facility. The goal is to help objectively state, document, and rank risk, and prepare a plan for implementation.
> —The American Society of Heating, Refrigerating and Air Conditioning Engineers report, "Risk Management Guidance for Health, Safety and Environmental Security Under Extraordinary Incidents."

So 9/11 and the natural disasters of 2004 and 2005 have occurred, the Federal and state governments and the engineering community have conducted and released major studies and issued their recommendations for possible changes in our construction codes, standards, and practices to address those findings, and some segments of the previously mentioned community have begun to work on considering them. But you as an owner, architect, engineer, or other member of the construction team pursuing the design and construction of a new building or renovation do not have access to any of the pending new codes, standards, and guidelines. What is out there to guide you in your decisions regarding the safety and security of the future occupants of your structure?

Beginning with the End in Mind: To Know What To Do We Must Assess Risk

Every building, from a single family residence to an iconic high-rise commercial building over the course of the 50 to 100 years that they are used are going to be subjected multiple times to natural and/or man-made events that stress that structure perhaps to the very limits of one or more aspects of its design. The highest probability is that these events will be by "natural" and not man-made causes: floods, heavy snowstorms, hurricanes, tornadoes, and earthquakes. On the man-made side, fires accidentally or deliberately set also are a realistic event in the life of any building.

Acts of domestic or foreign terrorism, be they blast, biochemical, or even radiological, while they have an extremely low probability of occurring in any building's life, nonetheless can occur as we have seen and can impact some buildings somewhere in this nation either as the direct target of an attack or as they are impacted by collateral damage.

Our building codes and standards include within their provisions requirements for a known level of risk from natural disasters and accidental fires and provide the building owner with a set of design minimums. Elected officials at either the state or local level through their police powers adopt and mandate the enforcement of such codes at levels of safety that they deem appropriate to their community (e.g., wind and snow loads and seismic design).

In some cases, elected officials have chosen to either not adopt such codes and standards or have chosen to adopt codes and standards with provisions below those that are recommended for their particular region of the country. In those cases, building owners (and their financial backers and insurance providers) rely upon their architects, engineers, and other members of the construction team to either draw on best practices elsewhere in the nation or at a minimum use the "standard of care" and design or renovate buildings using appropriate levels of safety for the design and construction of their building.

Living in the post 9/11 world and given the lessons from the 2004 and 2005 hurricane season, there is a growing sense that best practices and the "standard of care" doctrine coupled with the litigious nature of the United States today warrant building owners to undertake some form of analysis of what are the potential risks to their building during its lifetime, and assess whether or not additional levels of safety should be designed into those structures to accommodate or mitigate that risk.

Originating in the financial and insurance communities, the field of risk analysis has evolved rapidly in the closing decades of the last century to now include the field of terrorism and natural disasters. Today different public and private sector groups have different names for their assessment tools. To name but a few: the General Services Administration (GSA) has a security risk assessment system, Federal Emergency Management Agency (FEMA) offers several risk assessment tools, the National Institute for Justice at the Department of Justice created a vulnerability assessment model, the National Institute of Standards and Technology (NIST) working with the private sector established the Building Security Rating Index, and the American Society of Heating Refrigerating and Air Conditioning Engineers (ASHRAE) produced their own risk management guide.

Regardless of their names, the purpose of risk-threat analysis or vulnerability assessment models (VAM) is to provide building owners and their design and construction team with a tool to ascertain whether actions should be taken or features should be built into their buildings beyond the mandated minimums to protect the occupants of those buildings and the structure from natural and man-made stresses to which their structure may be subjected during its lifetime.

Figure 4-3

Residential construction, Washington, D.C.

This chapter provides an overview of a number of existing methodologies and takes a more detailed look at four different methodologies: GSA's building classification and risk assessment system, FEMA's risk assessment model, NIST's more complex "Cost Effective Responses to Terrorist Risks in Constructed Facilities" and ASHRAE's "Risk Management Guidance for Health, Safety, and Environmental Security under Extraordinary Circumstances." The chapter includes links to access each of these methodologies enabling the reader to determine which one may be most appropriate to use for their building or buildings.

As will be noted in Chapter 6, these same tools aid the owner of an existing building by providing them with guidance for making a determination as to what actions they may want to take and in what time frame to modify an existing structure to enable it to withstand a natural or man-made disaster event that goes beyond the structural and safety provisions in the codes and standards to which that building was constructed.

Background on Risk Assessment

Dating back to the early and mid-1980s, several Federal agencies and national professional societies began wrestling with the question of the need for enhanced building safety and durability in the face of man-made events. Given attacks on U.S. embassies and military installations overseas, the U.S. Department of State and the Department of Defense (DoD) began in the 1980s to develop not only design guidelines and requirements to protect their employees and properties from terrorist events, but also a set of criteria through which to assess and make determinations as to which buildings were most at risk and from what threats. These efforts subsequently enabled these federal agencies to prioritize upgrades in building security and rehabilitation (like that completed on the west side of the Pentagon), and in new building design to address the most credible risks, threats, and vulnerabilities to those structures and their employees.

Figure 4-4

Hospital renovation and addition

Figure 4-5

U.S. Information Service, New Delhi, India, 1975

It is here that current building owners and their architects, engineering firms, contractors, and other members of the construction team should start. Beyond the protection that exists in the building codes and standards that are adopted and enforced within our community, what realistically are the risks, threats, and vulnerabilities that my structure may be subjected to during its life? If no such codes and standards have been adopted, then what codes and standards are available that can be used?

Federal Risk Assessment Tools: General Services Administration, Federal Emergency Management Agency, National Institute of Justice, and National Institute of Standards and Technology

The General Services Administration's Approach toward Risk Assessment

The U.S. General Services Administration is responsible for the design, construction, operation, maintenance and, in some cases, the lease of over 45% of the buildings that are used by Federal agencies to house their employees or perform their job functions.

Annually GSA oversees over 1,800 government-owned and 6,200 leased properties nationwide, with a replacement value of $35 billion. In addition, each year GSA designs and constructs approximately $650 million in new buildings ranging from warehouses to Federal court houses.

In wake of the domestic unrest of the 1960s and 1970s, GSA became increasingly more involved in looking into and including basic physical security provisions for their properties that might have a higher exposure to such unrest. These concerns were largely based on the early principles of crime prevention through environmental design (CPTED) and resulted in enhanced security by allowing for "gates, guards, and guns." The GSA also began reviewing work by the Department of State and DoD from their experiences overseas to begin to consider possible incorporation of more security considerations into the design and construction of their buildings.

The horrific bombing of the Alfred P. Murrah Building in 1995 focused attention on the vulnerability of our public institutions to terrorist threats and forever altered the way the Government views security in its buildings.

—Joseph Moravec, Public Building Service Commissioner, GSA, July 27, 2005

Prior to April 1995, however, the Federal government did not have any formally established risk assessment tools for its domestic buildings or any building security standards for Federally owned or leased facilities here in the United States.

Within days after the April 19, 1995, Oklahoma City bombing took 168 lives, President William Clinton's Executive Order 12977 created the Interagency Security Committee (ISC) and directed the Department of Justice to assess Federal building and facility vulnerability to acts of terrorism or violence and to establish recommendations for minimum security standards for such structures.

Comprised of 21 Federal agencies including the GSA, the ISC drew upon the experiences and expertise of both the DoD and the State Department and established five different categories for all Federal facilities and created minimum security requirements for each level, which will be discussed later in this chapter. At approximately the same time, based upon the work of the ISC, GSA initiated a program to both immediately upgrade security in those facilities it controlled and also to develop and put in place more well-defined tools for assessing the risk, threat, and vulnerability of all of its owned (and subsequently leased) facilities.

Department of Justice and General Services Administration Risk Assessment and Building Classifications

Based upon the work of the Department of Justice, five levels of Federal building security classifications were developed and GSA began assessing all of their properties against those classifications. Criteria for setting these levels included the mission function of the facility, agency sensitivity, volume of public contact, building size, and the nature of the tenant population. The classifications ranged from level 5, those with the highest risk level to level 1, those with the lowest.

As extracted from GSA documents, the five classifications are as follows:

- Level 5: A building that contains mission functions critical to national security (e.g., Pentagon, Central Intelligence Agency, and Department of Homeland Security headquarters), has 451 or more federal employees and more than 150,000 square feet of space (same provision for level 4), and includes the same security provisions as a level 4 facility with each Federal agency securing the site according to their own requirements.

- Level 4: A building that may include high-risk law enforcement and intelligence agencies, courts and judicial offices and highly sensitive government records and have a high volume of public contact, has 451 or more federal employees, and more than 150,000 square feet of space.

- Level 3: A building that has between 151 and 450 federal employees with between 80,000 and 150,000 square feet of space and moderate to high volume of public contact; tenant agencies may include law enforcement agencies and government records and archives.

- Level 2: A building that has between 11 and 150 federal employees with between 2,500 and 80,000 square feet of space, moderate volume of public contact, and federal activities that are routine in nature and are similar to commercial activities.
- Level 1: A building that has 10 or fewer federal employees, 2,500 or less square feet of space such as a small storefront type of operation, and low volume of public contact or contact with only a small segment of the population.

In 1996, GSA began evaluating all of its existing facilities against the preceding classification levels and taking steps to prioritize, fund, and put in place within these structures the appropriate minimum security standards called for in the June 1995 Department of Justice report. That report contained 52 minimum security standards in four separate categories: perimeter security, entry security, interior security, and security planning.

Tables 4-1 to 4-4 below describe the minimum security standards that the Department of Justice issued in June 2005 for application against each of the five levels of building classifications.

By 2002, GSA had completed their assessment of all their facilities against these criteria and had applied, where necessary, the appropriate security upgrades for their buildings. In addition to applying these standards, in 2002, GSA issued more detailed "Protective Design and Security Implementation Guidelines" for application to their facilities. This incorporated additional work of the ISC for new and existing buildings and for GSA leased facilities.

The Protective Design Security Implementation Guidelines also included details on handling different types of threats, both man-made and natural events. Among the man-made events were crime and terrorism; incorporated provisions for explosives, ballistic and forced entry threats; and chemical, biological, and radiological threats. The provisions for natural disasters included: wind, water, fire, and earthquakes.

Figure 4-6
Bollards, Pennsylvania Avenue, Washington, D.C.

Table 4-1

Department of Justice, Recommended Minimum Security Standards, Perimeter Security

	Level of security				
Perimeter security	I	II	III	IV	V
Parking					
Control of facility parking	□	□	●	●	●
Control of adjacent parking	□	□	□	○	○
Avoid leases in which parking cannot be controlled	□	□	□	□	□
Leases should provide security control for adjacent parking	□	□	□	□	□
Post signs and arrange for towing unauthorized vehicles	○	○	●	●	●
Identification system and procedures for authorized parking (placard, decal, card key, and so on.)	□	□	●	●	●
Adequate lighting for parking areas	□	□	●	●	●
Closed circuit television (CCTV) monitoring					
CCTV surveillance cameras with time lapse video recording	□	○	○	●	●
Post signs advising of 24-hour video surveillance	□	○	○	●	●
Lighting					
Lighting with emergency power backup	●	●	●	●	●
Physical barriers					
Extend physical perimeter with concrete and/or steel barriers	N/A	N/A	□	○	○
Parking barriers	N/A	N/A	□	○	○

Legend:

Minimum standard = ●; Standard based on facility evaluation = ○;

Desirable = □; Not applicable = N/A

Source: http://www.fas.org/irp/gao/ggd-98-141-4.htm

The guidelines described "Disaster/Emergency Management Considerations" including:

- Definition of a disaster, planning/preparedness, response, recovery, and occupant emergency plans. The planning and preparedness section included provisions for identification of hazards and risk management, developing a disaster management plan, logistics and facilities, training, exercises, evaluations, and corrective actions and other planning and preparedness actions.

In Sections 5 through 12, the guidelines provided details on the following areas:

- Section 5: Security risk management (including "What is a security risk assessment?" and "When should such assessments be performed?")
- Section 6: Physical security concepts/approach

Entry security	Level of security					
	I	II	III	IV	V
Receiving/Shipping					
Review receiving/shipping procedures (current)	●	●	●	●	●
Implement receiving/shipping procedures (modified)	□	○	●	●	●
Access control					
Evaluate facility for security guard requirements	□	○	●	●	●
Security guard patrol	□	□	○	○	○
Intrusion detection system with central monitoring	□	○	●	●	●
Upgrade to current life-safety standards (fire detection, fire suppression systems, and so on.)	●	●	●	●	●
Entrances/Exits					
X-ray and magnetometer at public entrances	N/A	□	○	○	●
Require x-ray screening of all mail/packages	N/A	□	○	●	●
Peepholes	○	○	N/A	N/A	N/A
Intercom	○	○	N/A	N/A	N/A
Entry control with closed circuit television and door strikes	□	○	N/A	N/A	N/A
High-security locks	●	●	●	●	●

Table 4-2

Department of Justice, Recommended Minimum Security Standards, Entry Security

Legend:

Minimum standard = ●; Standard based on facility evaluation = ○;

Desirable = □; Not applicable = N/A

Source: http://www.fas.org/irp/gao/ggd-98-141-4.htm

- Section 7: Protecting against explosive attack
- Section 8: Protecting against progressive collapse
- Section 9: Protecting against other weapons of mass destruction
- Section 10: Applying the ISC security design criteria—balancing risks and costs
- Section 11: Available tools for implementing the ISC (including classified software)
- Section 12: Considerations for procurement

Components of General Services Administration Risk Assessment and Their Relevance to Public and Private Sector Construction: New and Existing Buildings

GSA's risk assessment process includes the "entire process of asset and mission identification, threat assessment, vulnerability assessment and impact assessment, and risk analysis." In new construction (for example, of a post office), GSA notes that the first

Table 4-3

Department
of Justice,
Recommended
Minimum Security
Standards, Interior
Security

Interior security	Level of security				
	I	II	III	IV	V
Employee/Visitor identification (ID)					
Agency photo ID for all personnel displayed at all times	N/A	□	O	●	●
Visitor control/screening system	□	●	●	●	●
Visitor identification accountability system	N/A	□	O	●	●
Establish ID issuing authority	O	O	O	●	●
Utilities					
Prevent unauthorized access to utility areas	O	O	●	●	●
Provide emergency power to critical system (alarm system, radio communications, computer facilities, and so on.)	●	●	●	●	●
Occupant emergency plans					
Example occupant emergency plans (OEP) and contingency procedures based on threats	●	●	●	●	●
OEPs in place, updated annually, periodic testing exercise	●	●	●	●	●
Assign and train OEP officials (assignment based on largest tenant in facility)	●	●	●	●	●
Annual tenant training	●	●	●	●	●
Day care centers					
Evaluate whether to locate day care facilities in buildings with high threat activities	N/A	●	●	●	●
Compare feasibility of locating day care in facilities outside locations	N/A	●	●	●	●

Legend:

Minimum standard = ●; Standard based on facility evaluation = O;

Desirable = □; Not applicable = N/A

Source: http://www.fas.org/irp/gao/ggd-98-141-4.htm

step in conducting a risk assessment is to develop a site-specific risk assessment of the new facility and its operation to determine the likelihood that identifiable threats will harm a federal agency or its mission. GSA calls for this to be done by Federal agencies in conjunction with their agency specific programs. (These agency-specific programs often contain security features that are unique to that particular agency.)

There is no "one-size-fits-all" approach toward risk assessments. Each site for each building and for different agencies has different threats and risk levels leading to different security measures for each site.

Security planning	Level of security				
	I	II	III	IV	V
Intelligence sharing					
Establish law enforcement agency/security liaisons	●	●	●	●	●
Review/establish procedure for intelligence receipt and dissemination	●	●	●	●	●
Establish uniform security/threat nomenclature	●	●	●	●	●
Training					
Conduct annual sercurity awareness training	●	●	●	●	●
Establish standardized unarmed guard qualifications/training requirments	●	●	●	●	●
Establish standardized armed guard qualification/training requirements	●	●	●	●	●
Tenant assignment					
Colocate agencies with similar security needs	□	□	□	□	□
Do not colocate high- or low-risk agencies	□	□	□	□	□
Administrative procedures					
Establish flexible work schedule in high-threat or high-risk areas to minimize employee vulnerability to criminal activity	○	○	□	□	□
Arrange for employee parking in/near building after normal work hours	○	○	○	○	○
Conduct background security checks and/or establish security control procedures for service contract personnel	●	●	●	●	●
Construction/Renovation					
Install Mylar film on all exterior windows (shatter protection)	□	□	○	●	●
Review current projects for blast standards	●	●	●	●	●
Review/establish uniform standards for construction	●	●	●	●	●
Review/establish new design standards for blast resistance	○	○	●	●	●
Establish street setback for new construction	□	□	○	●	●

Table 4-4

Department of Justice, Recommended Minimum Security Standards, Security Planning

Legend:

Minimum standard = ●; Standard based on facility evaluation = ○;
Desirable = □; Not applicable = N/A

Source: http://www.fas.org/irp/gao/ggd-98-141-4.htm

While the following guidelines from GSA are pertinent to GSA-constructed (or leased) facilities, as will be noted later, GSA's risk assessment tools are similar to those prepared by other Federal agencies (including FEMA) and by the private sector. Data for the likelihood for each specific risk and threat are available from a number of sources including: crime—the police department; terrorism—Department of Homeland Security or State Homeland Security Director; natural hazards—FEMA and its HAZUS program (see page 109 of this chapter), U.S. Geological Survey, and National Weather Service.

Any risk assessment analysis addresses the following questions:

1. What assets and missions are we trying to protect within this building?
2. Given the tenants in this building (both known and potential), what credible natural and man-made threats or dangers could impact this building—externally or internally?
3. What is the likelihood of occurrence for each of those threats?
4. How vulnerable is this building to each of those threats?
5. How much damage might those threats cause given the planned design for this building, given the above assets, mission, threats, and vulnerabilities? (Or as GSA asks this question on performing an impact assessment—"What would happen if your security measures failed?")
6. What should be done in the design and construction of this building to protect its structure and occupants (including visitors) from credible threats and vulnerabilities?
7. What is the cost–benefit of including in the design and construction of the building various systems or materials to address those credible threats and vulnerabilities? (Or as GSA notes in their risk assessment questions—"How much security is enough?")

The preceding seven questions are applicable to any new or existing building and any building owner or member of the construction team. The structure for conducting this assessment is the filling in of a large number of boxes within a multilevel matrix that is generated by asking and answering these questions. Each area of risk is looked at for what the impact of that event might be on the structure and the functions performed within that structure.

The development of a mitigation strategy based upon the risk-threat assessment likewise is a matrix approach with boxes to be filled in to indicate the relative effectiveness and cost of taking various actions from guards and guns to strengthening the buildings columns and other structural elements against bomb blast.

Here is how GSA runs their Federal security risk management approach

- Step 1: Asset and mission identification—What are you trying to protect?
- Step 2: Threat assessment—What bad things could happen?
- Step 3: Vulnerability assessment—What are your weaknesses?
- Step 4: Impact assessment—What would happen if your (planned or existing) security measures failed?
- Step 5: Risk analysis—What does it all add up to?

$$Risk = Consequence \times Threat \times Vulnerability$$

- Step 6: Develop a mitigation strategy based upon cost and benefit to reduce level of risk to acceptable levels.

In addition to these five steps, Scandia National Laboratories also developed for GSA a software tool for their property managers to conduct risk assessments: RAMPART—Risk Assessment Method-Property Analysis and Ranking Tool.

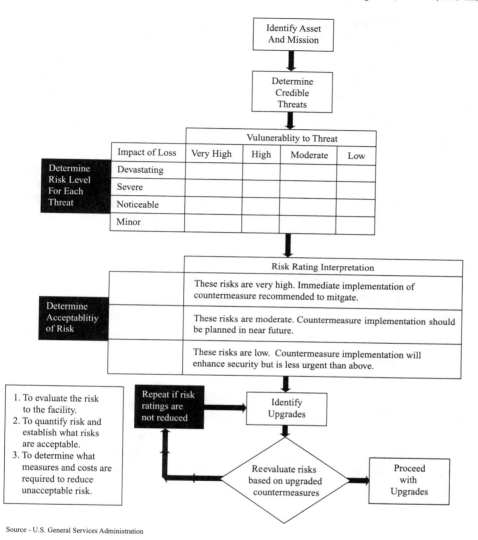

Figure 4-7

Diagram of
General Services
Administration
Federal Security
Risk Management
approach
(Source: GSA)

Source - U.S. General Services Administration

Addressing both natural and man-made disasters, RAMPART combines building and site-specific information provided by GSA facility managers with an expert system of rules and geography-based climatologic, seismic, and crime data to predict a building's vulnerability to several categories of consequences caused by man and by nature. The consequence categories include damage to property and contents and loss of use and mission.

The man-made hazards that are addressed include terrorism and crime inside and outside of the building. Hurricanes, flooding, winter storms, and earthquakes are covered by natural hazards. Terrorism values in the software are entered by the user, while the software provides the hazard data for crime and natural disasters based upon the building's geographic location.

Federal Emergency Management Agency Risk Assessment Tools and a Common Approach

The Federal Emergency Management Agency both prior to and after its integration into the Department of Homeland Security generated for the private sector and for state and local governments a number of useful guides (see list on page 43, Chapter 2, "Challenges Facing the Construction Team: Revising Codes and Standards, Redefining Roles and Responsibilities") to aid in both risk assessment and in helping communities to better withstand both natural and man-made disasters.

Designed for community use and not for application to individual buildings or businesses, the series of FEMA publications number 386-2 through 386-7 address various aspects of identifying and taking actions to mitigate risk from both natural and man-made disasters. FEMA 386-2, "Understanding Your Risks: Identifying Hazards and Estimating Losses" (August 2001), addresses natural disasters and includes a basic description of the risk assessment process.

Similar in structure to other Federal risk assessment methodologies, this publication describes a four-step process:

1. Identifying the hazards
2. Profiling the hazard events by magnitudes and looking at specific asset vulnerabilities
3. Inventorying assets
4. Estimating losses

Following from 386-2, FEMA 386-3 takes the next step by assisting the reader in "Developing the Mitigation Plan, Identifying Mitigation Actions, and Implementing Strategies," to address the risks identified in the previous document. In FEMA 386-4, "Bringing the Plan to Life: Implementing the Hazard Mitigation Plan," FEMA provides steps that can be taken to implement the strategies that were identified in the previous document.

FEMA 386-7, "Integrating Human-Caused Hazards into Mitigation Planning," was released in September 2003 and covers terrorism and "technological disasters" (e.g., major power failures). Covered later in Chapters 5 and 6, FEMA also has released a risk management series of publications, 426, 427, 428, and 429 that help building owners, architects, and engineers reduce physical damage and casualties from different types of terrorist attacks. The key elements to FEMA's assessment process model follow in the next section.

Common Steps in Risk Assessment: A Basic Approach for Building Owners and Owners of Companies

Using the preceding FEMA process as a model, here are the basic actions that any building or company owner can take to develop their own risk assessment and make a set of decisions regarding actions they will take to address and manage that risk.

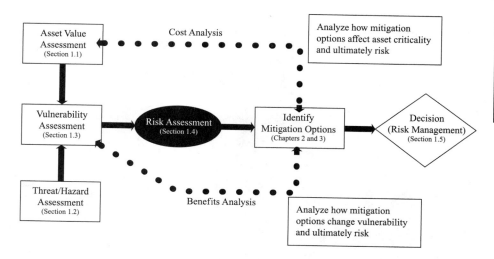

Figure 4-8

Federal Emergency Management Agency, Risk Assessment Process Model

Step 1: Assessing the Value of Your Asset

The building owner (and/or company owners) assesses the value of their building asset, the staff who work in that facility, and the value of the mission they perform. This assessment includes looking at what would be the cost to the owner, company, and perhaps community from the loss of that building and staff for a short period to long period.

Step 2: Scanning the Horizon: What Are All the Existing and Potential Threats and Hazards?

The building owner/company owner looks at all existing and potential man-made and natural threats or hazards. These may include action by a disgruntled employee, terrorist bomb, internal or external release of a biochemical agent, vandalism, and collateral damage from neighboring building that is likewise attacked or impacted by a natural disaster such as a hurricane, tornado, flood, earthquake, or fire.

Step 3: How Vulnerable Is My Asset (Building/Company) to Each of These Threats and Hazards?

The building owner/company owner under step 3 looks at the vulnerability of the building against each existing or potential man-made or natural threats or hazards. As noted earlier, data here to support this assessment may come from a variety of sources including the National Weather Service, police files, Department of Homeland Security, and State Homeland Security Director data (both unclassified and classified).

If it has not already been looked at under step 2, it is important to consider here the potential vulnerability of the building due to its location near neighboring buildings from collateral damage as a result of natural disasters, as well as potential man-made disasters. While collateral damage on 9/11 included the collapse of other structures on the World Trade Center (WTC) site, far more common is what occurs in fires or hurricanes. Common collateral damage in hurricanes has included flying debris (e.g., rooftop air conditioning units blown off one structure only to land on another below it, or gravel blown off a neighboring building's roof shattering windows in the owner's building).

Figure 4-9

Philadelphia,
Pennsylvania
office buildings

Step 4: Assembling the Risk Assessment

The combination of all of the information gathered under steps 1 to 3 constitutes the risk assessment for that particular structure and the people and companies it houses. The analysis shows the level of the threat, asset value, and vulnerability to each existing or potential hazard.

Step 5: Identification of Mitigation Options

Once a matrix has been developed ascribing the level of threat, asset value, and vulnerability to each hazard, the building or company owner gathers information from as wide a range as possible of actions that can be taken to mitigate those hazards. These actions may include physical security strategies (guards, gates, and guns), building setbacks, special materials or products (such as shatterproof windows), design considerations, or special details (e.g., making sure the air intake for the building is at least two stories above grade), (Chapters 5 and 6 offer a number of these mitigation options.)

Step 6: Cost-Benefit Analysis

Having assembled all of the preceding information, each of the mitigation options are reviewed for their effectiveness and costs and the benefits of taking one or more or a mix of those mitigation options. Mitigation options also need to include the cost of maintaining a feature once it has been put in place.

Step 7: Risk Management Decision

Based upon the earlier assembled data, the building or company owner can make a final risk management decision and put their mitigation plan in place.

The Federal Emergency Management Agency Hazard Risk Assessment Software Tool—HAZUS: Assessing Natural Disaster Risks

In the late 1990s, FEMA funded the National Institute of Building Sciences (NIBS) development of a software tool to provide individuals, businesses, and communities with information and tools to mitigate and reduce losses of life and property from natural hazards—HAZUS. Originally designed to cover seismic events, HAZUS was expanded to cover multihazards by incorporating modules for wind and water. Further

Figure 4-10

Federal Emergency Management Agency Hazard Risk Assessment tools, HAZUS modifications to HAZUS-MH (multihazard) will shortly include third-party model integration and access to a wider range of man-made and natural disaster models including biochemical, biological, and radiological events.

The original HAZUS earthquake model included the following:

- A building classification system based on the characteristics of building structure and frame
- Capability to compute damage to residential, commercial, and industrial buildings, essential facilities, and transportation and utility lifelines; and the capability to also compute damage to building structure, contents, and interior.
- Capability to estimate debris quantities, shelter needs and fire following the event and casualties, and estimate direct and indirect economic losses.
- A mechanism that enables the user to formulate and evaluate policy programs to reduce earthquake loss, including general mitigation strategies.

The HAZUS provisions for wind (Hurricane Preview Model) and water (Flood Model) provide similar information for these events for users.

Additional information on HAZUS and the HAZUS-MH tool can be accessed by going to the NIBS website www.nibs.org and by visiting the HAZUS User website at www.hazus.org.

National Institute of Justice: Assessment Tools

In November 2002, the U.S. Department of Justice's National Institute of Justice (NIJ) issued their version of a prototype risk assessment methodology in a document prepared for them by the Scandia National Laboratory, NCJ 195171, "A Methodology to Assess the Vulnerability of U.S. Chemical Facilities." Called the Vulnerability Assessment Model (VAM), the model was developed as a "systematic, risk-based approach in which risk is a function of the severity of consequences of an undesired event, the likelihood of an adversary attack, and the likelihood of adversary success in causing the undesired event."

The VAM methodology has twelve basic steps:

1. Screening for the need for a vulnerability assessment
2. Defining the project
3. Characterizing the facility being evaluated
4. Deriving severity levels (from the consequences of the event)
5. Assessing threats
6. Prioritizing those threats
7. Preparing for the site analysis
8. Surveying the building site
9. Analyzing the existing or proposed security system's effectiveness
10. Analyzing risks

11. Making recommendations for risk reduction

12. Preparing the final report

National Institute of Standards and Technology: "Cost-Effective Responses to Terrorist Risks in Constructed Facilities"

The National Institute of Standards and Technology (NIST) in the wake of 9/11 not only undertook the massive effort to research and report on the collapse of the WTC's buildings, it also began to look at ways to provide tools to the private sector and to state and local governments to conduct a more complicated risk-threat analysis to describe best practices and determine the most cost-effective responses to terrorist risks. This is a more complex risk assessment tool than that provided by FEMA.

In March 2004, NIST released its report on "Cost-Effective Responses to Terrorist Risks in Constructed Facilities," and in July of that same year NIST issued its "Best Practices for Project Security." The former document was accompanied by a software tool to facilitate the conduction of the risk-threat analysis and determination of what mitigation techniques and construction design approaches to take to reduce a building's vulnerability to a terrorist attack. An updated version of that software will be issued in the fall of 2006 and will include a financial risk model to enable users to conduct "a rigorous, probabilistic financial risk assessment of alternative mitigation strategies." You can access the NIST model by going to www.nist.gov.

Step by Step through the National Institute of Standards and Technology Processes

In their March 2004 report on "Cost-Effective Responses to Terrorist Risks in Constructed Facilities," Robert E. Chapman and Chi J. Leng from NIST's Office of Applied Economics with NIST's Building and Fire Research Laboratory addressed terrorism threats on three risk mitigation strategies:

1. Engineering alternatives

2. Management practices

3. Financial mechanisms

While addressing terrorism per se, these same three strategies can be applied to natural hazard risk mitigation strategies as well. The NIST "Cost-Effective Responses" process is an especially useful tool in that it looks at four complicating factors in the capital asset decision-making process. These factors address the following questions:

- "What mitigation strategies should we employ, and how will they operate, both singularly and in combination?"

- "How do we produce a risk mitigation plan that demonstrates superior economic performance?"

- "How do owners and managers of multiple properties identify which constructed facilities to protect and why?"

- "Who bears which costs?"

Figure 4-11

Cover of National Institute of Standards and Technology, "Cost-Effective Responses to Terrorist Risks in Constructed Facilities"

To answer these questions, NIST in its report and in its accompanying software program established a more formal risk assessment methodology than that provided by FEMA in their model. The purpose of the NIST methodology was to "insure that all relevant costs are captured and analyzed using well-defined metrics to identify an economically superior risk mitigation plan." The NIST model includes "life-cycle cost analysis," "present value to net savings," "savings-to-investment ratio," "adjusted internal rate of return," and links it all to a "detailed cost-accounting framework."

In its seven chapters, the NIST report lays out the preceding methodology as follows:

Chapter 1 provides an overview of the process and the work done by NIST's Office of Applied Economics to produce the report and its companion software product. Chapter 2 goes into detail on the three types of risk mitigation strategies (engineering alternatives, management practices, and financial mechanisms). These are defined as follows:

Engineering Alternatives are "design, material, or component choices in the construction or renovation of constructed facilities, their systems, and subsystems." Management practices "include the security, training, communications, and emergency procedures that an organization establishes and implements to prevent or respond to terrorist attacks" and "the decisions about facility location as well as access to its systems."

Financial mechanisms include "a set of devices that facility owners and managers can utilize to reduce their exposure to terrorist risk," including the "purchase of insurance policies and responding to external financial incentives to engage in engineering-based or management-based risk mitigation." The latter may include "government subsidies for investments to harden a facility or rental premiums paid by tenants who valued the facility's added safety features."

Chapter 3 reviews the NIST three-step risk mitigation plan protocol: "risk assessment, identification of potential mitigation strategies, and economic evaluation of risk mitigation strategies." This follows steps similar to those in other Federal agency risk assessment methodologies covered earlier in this chapter, leading the owner through to an economic evaluation of various risk mitigation alternatives and determining the most cost-effective combination of mitigation strategies to employ for their facility.

Chapter 4 provides "the decision methodology which provides the technical basis for the economic evaluation of risk mitigation alternatives" that were explored in Chapter 3. NIST bases its decision methodology on "two types of analysis, four standardized economic evaluation methods, and a cost-accounting framework." Designed to reinforce each other, the two types of analysis are baseline and sensitivity. The four economic evaluation methods are life-cycle cost analysis, present value to net savings, savings-to-investment ratio, and the adjusted internal rate of return. The report's main focus is on the life-cycle cost method and provides guidance on using the other three methods.

NIST includes a discussion on "how to identify, classify, and estimate on a year-by-year basis the key benefits and costs entering into the economic evaluation." The chapter ends by providing building owners and managers with an additional decision-making tool. That tool helps them understand "how the cost-accounting framework facilitates the decision-making process by identifying unambiguously who bears which costs, how costs are allocated among several widely-accepted budget categories, and how costs are allocated among key building components and the three types of risk mitigation strategies" (engineering alternatives, management practices, and financial mechanisms).

The last three chapters of the NIST report describe the software product now available to implement the economic evaluation methods described in Chapter 4 and areas for future research (Chapter 7). Six Appendices (A-F) provide additional support information for the overall methodology, a sample economic representation of the negative externalities that arise when some, but not all, facility owners and managers implement risk mitigation plans, and a glossary of terms.

Appendix A, "A Nation at Risk," provides an excellent summary of constructed facilities that are at risk, a classification of those facilities, a summary of critical infrastructure and assets in the United States in 2003, a classification of hazards, and information on the general national responsiveness to different hazard classifications.

Tables A-1, A-2, and A-3 from that report are provided in Chapter 5 of this book.

PRIVATE SECTOR ASSESSMENT GUIDES

Derived in part upon previous work by Federal agencies, the private sector in the wake of 9/11 and the anthrax attacks developed tools to assist their members in assessing and considering actions that could be taken to reduce their exposure to losses of life and property from future terrorist events. Following are four such assessment tools. The first of these, the one developed by the American Society of Heating, Refrigerating and Air Conditioning Engineers (ASHRAE), will be covered in detail to serve as a model for similar tools by the other groups listed in this chapter.

Risk Management Methodology from the Report of the American Society of Heating Refrigerating and Air Conditioning Engineers

> The amount of time that buildings function under normal conditions far exceeds the amount of time under extraordinary incidents.
>
> —ASHRAE Guide, 2003

As noted in Chapter 2, a number of professional societies took immediate action after 9/11 to identify products that would address their members' future concerns with future terrorist attacks upon the American public and the built environment. ASHRAE immediately responded by the appointment of a Presidential Ad Hoc Committee, which produced "Risk Management Guidance on Health, Safety, and Environmental Security under Extraordinary Incidents" (both man-made and natural hazards) as a tool to provide guidance on building construction and operations to the owners and operators of buildings and those who design such structures.

The ASHRAE document drew upon that association's and its members' "expertise in HVAC & R, its knowledge of building envelope performance, intake and exhaust air control, air and water treatment, and food preservation," elements that are critical to environmental security and building occupant survival and safety. Released in January 2003, ASHRAE's document divided "extraordinary incidents" into three categories.

1. Natural incidents, which included flood, wind, storms, and seismic damage

2. Accidental incidents, generally caused by humans, and including fire, chemical (and other) spills and infrastructure damage

3. Intentional incidents, criminal actions, and acts of terrorism that include fire, explosion, biochemical and radiological events, and infrastructure damage

Noting that most of their members had little experience with risk management, ASHRAE built its report based upon lessons learned from the events of both 9/11 and the distribution of anthrax through the mails, and preventative actions taken in the wake of those events by ASHRAE members and the owners of buildings.

Among those lessons learned were the following:

- Methods of protection developed and implemented in buildings for accidental and naturally occurring "extraordinary incidents," often also are effective for "intentional extraordinary" events.

- Our nation's existing building codes and standards, where they are effectively followed and enforced contain "factors of safety," that already have been proven to be effective against many threats (natural and man-made).

- We must not negatively impact the performance of buildings under normal conditions by the control strategies we adopt and put in place to increase our ability to prepare for and respond to extraordinary incidents.

- To successfully address both internal and external "aerosol attacks" on/in our buildings, our internal and external ventilation systems must have effective and timely controls that either isolate the building from external attack or expel aerosols that have been internally released.

- Enhanced egress systems and isolation of contaminated areas in buildings must be considered where areas of refuge within buildings are not economically viable.

- Improved building envelop air tightness cannot rely solely on enhanced air filtration systems. Building owners and designers also need to look at employing a comprehensive strategy that includes pressurization of the building's interior relative to the outdoors.

Chapter 5 will review in detail ASHRAE's recommendations in their "Risk Management Guidance" document as it applies to the preceding HVAC & R considerations for new construction. The following section looks at the structure of ASHRAE's suggested approach to conducting a risk analysis portion of their risk management analysis methodology.

American Society of Heating, Refrigerating and Air Conditioning Engineers' "One Approach to Risk Management"

In their 2003 Guidance document, ASHRAE notes that the risk management process has four steps (see Figure 4-15).

- Step 1. Risk analysis
- Step 2. Risk treatment planning
- Step 3. Risk treatment implementation
- Step 4. Reevaluating the plan after implementation, and modifying it as needed

Figure 4-12

Diagram
of American
Society of Heating
Refrigerating and
Air Conditioning
Engineers Risk
Management
Analysis
Methodology

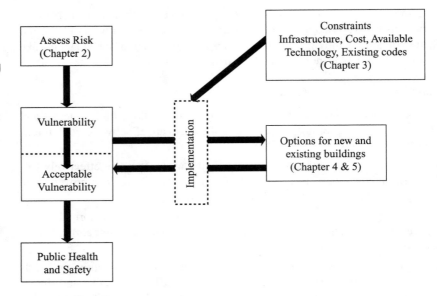

Step 1: Risk Analysis

As with the FEMA approach, ASHRAE noted that there are six actions that must be undertaken to conduct step one, the risk analysis of a facility or an organization. The six actions are as follows:

1. Determining the organization's or building's level of exposure
2. Identifying the different man-made and natural risks
3. Estimating the probability of each risk occurrence
4. Determining the value of loss from each risk
5. Ranking those risks
6. Identifying the organization's or buildings vulnerabilities against those risks

Step 2: Risk Treatment Planning

The second step in ASHRAE's overall risk management methodology is developing a risk treatment plan. This step requires the building owner or manager (organization's leader) to look at options, methods, costs, and procedures developed to mitigate or counter each risk or vulnerability that were identified under step one, and then rank the options. This includes the concept of "loss control," or taking actions (including building design features) that reduce the probability or scale of losses that occur from a natural, accidental, or deliberate man-made event. "For example, in heating and air conditioning terms, moving the location of an outside air intake (from grade level to two stories above grade) could significantly mitigate the risk of a chemical or biological attack on a facility by reducing the probability of the loss occurrence."

To complete this second step, the owner/manager must then use the preceding information to "Develop Options to Mitigate the Risk and Cost to Implement." This entails looking at the list of vulnerabilities that were developed under step 1 and the list of solutions to address those vulnerabilities and compare the costs of implementing each solution against the relative ranking of those vulnerabilities.

As described in NIST's "Cost-Effective Responses to Terrorist Risks," the preceding costs should be looked at and ranked on the basis of life-cycle cost. Other methods that ASHRAE notes that can be considered include cost-benefit ratio, return-on-investment, and simple payback.

The earlier information then is used by the owner/facility manager to prepare a comprehensive cost-sensitive risk treatment plan that addresses the mitigation of the areas of highest vulnerability.

Step 3: Implementation of the Risk Treatment Plan

The owner/facility manager then implements the preceding plan, either all at one time (as in the case of a new building design) or over a phased-in time frame (as may be the case for an existing building).

An important element within this plan should be steps to as effectively as possible address the issue of business continuity of operations. As ASHRAE notes on page 12 of their report:

One way to significantly reduce the magnitude of loss is for the organization (building) to return to normal business (operations) as quickly as possible. This is accomplished by the organization's (building owner's) business resumption plan.

As will be noted in Chapter 7, "Homeland Security and the Issues of Energy Sustainability, Environment, Accessibility, and New Products, Materials and Techniques," one of the key elements to helping buildings get operational again as quickly as possible after an "extraordinary incident" (disaster event) is for the community, where that building is located to have an effective disaster preparedness, response, and recovery plan that includes adequate staffing and funding of the building codes administration and enforcement program which will conduct building damage assessments and issue building construction permits.

In their report, ASHRAE also recommends that the selected "set of prioritized options should be designed into a coherent plan, installed, and commissioned, using procedures such as the ASHRAE Guideline O-P, the Commissioning Process."

Step 4: Reevaluation of the Plan

The fourth step to the ASHRAE process is a feedback loop—the reevaluation of the risk treatment plan after it has been implemented and the modification of that plan as needed. This should be performed on a regularly scheduled time table but also should be undertaken when parameters surround a risk change, such as when a new, previously unused, biochemical agent is used by terrorists somewhere in the United States or overseas or when there are new data regarding the severity of the hurricane season cycle specifically affecting buildings along the Gulf or East coasts.

In addition to its release in 2003, of equal value to building owners, operators, and members of the construction team will be ASHRAE's completion and issuance later in 2006 of a more detailed risk management document: "Guideline for Risk Management of Public Health and Safety in Buildings." Building upon the contents of the 2003 risk management guidance publication, this new document will contain qualitative and quantitative methods for the management of risk of extraordinary incidents in buildings. "The extraordinary events addressed in this guideline include fire, seismic events, chemical and biological releases, blasts, and other extraordinary hazards. The Guideline will address extraordinary incidents from a multihazard perspective and will cover both intentional and accidental occurrences."

Other Current Private Sector Risk Management Processes

American Society for Industrial Security

The response of the 32,000 member American Society for Industrial Security (ASIS), International, to 9/11 was to form a guidelines commission in 2001 to "advance the practice of security through the development of risk mitigation guidelines within a voluntary, nonproprietary, and consensus-based process utilizing to the fullest extent possible the knowledge, experience, and expertise of ASIS membership and the security industry."

In 2003, the Society issued its guideline "General Security Risk Assessment." The guideline provided a seven-step process that provides security professionals with a methodology by which "security risks at a specific location can be identified and communicated along with appropriate solutions." Available on the internet for free downloading (www.asis.org), the guide's seven steps parallel those already described in this chapter.

- Identify assets (understand your building/organization)
- Specify loss events/vulnerabilities (hazards/threats)
- Establish the probability of loss risk and frequency of loss events ("virtually certain, highly probable, moderately probable, less probable, possibility unknown")
- Determine the impact of loss events ("permanent replacement, temporary substitute, related or consequent cost, lost income cost") including "cost-to-loss formula," and "criticality ratings"
- Develop options to mitigate risks losses
- Study the feasibility of those options
- Conduct a cost-benefit analysis of each mitigation option that leads to establishing and implementing a hazards mitigation plan
- Conduct period reassessments of the preceding seven steps

American Management Association

In 2004, the American Management Association released, "The Facility Managers Emergency Preparedness Handbook" to provide checklists, guidelines, and tools to help prepare for different types of emergencies including terrorism, fire, and workplace lock-outs or violence. Chapters in the book include sections on damage assessment, electrical power requirements, elevators and escalators, hazardous materials and spills, indoor air quality, and terrorism.

RS Means: "Building Security: Strategies and Costs"

To assist building owners and facility managers in assessing risk and vulnerability to their new and existing buildings, in 2003 R.S. Means, one of America's suppliers of construction cost information, produced "Building Security: Strategies and Costs."

The guide also assists in the development of emergency response plans, and in making decisions about protective measures and designs and pricing information for several security-related systems, components, and equipment. The guide also includes information on labor costs to install that equipment.

COMBINING TOOLS FROM PUBLIC AND PRIVATE SECTOR TOOLS

This chapter has either highlighted or described in detail, eight different risk, threat, and mitigation methodologies. Most have common steps. All have slightly different emphasis based upon the nature of the risks and hazards from the developing agencies or organization's perspective.

Depending upon the nature and location of the building being constructed or renovated by the building owner and the construction team, different risk, threat, and mitigation analysis may be of greater practical use than others. Owners wanting great detail in cost-risk analysis may, for example, want to apply the NIST's "Cost-Effective Responses to Terrorist Risks in Constructed Facilities" methodology. An owner concerned with remodeling an existing structure may, however, want to look at the cost-risk features of the preceding NIST methodology but also apply the steps of the ASHRAE, "Risk Management Guidance for Health, Safety, and Environmental Security under Extraordinary Incidents."

SUMMARY OF BENEFITS OF CONDUCTING A RISK-THREAT ANALYSIS

Given the realities of the post-9/11 world, the concept of organizations, companies, building owners, facility mangers, and other members of the construction team undertaking a risk-threat analysis and developing a hazard mitigation strategy is no longer an alien concept. Hurricane Katrina in August 2005, coupled with the 1995 Oklahoma City bombing, demonstrated that such analyses are not just for those organizations or buildings that are located in areas such as Washington, D.C., and New York City where international terrorists have caused death and destruction.

As documented in this chapter, numerous public and private sector organizations provide building owners with a wide-range of tools to conduct such assessments. In "Risk Management Guidance for Health, Safety, and Environmental Security under Extraordinary Incidents," ASHRAE provides one of the clearest lists of reasons why building owners and facility managers should use a risk management approach. Those reasons are as follows:

- Identifies which risks are the most critical and need the most resources.
- Is flexible and can be adapted to any organization's needs and resources.
- Creates a written history of risk analysis, mitigation evaluation, and implementation.
- Encourages a discussion about risk, requirements, and technologies.
- Promotes a periodic review to ensure the organization's (building owners) needs are met.

- Can involve a diverse group, to bring broad range experiences and expertise to solve the problem. This is especially true of engaging many members of the construction team including building product manufacturers, suppliers, contractors, and regulators in developing and implementing cost-effective mitigation plans.

Despite the preceding reasons, most owners are not undertaking such analyses before they have new buildings designed or existing structures renovated. Why?

Constraints on Undertaking Risk-Threat Analysis

In a survey conducted by *TEC* International and reported in the *Wall Street Journal* in March 2003, it was noted that 73% of 1,090 chief executive officers (CEOs) responding to the survey reported that in the wake of the events of 9/11 they had taken no actions to protect their firms from attack. Contributing to the lack of action were several factors. The first is the obvious one; just how do you protect your employees from another attack by a fuel-laden hijacked aircraft? There are no guidelines or standards, and how likely is the repeat of such an event?

The secondary factor has been the lack of access until relatively recently to good, low-cost risk assessment tools. But now that such tools as those described in this chapter are available, what holds CEOs back?

As was noted in Chapter 1 of this book, the very litigious nature of our society has limited the ability of owners, architects, engineers, contractors, product manufacturers and suppliers, and building officials and managers to work together as a more effective construction team and also has made many members of that team shy away from undertaking such an analysis in the first place.

Consider the following, on October 26, 2005, a Manhattan jury found the Port Authority of New York and New Jersey negligent in the 1993 terrorist bombing of the WTC parking lot that killed six persons. In assigning liability, the jury found the Port Authority 68% liable and the terrorists only 32% liable.

While the Port Authority is appealing the case and hopes to have it overturned, it is important to note what the basis of the assignment of that liability was. The Port Authority's liability was based upon the fact that in 1985 the Port Authority commissioned a security report that included within its list of possible recommended actions the agency close the WTC garage to public use and/or have guards conduct random searches of vehicles. These recommendations were not acted upon and thus the terrorists had access to the parking garage where they set off their bomb hoping to bring down one of the towers.

Engineering News Record, in an article on the case in the November 7, 2005, edition of their publication, quoted Daniel Ansell, a lawyer at Greenberg Trany LLP, as saying, "Accordingly, property owners face a dilemma in determining how to respond to security recommendations because failure to implement such recommendations, regardless of cost or inconvenience, could result in substantial liability."

Figure 4-13
Tower of London, England

While this problem has been discussed within the business community, Congress has not adequately addressed it. Neither the passage in November 2002 of Public Law 107-297, "The Terrorism Risk Insurance Act of 2002," nor the Department of Homeland Security's announced intention to adopt "Regulations Implementing the Support Anti-Terrorism by Fostering Effective Technologies Act of 2002," which limits liability for putting in place "qualified anti-terrorism technologies," have thus far removed this potential litigation barrier to conducting and acting on risk, threat, and mitigation assessments.

Additional legislation and perhaps even the much discussed but never acted upon need for tort reform, are the only meaningful ways to remove this significant constraint that still blocks many owners from "beginning with the end in mind," and conducting risk-threat assessments of their buildings before they are designed, built, or renovated.

While this is true, it is equally true that as an owner or member of the construction team, it is extremely difficult to determine what added provisions from existing building codes and standards and construction guidelines (outlined in the next two chapters) can be followed without undertaking one or more of the risk-threat mitigation analysis described in this chapter.

Certainly we have the technical ability to build the twenty-first century equivalents of Britain's fourteenth century Bodiam Castle or the Tower of London, but armed with a risk-threat mitigation plan and following the provisions noted in Chapters 5 and 6, in very few cases will structures need to be built that way to increase our public's safety in the built environment.

5 Existing Construction Standards, Codes, Practices, and Guidelines that Promote Security and Disaster Resilience in New Construction

Architects, building officials, contractors and other practitioner fields related to the built environment have traditionally approached their particular tasks without having to address issues deemed beyond their own professions.

Seemingly discrete tasks such as the design of construction of a shopping center are thought relatively straightforward to deal with; there is a beginning and an end; there are codes and guidelines to follow. However, it is increasingly evident that every aspect of the built environment is indeed an integral part of a larger context. No action or element exists disconnected or in isolation from a larger web of activity. Our world is increasingly a smaller place and people, ideas and events are more interconnected.

—Paul Knox, Peter Ozolins, eds., *Design Professionals and the Built Environment*, Preface, John Wiley & Sons, 2000.

Every American since the events of 9/11 lives in a heightened state of concern as to where (and when) foreign or domestic terrorists will next strike on our shores. Fortunately, an extremely small number of the buildings currently planned, designed, or under construction in our nation will ever be the target of a direct attack by terrorists.

The vast majority of our buildings, instead, will be subjected during their expected 50 to 100 years of life to one or more events, natural (earthquakes, storms, flooding) or man-made (fires, forced entry and so on), which do indeed test the building to the full extent of one or more of their design capacities. With modern building codes and standards constantly undergoing updates based upon lessons learned from past disasters and revised to address new construction materials, products, and techniques, the vast majority of new construction that is being built in communities that adopt and effectively enforce such modern building codes and standards will perform quite adequately to these future safety hazards.

This chapter offers guidance to owners and their construction team regarding design resources from which to select provisions to enhance building safety either where such modern codes and standards are not in place (or are not being effectively enforced) or where the owner has concluded from their risk-threat analysis and disaster mitigation strategy that they want to include safety provisions beyond the minimums in the mandated building codes and standards adopted in their community.

As reflected in Chapter 3, "Findings from the World Trade Center Towers' Collapse and Other Post-9/11 Disasters," the preceding pre-9/11 statement by Knox and Ozolins is even truer today than it was when they wrote that preface to their book. Considering the lessons learned from 9/11 (and other man-made and natural disasters), and having used one (or more) of the risk-threat analysis tools outlined in Chapter 4, the person or company planning on building a new structure may have determined that they indeed wish to include within and around that building, design and safety features that exceed those required by the jurisdiction in which the structure is to be erected.

Addressing risks by their level of severity and by hazard areas, this chapter lays out building guidelines and construction codes and standards that are currently available to both the public and private sector owners and their partners in the building construction team. Starting with basic external building security, the chapter moves on to cover the issues of blast and progressive collapse and internal building issues including HVAC (heating, ventilation, and air conditioning) systems and both internal and external releases of biochemical hazards. Natural hazards of wind, flood, and seismic events are then briefly addressed.

Recently adopted ordinances and guidelines by major cities concerning building evacuation drills and high-rise construction are covered, and the chapter closes with a review of proposed changes from parties participating on the National Institute of Building Sciences (NIBS)/MCC Committee on World Trade Center (WTC) recommendations in response to the findings from the National Institute of Standards and Technology (NIST) investigation of the collapse of the WTC Towers.

Chapter 6, "Existing Buildings: Inspections and Retrofitting" will take up these same hazard areas as they regard codes, standards, guidelines, and procedures applied to the nation's existing building stock.

OVERVIEW OF GUIDELINES, CODES, AND STANDARDS FOR BUILDING SECURITY IN NEW CONSTRUCTION: CRIME AND TERRORISM

Building security involves more than bars on windows, a guard in a booth, a camera on the ceiling, or locked doors and gates. Effective security solutions call for systematic integration of design, technology, and facility operation and management. By understanding building use and operation, recognizing relationships between architecture and human behavior, and applying a mix of technologies that can enhance operational functions, architects and building design professionals can create environments that meet the security requirements of their clients.

—Randall I. Atlas, "Security Design Concepts," Chapter 3. In *Security Planning and Design—A Guide for Architects and Building Design Professionals*, AIA. J Wiley & Son, 2004

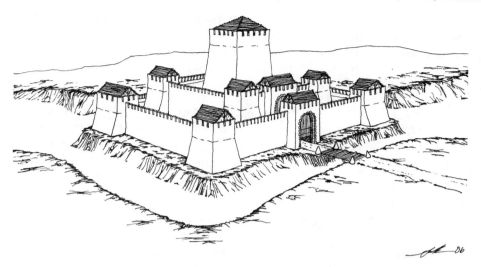

Figure 5-1

Original castle sketch by Andrew Corcoran, Portland, Oregon

Basic Security Principles

Rings of Defense

The age-old concept of "rings of defense," or layering security, grew beyond the crime prevention through environmental design (CPTED) movement and into a more sophisticated system of building security in the 1980s and 1990s, expanding on the lessons learned from attacks on American embassies and military bases overseas. The federal

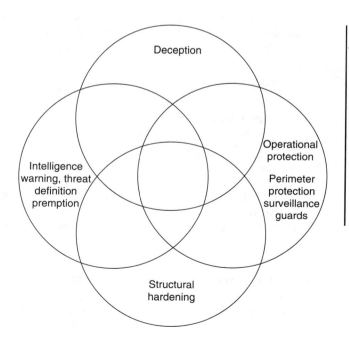

Figure 5-2

Federal Emergency Management Agency, "Components of Security," from FEMA Publication 427, "Primer for Design of Commercial Buildings to Mitigate Terrorist Attacks." Figure 5-1

response to the bombing of the Alfred P. Murrah Building in Oklahoma City, in April 1995 brought the General Services Administration (GSA) and Federal Emergency Management Agency (FEMA) into the heart of the problem which was expanded to incorporate all federal facilities through the initial efforts of the Interagency Security Committee (ISC; see Chapter 4, page 98).

The FEMA chart in Figure 5-2, taken from the FEMA Risk Management Series publication 427, "Primer for Design of Commercial Buildings to Mitigate Terrorist Attacks," stresses the following three basic principles of security that have evolved over the past four decades:

- Prevent the attack
- Delay the attack
- Mitigate the effects of the attack

Preventing the Attack: Intelligence and Deception—Beyond the Outer Ring This basic concept for the building owner or architect is to make it more difficult for obvious attack scenarios ranging from burglary by smashing a window or the taking of lives through a car or truck bomb attack to be implemented. This includes making the target appear to be less desirable or of low value to the would-be criminal or terrorist.

As FEMA cautions, however, this concept, with some risk, also can be applied the other way, by making the facility look too well-protected and thus more hazardous to the criminal or terrorist to target. The risk, here, is that some criminals and terrorists would only be encouraged by such obvious enhanced physical security to go ahead and attack the facility.

Examples of defensive mechanisms that are "beyond the outer ring," include gathering and maintaining close contact with public safety and state or local homeland security personnel, the location of the building on the building site, and the visibility to the street of obvious levels of physical security provided for the outer and inner rings, and signage—ranging from "Trespassers will be Prosecuted," to stronger statements.

Delaying the Attack: Operational Protection—The Outer Rings By creating a "buffer zone," between the public areas and the vital areas of a building, the attack can be delayed by either discouraging the attacker from making such a strike or giving security forces more time to respond to the event.

Effective design also has been applied to delay the attack by guiding the attacker into noncritical areas of the facility. Examples of outer ring protections include building setbacks, parking, physical barriers (landscaping, fences, bollards, security gates), protective lighting, cameras with closed circuit television, and guard posts with clear lines of sight.

Mitigate the Effects of the Attack: Structural and Other "Hardening" The Inner Rings of Defense The first two approaches, preventing and delaying attack can be relatively inexpensive approaches toward enhancing building security as opposed to this third area—the actual hardening of the building's exterior and interior design to reduce the physical and loss of life or injury consequences of either a criminal or a terrorist breaching the outer rings of the building's defense. Here is where the use of one or more of the risk, threat, and mitigation methodologies covered in the previous chapter are of vital importance.

Examples of the inner ring defenses include limitations on public access to portions of the building, shipping and receiving areas, high security locks, internal gates and guard stations, magnetometers, blast-resistant windows, mullions and doors, blast-resistant building structural features, and features in the HVAC system (possibly including filters) to protect the building from internal (and external) releases of bio-chemical agents.

Applying Risk-Threat Analysis and Mitigation Plan to New Building

As a result of conducting one of the risk-threat analysis methodologies covered in the previous chapter, the owner and his or her construction team determine the level of acceptable risk for their new structure. They also have developed a mitigation strategy that will be incorporated into the building's site, design, construction, and operation, and addresses one or more of the following criminal or terrorist threats.

The criminal threats that are mitigated by the plan may include the following:

- Assault
- Vandalism
- Threat of property
- Threat of information
- Workplace violence
- Kidnapping and hostage-taking
- Demonstrations

The terrorist (domestic and foreign) threats that are mitigated by the plan may include the following:

- Surveillance
- Hostage-taking
- Blast
- Biological–Chemical–Radiological events (both internal and external to the structure)
- Ballistic
- Aerial attack (9/11)

Depending on whether the threat analysis has identified a relatively moderate risk from the list of criminal activities and a minimal risk of ever being subjected to a terrorist event, or a low to moderate risk of being subjected to a criminal event but a moderate to high risk level to terrorism, the following guidelines and standards afford the building owner and design and construction team a range of options from which to select in providing for the relative safety and security of the occupants of their structure.

The GSA's five building classifications provided on pages 98 to 99 in Chapter 4, and Tables 4-1 through 4-4, offer the building owner a point of departure for determining what security features they may wish to include within their new structure for each of the rings of defense: external (GSA perimeter security, Table 4-1), and internal (GSA's entry and interior security, Tables 4-2 and 4-3). Table 4-4, "Recommended Minimum Security Standards, Security Planning," describes the operational issues and a few of the building maintenance issues that the building owner and designer must be cognizant of in selecting different security elements to include within the building's design.

Selecting the Best Approach or a Blend of Guidelines, Standards, and Codes

The level of determined risk and the risk mitigation plan lead the owner and the construction team to a wide-range of guidelines, standards, products, and services from CPTED, Department of Defense (DoD), GSA, NIST, FEMA, International Code Council (ICC), and National Fire Protection Association (NFPA), with which to select what works best for them both on the basis of cost, as well as on the purpose and function of the building. Here are three examples:

Example 1

A builder of a shopping center in a small midwestern town may want to look at CPTED guidelines for security but, if the shopping center is located in "Tornado Alley" he or she may also want to look at some of the guidelines for hardening a structure against wind damage (including perhaps providing tornado shelters for shoppers and workers) covered later in this chapter.

Example 2

A builder of a new high-rise structure, which may become an icon itself or will be located next to an iconic building within a major city such as New York City, San Francisco or Chicago, may want to look at a number of the GSA's level 5 security features,

Figure 5-3

Publications: Federal Emergency Management Agency 427, National Fire Protection Agency, International Code Council

FEMA's "Reference Manual," and "Primer for Design of Commercial Buildings to Mitigate Terrorist Attacks" (FEMA 426 and 427), as well as the enhanced structural provisions of the International Building Code and perhaps even some of the egress-related recommendations from the NIST report on the WTC Disaster.

Example 3

An owner of a new building may hope to lease space to one or more federal agencies either upon opening or sometime in the immediate future. Depending in part on its location and on the federal agencies involved, that owner and his or her construction team may also want to select provisions from GSA's construction guidelines.

A variation on this last example is a situation where the owner recognizes that while the building and its location may have a low-risk profile at the present time, some higher levels of security features may be incorporated into the building as a marketing advantage, given either the climate of the times, potential higher risk buildings, and tenants coming into the area or just wanting the flexibility to one day have a federal, state, or local government agency as a tenant.

In addition to the earlier example, before selecting which codes, standards, and guidelines to use in your building above those that are mandated by the adopted state or local building code in your jurisdiction, it is useful to run through the following screening checklist.

Screening Checklist: Rechecking What Level of Security and Security Design, Materials and Operation Features Are Wanted in the New Building

The following is a checklist of questions to ask in selecting provisions above those mandated by state or local building codes.

1. Do these more stringent codes, standards, and guidelines interfere with the overall function of the building?

2. Are these additional features sustainable? Do they require significant education and training of personnel to provide them or service them? Are such skilled personnel available? Were these costs included in the cost-benefit analysis that was conducted before selecting these provisions?

3. How readily upgradeable are these security features? At what cost? Will such an upgrade require retraining?

4. If the level of risk was to suddenly increase and security was desired or needed to be upgraded, how expensive would it be to upgrade these features now? Given present knowledge, how likely is it that an event (terrorism or building of an iconic or high-risk building next door) will require upgrading of this building's security features?

5. How big is the market from which to select these products, materials, or services? Are these products or materials likely to be available in the future when they need to be serviced or replaced?

Building Security Design Guides

- What design guidelines, standards, and codes are available to apply to different types of buildings with different levels of risk in each of the three rings of security areas?

- What resources are available to determine the costs of incorporating these design features into a new structure?

Starting with the outer ring of security and moving into the inner ring here are the guidelines, standards, and codes that are currently available from the federal government and from the codes, standards, and construction community for use in the following two types of building groups with varying degrees of risk from criminal and terrorist events:

- Building Group 1: Buildings with low levels of risk from terrorism but a range of levels of risk from crime

- Building Group 2: Buildings with moderate to high levels of risk from terrorism and a range of risks from low to high for crime

GUIDELINES FOR EXTERNAL PROTECTION OF THE NEW BUILDING: THE OUTER RING OF DEFENSE

Perimeter Security to Prevent or Delay Attack

Building Group 1: Buildings with Varying Levels of Risk from Crime but Low Level of Risk from Terrorism

"Security design can and should protect the public in a manner that preserves the integrity of our buildings, public spaces, and communities, while demonstrating the values of an open and accessible society."

—Nancy Somerville, Executive Vice President of the American Society of Landscape Architects (ASLA) during the July 2004, "Safe Spaces: Designing for Security and Civic Values Symposium," Chicago, Illinois

If all buildings under design and construction in the United States today were run through a risk-threat analysis, the vast majority of them would fall into this security category – low

Figure 5-4

Original castle schematic of external, outer most ring of defense by Andrew Corcoran

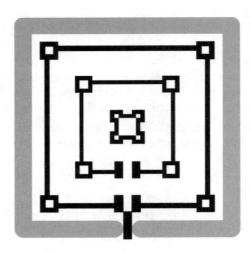

risks from terrorism but low to moderate risks from crime. Where owners have run that risk threat analysis and determined that while not at a moderate or high risk from terrorism, they do want to include in the siting, design, construction, and operation of their building, features that enhance the safety and security of the occupants and visitors to their buildings, they will want to follow the guidance expressed by ASLA Vice President Somerville in her above July, 2004 remarks. The principles of CPTED, "Crime Prevention through Environmental Design," offer a basic design principle for enhancing public safety.

Drawing from a wide range of resources including the publications and guidelines from FEMA, GSA, the American Planning Association's "Policy Guide on Security," and the earlier mentioned works of Barbara Nedel and Joseph Demkin, here are the basic principles of CPTED that owners may find adequate to address the added level of security they have determined that they need to include in their new building.

Crime Prevention Through Environmental Design

The fundamentals of physical security for buildings, as evidenced by Figures 5-1 and 5-2 have been relevant throughout human history. CPTED, "Crime Prevention through Environmental Design," is a modern effort to create a "climate of safety" for a community through the design of a new or modification of an existing physical environment that has a positive influence on human behavior. Pioneered in his 1972 book, "Defensible Space, Crime Prevention through Urban Design" by the late urban planner, Oscar Newman (1935–2004), this concept evolved in the United States in response to the rise in urban crime in the 1960s and 1970s.

Better lighting of neighborhoods, improved lines of sight, setbacks from roadways, and even the growth of gated communities all enhanced public safety through the application of the CPTED principles and its three strategies:

- Territoriality—the expression of ownership through the use of landscape, pavement, fences, signs, and buildings to convey psychologically to potential criminals that they are at risk apprehension if they try to undertake a criminal act at this location.
- Surveillance—maximizing visibility of people, physical features (cars, trucks), and activities going on around the building by arranging it so they are within easy view of an observer inside the building. Features include clear lines of sight, lighting, and closed-circuit television (which also contributes to the strategy of territoriality).
- Access control—through the strategic placement of landscaping, lighting, fencing, entrances, and exits.

The features of territoriality, surveillance, and access control and those noted in the following checklist can be developed and incorporated into building design and operation under the CPTED 3D process:

- Designation—clearly denoting the purpose and intended use of every space on the building site and inside the building.
- Definition—defining each space on the basis not only of its physical structure but also on its "social, cultural, legal, and psychological basis."
- Design—how well does the space support its intended functions and the psychological behaviors of the people who will pass through or occupy it?

A building owner and members of the building design and construction team can follow the following CPTED provisions to strengthen the level of security of their building from crime and at the same time provide a minimum level of protection from a terrorist event.

CPTED Provisions for Consideration of Incorporation into Building Site and Building Design to Reduce Threat of Criminal Activity

LOCATION OF THE BUILDING ON SITE

Layering of Security

1. Does the building's location on the site contribute to the layering of security in several of the following areas?
2. Is the building sited on the property so as to maximize natural surveillance with clear direct lines of sight for occupants of the building or a guard station?
3. Is the building located so as to take advantage of natural lighting to help surveillance and where necessary has adequate artificial light been provided?
4. Does the building's location on the site and the use of natural plantings provide police, neighborhood watch (if one is available) and the general public with a clear direct line of sight of the entrances and exits to the building?
5. Does the building's location on the site facilitate the use of natural (trees, berms) and man-made barriers (fences, bollards, gates) to provide obstacles limiting access to the structure?
6. Does the building's location on the site lend itself to using features such as low bushes or garden edging to the sidewalks that give people "psychological ownership" of the space and thus discourage vandalism or other criminal activity?

BUILDING DESIGN

Security Zoning

1. Has the building been designed and landscaped to reduce potential for criminal activity, thus enabling building occupants and visitors to enter, leave and move within the building to their various destinations without fear of attack?
2. Does the building's design include physical barriers that enable building tenants to control access to certain portions of the building (security desk, keyed entry systems, metal detectors, and so on)?
3. Does the building's design include features that clearly separate zones for public access and unrestricted use, such as lobbies, public restaurants, or public meeting rooms, from those areas that require restricted access?
4. Does the building's design and operation facilitate limiting access to fire control, HVAC equipment and controls, loading docks, mail rooms, and other sensitive areas from anyone other than appropriate authorized personnel?

CPTED in Your Community's Existing Site Standards   A growing number of communities have adopted CPTED standards into their zoning, land use, and site development standards. Among those are Cincinnati, Ohio; SeaTac Airport, Washington; Knoxville, Tennessee; Houston, Texas; Tempe, Arizona; Sarasota, Florida; Tempe, Arizona (from Nadel, "Building Security").

CPTED has proven to be especially useful in its application to buildings with low threat risks from terrorism and to the nation's older building stock (i.e., buildings built before security became a design feature in new construction). Basic CPTED design principles as applied to existing structures will be covered in Chapter 6.

In addition to CPTED, a number of communities have adopted land use and design regulations and guidelines that are based on creating a sense of community rather than reducing crime. Called "SafeScape" this American Planning Association approach, in addition to modifying the physical environment, also involves design elements to help people change how they "think of and interact with the physical environment thereby enabling a sense of community" and maintaining and sustaining a sense of livability.

The Inner Ring for the Low-Risk Building

Provisions in Model Codes and Standards   In addition to CPTED, provisions in our existing codes and standards also offer enhanced protection from criminal activities and some degree of protection from low levels of perceived threats from terrorism. Provisions regarding the outer ring of safety for buildings are not contained in the provisions of either the ICC's "International Building Code" (IBC) or in the provisions of the NFPA's "Building Construction and Safety Code," NFPA, 5000, and the NFPA "Life Safety Code, NFPA 101."

Regarding "inner ring defenses," the NFPA produces two documents that are relevant to building owners and designers: NFPA 730, "Guide for Premises Security," and NFPA 731, "Standard for the Installation of Electronic Premises Security Systems."

National Fire Protection Association Guides and Standards: 730 and 731

In August 2005, the NFPA issued two documents concerning external building security for adoption and use by communities that incorporate a number of the principles of CPTED: NFPA 730, "Guide for Premises Security," 2006 edition, and NFPA 731, "Standard for the Installation of Electronic Premises Security Systems," 2006 edition. These standards were compiled after a request was made to NFPA in 1994 to develop a set of burglary/security documents. That request did not move forward into action until 2000 when the NFPA Standards Council appointed a committee to develop these documents.

The "Guide for Premises Security" provides criteria for the selection of a security program to reduce vulnerabilities of buildings from criminal activity and also considers the protection of building occupants from those activities. In that regard it also covers a number of "protective features and systems, building services, operating features, maintenance activities… in recognition of the fact that achieving an acceptable degree of safety depends upon additional safeguards to protect people and property exposed to security vulnerabilities."

Referenced within the guide are standards or portions of standards and other documents from NFPA and the following other organizations:

- American Society of Testing and Materials (ASTM)
- Builders Hardware Manufacturers Association (BMHA)

- Illuminating Engineering Society of North America (IESNA)
- Steel Door Institute (SDI)
- Underwriters Laboratory (UL)
- U.S. Army Corps of Engineers (USACE)
- Department of Justice

Containing nonmandatory language, the Guide is advisory in nature but NFPA reports that it is being considered for adoption by reference by a number of jurisdictions.

The Guide's provisions include the following:

- exterior security devices:
  - Physical barriers
  - Protective lighting
  - Walls, floors, and ceilings
  - Ironwork
  - Glazing materials
  - Passive barriers (including concrete planters, bollards, and Jersey barriers)
  - Electronic perimeter protection (including fence-mounted sensors, electronic vibration detectors, shock sensors, buried sensors, and other devices)

- Physical security devices:
  - Locking hardware
  - Exit devices
  - Security vaults
  - Strong rooms
  - Safes

- Interior security systems (including controlled and restricted areas)
  - Intrusion detection systems
  - Sensors
  - Annunciators
  - Holdup, duress and ambush alarms
  - Electronic access control systems

- Security personnel and security planning

The guide covers all types of construction including educational, health care, one- and two-family dwellings, multifamily dwellings, lodging, apartment buildings, restaurants, shopping centers, retail establishments, office buildings, industrial facilities, parking facilities, and special events.

Companion Standard 731, "Standard for Installation of Electronic Premises Security System" includes mandatory language to facilitate its adoption and use by state and or local governments. The standard "establishes minimum required levels of performance, extent of redundancy, and quality of installation but does not establish the only methods by which these requirements are to be achieved."

Figure 5-5
Security station
and road barriers,
Washington, D.C.

Among the electronic premises security systems covered by the standard are intrusion detection systems, access control systems, video surveillance systems, asset protection systems, environmental protection systems, holdup and duress systems, and integrated systems. A copy of NFPA 730 and 731 can be obtained by visiting the NFPA Web site at www.nfpa.org.

Perimeter Security Building Group 2: Buildings with Moderate to High Risk from Terrorism and Varying Levels of Risk from Crime

As noted in Chapter 2, the overseas terrorist events of the 1970s, 1980s, and early 1990s, coupled with the 1993 WTC bombing and 1995 bombing of the Murrah Building, brought into sharp focus for the federal government the need to develop special security provisions to better protect our public buildings from terrorism—both domestic and foreign. Among the critical deficiencies identified regarding building security in these disasters were site access, standoff distances, setback requirements, antiram barriers, glazing and hardening the buildings from blast and, ultimately from progressive collapse.

Recognizing the need to provide the other federal agencies, state and local governments, and the private sector with design guidance to be used in providing enhanced terrorism protection in the previously mentioned areas, DoD immediately after 9/11 began developing an unclassified version of its own minimum antiterrorism standards.

In July 2002, DoD issued for public release an unclassified version of their May 2002, "Unified Facilities Criteria—DoD Minimum Antiterrorism Standards for Buildings." Among the provisions contained in this document are those covering site planning, minimum standoff distances, parking and roadways, structure separation, and unobstructed space.

In March 2005, the GSA updated their security design requirements within the GSA's "Facilities Standards for the Public Building Service," and incorporated materials from DoD and the previously described CPTED concepts.

Beginning with the outer ring of defense, this section looks at each of these layers of security for buildings that are deemed at higher levels of risk from terrorism.

Outer Ring Security for Buildings with Moderate to High Risks from Terrorism

Beyond the Outer Ring: The Role of Site Selection and Building Location in Preventing and Delaying Attack With approximately 80% of terrorist attacks relying on explosive devices (truck and car bombs), site selection, and orientation of a building on that site can be an important strategy to mitigate risk. Wherever possible in conducting the risk assessment and developing the appropriate mitigation strategies it is critical to start first by looking at the site that is being developed.

Does the owner or builder have a broad range of possible sites to choose from for this building or is there a fixed site? In selecting one site over another does the owner reduce

Figure 5-6
Outer defenses

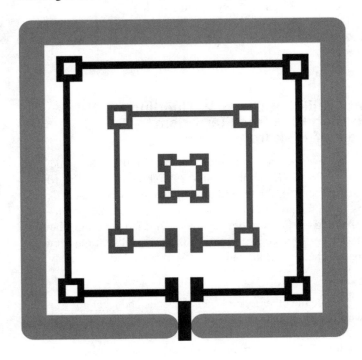

the potential level of risk for the structure and its occupants? Does the site provide more natural features to either reduce the likelihood of attack or delay the attack to allow more time for assistance to arrive to thwart or lessen the threat?

Second, within that site (or sites) does the owner or builder have any latitude as to where to place the building? The building's orientation? Or is this, for example, an already heavily developed urban site and both the boundaries of the site and the site itself require that the building's footprint fill the entire site.

Where the owner has a wide range of locations to site their building and orient the building on that site, basic principles of standoff security (including those from CPTED) can be applied. These also involve the use of fences, bollards, and natural barriers to provide maximum setbacks from streets and alleys that may border the property.

The section on blast (pages 153 to 163 and Figure 5-18) details information on how far back from roadways a building needs to be to minimize the effects of various sized explosions. In general, however, to emphasize the importance at this stage in considering the need for standoff distances, federal agencies recommend for cars to be 50 ft from the building and for trucks to be 100 ft. Car bombs tend to run around 500 lb of explosives and small trucks 2000 to 4000 lb. As will be noted later building design and construction materials play a critical role in the impact of blasts of these sizes from even these distances.

Drawn from FEMA, DoD, and AIA publications, there are two basic checklists that follow offering a useful starting point in helping the owner maximize the benefits of security from the layer that lies "beyond the outer ring":

1. Choose between the best of several possible locations for their facility
2. Choose the best location on the site in question taking into account limited sites or a single site for their building.

Guidelines for Site Selection: Multiple Options

One of the most fundamental recommendations for enhancing security in buildings is wherever possible include the risk-threat analysis process in determining which of possible multiple sites for a building is the best one to maximize the security of the building tenants and guests.

The following screening questions (similar to those for Type One buildings) form a checklist for helping the owner make such a determination.

1. Does the site meet the business and financial requirements of the owner?
2. Is access to needed transportation (roads, rail, airport, waterway, and so on) available and are any of these critical transportation lines themselves subject to high risk from natural or man-made disasters (e.g., rail line located within and lying lower than storm surge in coastal area subject to hurricanes)?

3. What uses and kinds of buildings are on properties bordering or in immediate area of the site? Are any of these hazardous use facilities? Do any of these have potential high risk for terrorist activity? (Data are available from fire, police, and possibly from local homeland security agency.)

4. What has been the crime rate in this area? (Police departments can supply this information.)

5. Are there any aspects of this site that pose potential problems in assuring security on the building site during the construction process?

6. Is topography conducive to providing security? Does it provide natural barriers for protection, e.g., good lines of sight for observation of potential criminal activity; multiple access points to highways; trees or other landscaping features that set site apart from other properties.

7. Does the site allow for adequate standoff distances between the building and access roads, parking lots, and passenger drop-off zones if vehicular access is not otherwise controlled on the site?

8. Where are the utilities located? Are they vulnerable to natural or man-made hazards?

9. Will any problems in the previously mentioned areas require special consideration in the building's design, construction or operation to reduce potential risks?

10. What are the relative costs of mitigating those risks in the siting, design, construction, and operation of the building on each site considered?

Unfortunately, the reality is that it is increasingly less common for owners to have the luxury of having multiple sites to consider for their buildings. More often than not, the financial realities limit the owner to only one or at most two sites and often within a confined environment, be it rural or, increasingly, more densely populated suburban or urban parts of our nation.

This being the case the owner will need to consider the following factors as they not only select the site for their building but also the location within that site for the building itself.

Guidelines for Building Location with Restricted Options: Urban Environment

1. Does location of the building on its site impact the business and financial requirements of the owner? If so, how does it?

2. Does the location of the building on the site increase or decrease secure access to needed transportation (roads, rail, airport, waterway, and so on) available and are any of these lines of access to critical transportation lines themselves subject to higher degrees of risk from natural or man-made disasters?

3. Does the nature of the building or of the site require that any special security features need to be in place during the construction process?

4. Can the building be placed on the site to afford maximum standoff distances from streets, alleys, or other potential access points for a car or truck bomb?

5. What uses and kinds of buildings are on properties bordering or in immediate area of the property? Are any of these hazardous use facilities? Do any of these have potential high risk for terrorist activity? (Available from fire, police, and possibly from local homeland security agency.)

6. If neighboring structures are possible targets for criminal or terrorist activity, does the location of the building on the site in one place or another reduce potential risk of collateral damage from attack on that neighboring structure?

7. Are there any plans before the jurisdiction to change the zoning for this area and thus increase the potential hazard level within this area?

8. What has been the crime rate in this area? (Police departments can supply this information.)

9. Are there natural security barriers that can be taken advantage of by virtue of the buildings orientation on the site (e.g., good lines of sight for observation of potential criminal activity; trees or other landscaping features that set site apart from other properties)?

10. Where are the utilities located? Are they vulnerable to natural or man-made hazards?

11. Will any problems in the previously mentioned areas require special considerations in the building's design, construction, or operation to reduce potential risks?

12. What are the relative costs of mitigating those risks in the siting, design, construction, and operation of the building for each different possible orientation of the building on that specific site? For example, in an area with determined high risk for terrorism and limited setback space, given the building's footprint, what are the costs for blast-proofing? What are the costs for restricting access to the street adjacent to the building? For using security cameras and blast-resistant fencing around the facility?

13. Does putting any of these special security features into one of these buildings provide increased value to the owner in terms of tenants? Future resale of the building?

14. Does placing any of these features into this building and the building's location on the site now as it is being built reduce the expense of perhaps upgrading that level of security at a later date as hazard conditions warrant?

Aiding the owner in completing either of the preceding two checklists are two documents: "Best Practices for Project Security" was issued by NIST in 2004 and is available online for downloading, and "Primer for Incorporating Building Security Components in Architectural Design," pending FEMA 430, that is due to be released in the fall of 2006.

These two publications are useful tools in making site selection and building location decisions. The NIST publication provides additional cost-analysis information for choosing different risk-reduction designs. The FEMA primer will offer additional detailed guidance on building orientation and design features.

"Best Practices for Project Security": Cost of Security Features, Constructability, and Construction Site Security

Figure 5-7

Rings of defense, bollards, natural barriers, raised entrance of a federal building in Seattle, Washington

In Chapter 4, the contents of NIST's report on "Cost-Effective Responses to Terrorist Risks in Construction Facilities," released in March 2004 were covered. In addition to that tool, NIST's Building and Fire Research Laboratory through a contract with the Construction Industry Institute (CII) in July 2004, issued a supportive document for building owners and managers that provides guidance for "implementing security-related practices during the delivery of chemical manufacturing and energy production and distribution projects," two industries that are vital to the economic viability of our nation.

While designed for the aforementioned two industries, the NIST Guide offers tools that are useful to other segments of the construction and critical infrastructure community, especially as they relate to issues that impact the decision on where to site, how to locate a building on a property site and the security issues that should be considered during the construction process itself. NIST's best practices document specifically looks at the planning through start-up phases of the life-cycle of buildings in a manner designed to increase "the likelihood that cost-effective protective measures will be implemented."

These are protective measures that CII research has documented to enhance a facility's security throughout the life of that facility if the measures are properly maintained.

The best practices document includes a "security risk index," (SRI) that "provides a quantitative means for determining the level of use of different security-related practices and for assessing their impacts on key project outcomes—cost, schedule, and safety." NIST notes that the "understanding of these impacts should lead to a management philosophy which fully integrates security into the project delivery process."

The basic screening questions asked in the best practices document is, "If (this) security (feature) were omitted from this practice, could its omission result in adverse consequences if the facility were attacked?" and is that feature affordable and constructable within that facility? NIST includes within the affordability calculations the issue of whether or not including this feature in the design and operation of the building may help reduce insurance premiums for the structure.

Appendix B of the NIST publication offers "Construction Security Guidelines," which are helpful not only in reducing losses of construction materials from theft but also in assuring protection to a building that requires special security during its construction process because of the nature of the building's purpose and/or of the future occupants. These NIST guidelines cover the areas of policy and program, organization, access control, barriers, lighting, locks and keys, alarms, communications, property control, emergency planning, and personnel.

FEMA 430: "Primer for Incorporating Building Security Components in Architectural Design"

FEMA 430 has been in development within the agency for over two years and has gone through two name changes (its original title was "Building, Site and, Layout Design Guidance to Mitigate Potential Terrorist Attacks"). Scheduled to be available in the autumn of 2006, FEMA 430 follows the layered (rings) defense approach described in the opening of this chapter and offers guidance on appropriate ways to orient a building within its site to reduce the potential impact of a terrorist action.

In conjunction with other federal guidelines, FEMA's three layers of defense are as follows:

- The first layer (beyond the outer ring): the surrounding area, installations and infrastructure, neighboring buildings, and other risk management strategies including input from police and homeland security on threat levels.
- The second layer (the outer ring): the space and natural barriers that can be used to protect a building (including CPTED principles described earlier), the placement of the building on its site, and access points to the structure.
- The third layer (the inner ring): the building envelope that includes building hardening.

Figure 5-8 shows the three-layer approach in place in modern context. The design features and the guidelines, codes and standards that they are drawn from to help the owner provide these layers of security are covered in the pages that follow.

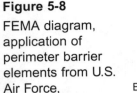

Figure 5-8

FEMA diagram, application of perimeter barrier elements from U.S. Air Force, Installation Force Protection Guide

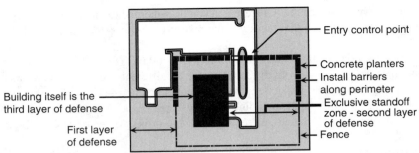

Building itself is the third layer of defense

First layer of defense

Entry control point

Concrete planters

Install barriers along perimeter

Exclusive standoff zone - second layer of defense

Fence

SOURCE: *U.S. AIRFORCE, INSTALLATION PROTECTION GUIDE*

BUILDING TYPE 2—GUIDELINES FOR PROTECTION: THE OUTER RING

Armed with the outcome of their risk-threat assessment and mitigation strategy and having selected the site where the new building is to be constructed, the owner and his or her construction team have a wide-range of final decisions to make concerning various security options. Drawn from FEMA, DoD, GSA, NIST, ASIS and other publications the following are a series of construction and design-guide checklists that owners can use to make their final determination as to which provisions work best for providing outer ring security to the new building.

At present, the biggest potential terrorist threats to buildings are bombs and the release of a biochemical agent. The best defense worked out so far to minimize potential attack by these means has been to deny access to the structure to inflict deaths, injuries, and damages to the building. The DoD and Department of State, as noted earlier, led the development of construction and design guidelines for natural, and man-made features designed either to deny access to or provide time for aid to come to the building to minimize the terrorist attacks with bombs, biochemical, or radiological agents.

The following checklists provide design considerations through which the outer perimeters of buildings are made more secure from such threats. The issues of design against bomb, blast, and biochemical attacks inside of and immediately outside of buildings are discussed later in this section.

Characteristics of the Surrounding Area: Beyond the Outer Ring and Their Impact on Determining the Level of Outer Ring Security for the Building

Whether the building that is being built is to be a secure government facility or private sector commercial structure, there are a wide range of security design considerations and guidelines for the owner to choose from to provide adequate levels of protection for the occupants of that building.

GSA's minimum security construction requirements for federal buildings were covered in Tables 4-1 through 4-4 in Chapter 4. Together with CPTED principles and FEMA and DoD documents the following are items that impact the security provisions that should be included in new construction.

Checklist for Surrounding Area Characteristics

1. What major structures surround the site where the new building is being built?
2. What are the potential risks, threats, and vulnerabilities associated with these surrounding buildings?_____high,_____medium or_____low for terrorism
3. Is the new building located in proximity to an outside building of high risk from terrorism and subject to potentially severe collateral damage from an attack (bomb, biochemical, radiological) from that neighboring structure?
4. Is the zoning in that area subject to change, which might bring a high hazard structure into the area where it could cause collateral damage to the new structure?
5. What is the proximity of the new structure to transportation hubs (highways, bridges, subways, tunnels, airports, ports)?
6. What is the proximity of the new building to telecommunications or utility service hubs or other critical infrastructure?
7. How close is the new building to hospital, police, fire departments, and their services?

These are all screening questions that should have been asked and answered when the risk-threat disaster mitigation determinations were undertaken as described in Chapter 4, but are asked again to determine which security features are to be selected for the site or included into the building.

Features to Include to Provide Outer Ring Security: Perimeter Control

If the information gathered in answering questions in the checklist is that the level of risk from neighboring structures (including utility and transportation infrastructure) is moderate to high, then the following security design features for perimeter control should be included in the new building.

Use of Natural Features for Perimeter Control As noted for low-risk structures covered earlier in this chapter, the CPTED principle of making use of natural topography or landscaping features afford some levels of security for buildings, especially from bomb attacks or in some cases biochemical or radiological attacks. The following features can be used to the owners' advantage, especially if they orient their building upon the construction site so as to make maximum use of these features.

- Raised elevations. Will the building sit higher than the base of surrounding buildings?
- Are there natural berms formed by the land that offer shelter protection or provide required standoff distances to ground floor of the building?
- Do trees or shrubs form natural barricades or lines of demarcation between public areas and areas that the owner wants to secure from general public traffic?
- Water features. Do streambeds and rivers form natural barricades or lines of demarcation between public and private access areas?

- Do these natural features still afford a clean line of sight for building security staff or occupants to observe behavior or actions of those approaching the building?

Use of Built Physical Barriers for Perimeter Control: Bollards, Fencing, and Gates
Where natural barriers do not exist to provide safe setback distances for the building to form a secure outer defense ring, man-made structures are provided. These features include the following:

- Bollards
- Planters
- Fences or walls
- Fences with gates
- Benches or decorative art that acts as bollards or barricades
- Other vehicle anti-ram devices
- Structures that preclude a high speed direct approach at the building
- Closed-circuit television
- Lighting

ANTI-RAM BOLLARDS   While bombings thus far in the United States have been done with stationary trucks and vans, overseas moving vehicular bombing attacks have been a major taker of lives in Lebanon, Israel, Saudi Arabia, and Iraq. Anti-ram bollards such as those in Figure 5-9 are designed to be anchored into the ground and at street corners or T intersections to be able to withstand the impact of cars and trucks striking them at speeds of 50 mph. The weight of these vehicles may vary between 4000 lb to 15,000 lb.

Figure 5-9

Design of typical anti-ram bollard, FEMA source, Design Guide, Figure 6-2

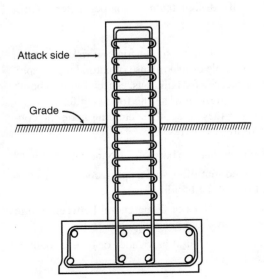

Attack side ⟶

Grade

Anti-ram bollards protecting portions of buildings that are parallel to adjacent streets are designed to withstand impact from vehicles of similar size but at lesser speed—30 mph.

In the first few years after 9/11, ugly Jersey wall concrete highway dividers were put up in Washington, D.C., New York City, Chicago, Los Angeles, and nearly every other major city to deter terrorist access to buildings, chemical and nuclear power plants, and other sensitive structures.

The American Society of Landscape Architects has initiated an effort to work with the building security industry, the GSA and later the Department of Homeland Security to encourage the design and installation of more aesthetically pleasing bollards or planters in place of the Jersey walls.

In addition to these resources, federal, state, and local government agencies can obtain from the joint Department of State/DoD Technical Support Working Group (TSWG) a classified software tool, "BIRM3D," for use by their physical security staff to test the vulnerability of a different types of vehicular security barriers against a wide range of vehicular bomb threats. (Visit the TSWG website at www.tswg.gov for more details.)

Use of Special Design Features and Location of Access Point Considerations for Perimeter Control   Since car and truck bombs have been the most common form of terrorist attack in the United States and in Europe, in addition to using the natural and man-made barriers to separate the building from vehicles, the location and operation of parking structures and the location of roadways, passenger drop-off, and truck delivery areas (loading docks) all are of critical importance to building security. Based upon DoD, GSA and other security documents including FEMA publication 426, "Reference Manual to Mitigate Terrorist Attacks Against Facilities" the following are lists of practices a designer should consider to provide protection to a building identified as being at high risk from a terrorist (domestic or foreign) attack.

Figure 5-10
Temporary protection, Jersey walls

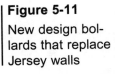

Figure 5-11

New design bollards that replace Jersey walls

PARKING

- Locate vehicle parking and service areas away from building to minimize blast.
- Restrict parking from interior of a group of buildings.
- Any parking within structure must be restricted and manned with guard who checks credentials of drivers of entering vehicles at safe standoff distance of the entrance to the building parking area.
- If possible, locate visitor or general parking area near but not on building site itself and locate that parking within view of the occupied building. This is for both stand-alone above-ground parking structures and surface parking lots to maximize surveillance of vehicles entering into, out of, and across the garage.
- If possible, design the parking lot with one-way circulation to facilitate monitoring for potential aggressors.
- Prohibit parking in the standoff zone.
- Provide parking areas with emergency communications systems (intercoms, telephones) at readily identified, well-lighted, closed circuit television monitored locations to permit direct contact with security personnel.
- In densely populated areas, require appropriate permits to restrict parking in curb lanes near building to only company-owned or key-employee vehicles.
- If parking within a building is required:
  —Do not permit uninspected vehicles to enter the parking structure.
  —Require an identification check if public or visitors must be allowed to park.
  —Restrict such parking to company vehicles and employees who work in that building only and check identifications prior to entry.
- Where parking inside the building is necessary and the building superstructure is supported by the parking structure:
  —Protect the primary vertical-load-carrying members by implementing architectural or structural features that provide minimum 6 in. standoff from the face of the member.

—Design columns in the garage area for an "unbraced length" equal to two floors, or three floors where there are two levels of parking.

—Avoid dead-end parking areas, as well as nooks and crannies and avoid landscaping that provides hiding places.

- Where parking garages are located within or adjacent to the building:

—Stairways and elevator lobby design should be as open as the code permits. Ideally make the stair or elevator waiting area as open to exterior as possible to ensure that people using the structure are readily seen and can easily see out.

—Elevator cabs should have glass backs wherever possible and lobbies should be well lighted to increase visibility to all.

- Pedestrian paths should be designed to concentrate activity (e.g., bringing all pedestrians, visitors, through a single secured portal into the building).

PASSENGER DROP-OFF ZONES

- Should be outside the secured stand-off zone and not within or underneath the building.
- Where necessary, provide covered walkways which do not restrict visibility of persons exiting vehicles and proceeding through the standoff zone to the building's entrance.

BUILDING DELIVERY AND SERVICE AREAS

- Provide signs that clearly mark separate entrances for deliveries and avoid driveways under or within the building.
- Separate by at least 50 ft from the utility rooms, utility mains, and service entrances from the loading docks and shipping and receiving areas. The utility areas include electrical, telephone/data, fire detection/alarm systems, fire suppression water mains, HVAC equipment room, or security station for the building.
- Locate shipping and receiving docks so that vehicles will not be allowed under the building.
- Where the first three items are not possible, shipping and receiving areas must be hardened to withstand blast from bombs that vehicles (trucks) could carry. Loading dock design should limit damage to adjacent areas and vent explosive forces to the exterior of the building but away from pedestrian traffic areas (do not vent into egress routes from building).
- Where possible, security personnel may be provided to inspect and clear entrance of delivery trucks to facility.
- If loading zones or drive-through areas are necessary, monitor them and restrict height to keep out large vehicles.

PHYSICAL SECURITY LIGHTING Security lighting should be provided to the entire site including the building perimeter, entrances, pedestrian walkway, and parking and loading dock areas to assure maximum surveillance by security personnel. Lighting systems should have a backup power system and power system should be located away from the loading docks or other places with vehicular traffic.

- Entry points require minimum surface lighting of four horizontal foot candles.
- High-mast lighting is recommended where practical to give broader and more natural lighting with fewer poles.
- Lighting of the entry control point should give any gate houses or security posts clear view of drivers and vehicles.
- One or more of the following four types of security lighting should be provided as needed:
  —Continuous lighting: flood a given area with continuous light during darkness with overlapping cones of light. Two primary methods are glare projection and controlled lighting. Glare lighting illuminates the area surrounding a controlled area with high-intensity light and keeps the guards in comparative darkness. Controlled lighting, best used outside the perimeter, provides limited lighting to a particular need, that is, it may either illuminate or silhouette security personnel.
  —Standby lighting: Similar to continuous lighting but lights are not always kept on. Lights are turned on by sensors or when suspicious activity has been detected.
  —Moveable lighting: Manually operated, moveable searchlights that usually are used as supplementary lighting system to continuous or standby lighting.
  —Emergency lighting: the backup power system that may duplicate one or all of the preceding lighting systems, as well as the lighting system for the interior of the building. May originate from batteries or generators (i.e., diesel, gasoline, or fuel cells).

SITE UTILITIES A high-risk building can only be as secure as its access to the utility services that support its operation—power and water (potable and sewer). These services can be particularly vulnerable to the effects of blast and (as with the WTC) their being severed can adversely impact the life safety of the building occupants in the aftermath of a terrorist attack.

- Wherever possible utilities should be protected, concealed and underground. Places where utility lines pass through the outer perimeter (fences, and so on) should be sealed to assure no one can pass through that security barrier through that opening.

Figure 5-12

New construction and layers of defense include high-mast lighting

- Redundant utility systems entering the building from different directions should be provided to support security, life safety, and rescue functions.
- Where possible provide quick connects for portable utility backup systems if redundant systems are not functioning or available. (This also is useful following natural disasters such as a seismic event that may severely damage or destroy a portion of or the entire power grid and water system.)
- Prepare a vulnerability assessment of all utility services to the site, including power lines, storm sewers, water lines, gas lines, and other utilities that the building is dependant upon and/or which cross the site perimeter.
- Secure manholes and underground utility conduits that enter the building grounds and building itself. This includes protecting water treatment plants and storage facilities from waterborne contaminates.
- Conceal incoming utility systems as much as possible and minimize signs marking them. Do, however, provide fire and building department emergency personnel with diagrams of utility feed locations and connections for use in response to emergency situations.
- Locate utility systems 50 ft or more from loading docks, front entrances, and parking areas and consider blast-resistant construction to harden utility rooms.
- Locate petroleum, oil, lubricant, or chemical storage tanks and operation buildings downslope from all other buildings. Where possible, locate fuel tanks at lower elevation than operational buildings or utility plants. Fuel-storage tanks should be a minimum of 100 ft from other buildings and away from loading docks, entrances, and parking.
- Provide utility systems with redundant loop service (especially electrical system).
- Decentralize a site's communications resources. When possible use multiple communications networks that will strengthen communications systems ability to work during disaster. Network control centers should be protected and, if possible, concealed.
- Route critical or fragile utilities so that they are not on exterior walls or on walls shared with lobby or mailroom (or loading docks).
- Fixtures and all overhead utilities weighing 31 psi or more should be mounted to reduce likelihood that they will fall during blast (or seismic event) and cause injuries. (Follow appropriate provisions for seismic portions of local building code.)

PEDESTRIAN TRAFFIC

- Use CPTED principles to design pedestrian traffic ways to maximize visibility and control physical access to building through main secured portal or entrance way. This includes both natural barriers and security devices including closed-circuit television, security lighting, and sensors or alarms that are set off when unauthorized personnel move into secured spaces.
- As necessary provide external security checkpoints for visitor access to the building.

Figure 5-13, prepared by FEMA, provides an example of how applying the preceding guidelines for setback, parking, and location of the loading docks can change an initial building design to reduce levels of risk from a potential terrorist attack. The original design layout (the top diagram) placed parking directly beneath the structure and the

Figure 5-13

Schematics of redesigning a building to increase layers and levels of security; Source: FEMA, Figure 6-4

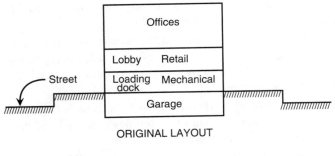

ORIGINAL LAYOUT

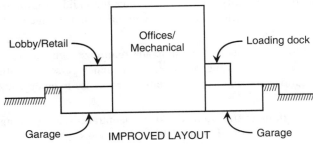

IMPROVED LAYOUT

loading dock next to the mechanical rooms, thus making the entire structure much more vulnerable to a bomb.

The "improved layout" (bottom diagram) moved the underground parking structure to the sides of the building and relocated the loading dock so it is not immediately adjacent to the vital mechanical room. The second design also moved public space, the lobby, and retail shops out of the main structure, thus potentially reducing the amount of nonbuilding occupant pedestrian traffic through the office building.

Other Resources for Defending the Outer Ring for High-Risk Structures

U.S. Department of Defense: Unified Facilities Criteria

In addition to the earlier guidelines, the following unclassified specification documents are available online for downloading from the U.S. DoD's Unified Facilities Criteria program via the Whole Building Design Guide (www.wbd.org), maintained by NIBS (UFGS-02821A: Fencing, published February 2002; UFGS-02840A, active vehicle barriers, February 2002; UFGS, 02841N, traffic barriers, August, 2001).

Codes and Standards and the Outer Ring

Other than the building code references, as noted earlier in this chapter, with the exception of NFPA Guide 730 and Standard 731, the nation's model building codes do not have specific security provisions governing perimeter access.

Building owners should consider following these two NFPA documents and other procedures and systems described in FEMA 426, for design guidance in offering increased security for buildings and for the installation of electronic security systems. NFPA Standards

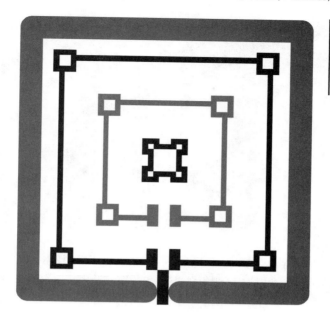

Figure 5-14

Original diagram, inner ring of defense by Andrew Corcoran

730, "Guide for Premises Security, 2006 edition, and 731, "Standard for the Installation of Electronic Premises Security Systems, 2006," are found on pages 133 to 135 of this chapter.

THE INNER RING—BUILDING TYPE 2

Security Inside the Outer Ring: Protection from Blast and Progressive Collapse

It is impractical to design a civilian structure to remain undamaged from a large explosion. The protective objectives are therefore related to the type of building and its function. For an office, retail, residential, or light industrial building, where the primary asset is the occupants, the objective is to minimize loss of life. Because of the severity of large scale explosion incidents, the goals are by necessity modest. Moreover, it is recognized that the building will be unusable after the event. This approach is considered a damage-limiting or damage-mitigating approach to design.

To save lives, the primary goals of the design professional are to reduce building damage and to prevent progressive collapse of the building, at least until it can be fully evacuated. A secondary goal is to maintain emergency functions until evacuation is complete.

—"Goals of the Design Approach," FEMA Document 427

Thanks to the declassification of earlier work by federal agencies, a building owner, and his or her construction team with a building site that either does not allow adequate standoff distances to mitigate the effects of a bomb blast, or whose risk-threat assessment strategy has led them to consider providing varying degrees of protection from similar attacks on a neighboring structure now have available to them a number of design approaches and building materials to use.

Figure 5-15

Fairfax County, Virginia Government Center uses multiple rings of security

Both the U.S. Departments of State and DoD have spent considerable time and effort between 1970 and 1990 researching and developing classified guidelines and practices addressing the issue of protecting buildings from blast.

Following the Oklahoma City Bombing in 1995, these federal agencies along with the GSA and the FEMA began producing declassified materials regarding blast and making them available to the private sector.

The primary FEMA document is "Primer for Design of Commercial Buildings to Mitigate Terrorist Attacks." Its companion documents are from FEMA's risk management series no. 426, "Reference Manual to Mitigate Potential Terrorist Attacks Against Buildings," and "Facts for Steel Buildings: Blast and Progressive Collapse" from the American Institute of Steel Construction (AISC). Released in December 2003, the FEMA documents built upon the Oklahoma City, Khobar Towers, and 1993 WTC bombings. The AISC document, released in April 2005, adds to the earlier information compiled from terrorist bombings in Iraq.

A unique resource that will be referenced several times in this chapter is the "Whole Building Design Guide" (www.wbdg.org). In 2003, several federal agencies came together and contracted with the NIBS to develop a "comprehensive guide for exterior envelope design and construction for institutional office buildings." Participating federal agencies included the U.S. Army Corps of Engineers, the Naval Facilities Engineering Command, the U.S. Air Force, GSA, Department of Energy, and the Department of Homeland Security's FEMA.

The guide is neither a building code nor a standard and does not contain mandatory criteria. It is available to both the public and private sectors to provide "design oriented information meant to assist designers in making informed choices of materials and systems to achieve performance goals in their buildings."

In addition to these unclassified resources, governmental agencies at the federal, state, and local levels also have available to them classified blast protection information, including details on blast-mitigating products, from the earlier mentioned TSWG. Originating under a 1982 National Security Decision Directive, TSWG operates today under the policy oversight of the Department of State's Coordinator for Counterterrorism and the technical oversight of the DoD's Assistant Secretary of Defense for Special Operations and Low-Intensity Conflict.

The mission of TSWG's physical security subgroup is to identify the physical requirements and conduct research and development to establish design requirements, construction methodologies, and products that can be effective in combating terrorism. Federal, state, and local government officials have access to this information via a secure section of the TSWG website.

Understanding Blast and Its Impact on Building Exteriors and Interiors

The three areas where the most research and design work have been done over the past 30 years have been in the areas of external security and mitigating the potential damage to buildings and their occupants from blast and biochemical attacks. Drawing from the DoD, GSA and FEMA documents are the major facts regarding blasts that the building owner, designer, engineer, and the rest of the construction team (including building maintenance personnel) must be aware of if they are to function as an effective team.

Blast 101

As described in the FEMA , risk management series publication no. 427, "Primer for Design of Commercial Buildings to Mitigate Terrorist Attacks," explosions involve an extremely rapid (at supersonic speeds) releases of energy as heat, light, sound, and a shockwave. Consisting of highly compressed air, a shockwave bounces off the ground surface and produces a hemispheric propagation of the wave that travels outward from the point of detonation at supersonic speeds. The incident, or overpressures of that wave, decrease as the shockwave expands.

A surface that is in the line-of-sight of the explosion that is struck by that wave reflects the wave, resulting in a tremendous amplification of the pressure. The supersonic velocity of the shockwave causes the amplification of pressure to be up to 13 times its original pressure (as opposed to sound waves that only amplify by two). The nearness or distance of the point of detonation and the angle of incidence that the shockwave hits that surface determine the magnitude of the reflection factor.

Pressures decay exponentially with time (milliseconds). Building features such as overhangs or internal corners of an l- or t-shaped building will trap the shockwave for a while, prolonging its duration and increasing its potential damage to that portion of the building.

As shown in Figure 5-16, late in the explosion, the shockwave becomes negative and is followed by a partial vacuum that causes suction behind the shockwave. A strong wind that picks up debris is then generated or drags pressure on the building as air rushes in behind the vacuum. When these detonations are outside, some of the blast energy goes into the ground creating a crater and generating a shockwave similar to that generated by a short-duration high-intensity earthquake.

Figure 5-16

FEMA diagram of air-blast pressure time history, Figure 3-1

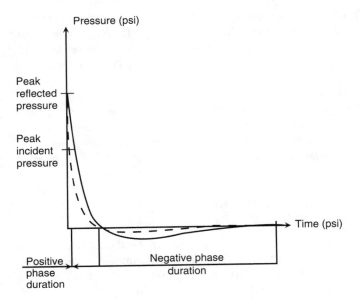

Figure 5-17 describes how the bomb's size (yield), which is expressed in pounds of TNT, and the cube of the distance from the detonation site determine the peak pressure of the blast. Standoff distances and blast-mitigation design considerations are determined based upon these functions of the size of the explosive device, peak incident and reflected pressures of the shockwave, and angle of impact.

The FEMA primer provides the following chart, Figure 5-18, as a guide to the building owner and designer concerning the impact of explosive devices delivered in a varying-sized vehicle and their overpressure as relates to standoff distances.

Blast and Exterior Building Damage

Different building shapes and different standoff distances have a significant effect on the relative impact of an explosive device. Shapes that dissipate air blast perform better than do those that trap or accentuate the air blast as shown in Figure 5-19. Impacts may range from shattered windows and cracked walls to the kind of catastrophic structural

Figure 5-17

FEMA diagram of pressure decay with distance, Figure 3-2

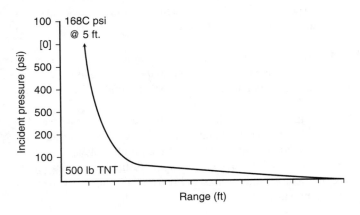

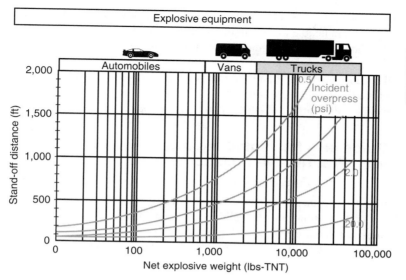

Figure 5-18

FEMA diagram of incident overpressure as a function of stand-off distance, Figure 1-4

failures witnessed in the Khobar Towers, Murrah Building, American Embassy and Marine Barracks in Beirut.

While injuries caused by flying glass and debris entering the building have caused deaths in bombings, the largest losses of life have been from progressive structural collapses caused by the spread of any initial localized collapse of a column, exterior wall,

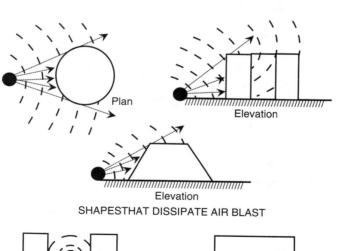

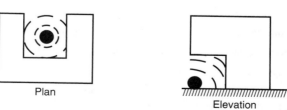

Figure 5-19

FEMA diagram, schematics showing the effect of building shape on air-blast impacts, Figure 6-3

roof, or floor system to other parts of the structure that may have received lesser damage but are unable to sustain the building load that has been transferred to them by the destruction of those localized columns, walls, and floor.

The close proximity of a powerful bomb to critical load-bearing columns produces progressive collapse, by propagating forces vertically upward or downward from the explosion's source and laterally from bay to bay.

Guidelines for Protecting the Structure from Progressive Collapse

The DoD, GSA, Department of State, and FEMA at the federal government level and from the private sector, the American Society of Civil Engineers (ASCE), AISC, and the Concrete Masonry Institute all have worked on and produced either construction guidelines or standards addressing technical issues regarding the design of new (and retrofit of existing) buildings to prevent or reduce the risk of progressive collapse from explosive devices.

In addition, in the wake of the Oklahoma City bombing, FEMA conducted a study to see if the Murrah building would have performed better had it been designed to a higher set of seismic structural safety requirements within the then existing model building codes. The results, while encouraging, were inconclusive that any definitive recommendation could be made that merely using an upgrade in the seismic requirements would be a successful design approach to propose to the construction community. FEMA instead moved forward with working on and supporting specific blast-mitigation design guidelines based on the work of DoD, GSA and the Department of State.

These guidelines were incorporated into FEMA's risk management series, no. 426, "Reference Manual to Mitigate Potential Terrorist Attacks Against Buildings" and GSA's "Progressive Collapse Analysis and Design Guidelines for New Federal Office Buildings." Drawing from those two documents, the design features that follow provide a more robust structure and decrease the potential for progressive collapse:

- Redundancy
- Use of ductile structural elements and detailing
- Capacity for resisting load reversals
- Capacity for resisting sheer failure

Consideration of one or more of the following engineering practices will determine its appropriateness:

- Internal damping into the structural system to absorb the blast impact
- Symmetric reinforcement that can increase the ultimate load capacity of the structure
- Wire mesh in plaster to reduce the incidence of flying fragments
- Avoid use of masonry when blast is a threat, evading potential problems experienced with masonry walls breaking up and becoming secondary fragments during the blast

- Multiple barrier materials and construction techniques that can sometimes accomplish the same goal with less expense than a single material or technique
- Lap splices to fully develop the capacity of the reinforcement
- Controlled deflections around certain members, such as windows, to prevent premature failure; additional reinforcement is generally required
- Minimal column spacing, in general, so that reasonably sized members can be designed to resist the design loads and increase the redundancy of the system
- Minimal floor-to-floor heights (unless there is an overriding architectural requirement, a practical limit is generally less than or equal to 16 ft)
- Fully grouted and reinforced concrete masonry units when CMU (concrete masonry unit) construction is selected
- Coordination of structural requirements for blast between the designer and other disciplines such as in architectural and mechanical areas
- One-way wall elements spanning from floor-to-floor to minimize blast loads imparted to columns
- Careful design approaches to ensure agreement between the elements (this may be true in use of ductile detailing requirements for seismic design and alternate load paths provided by progressive collapse design)
- Architectural and structural features that deny contact with exposed primary vertical load members (a minimum standoff of at least 6 in. from these members is required)

Building materials that are acceptable in the adopted building codes in the jurisdiction in which the building is being constructed are allowed, however, "special consideration should be given to materials that have inherent flexibility and that are better able to handle load reversals (i.e., cast in place reinforced concrete and steel construction)." "The construction type selected must meet all performance criteria of the specified level of protection."

The FEMA and GSA documents also note that all building components "requiring blast resistance should be designed using established methods and approaches for determining dynamic loads, structural detailing, and dynamic structural response." A designer or builder, working with a licensed structural engineer who has expertise in blast design and construction, should consult with the following design criteria and standards and, where applicable, incorporate them into the building's design.

- "Minimum Design Loads for Buildings and Other Structures," ASCE 7
- GSA, "Security Design Criteria"
- AISC, "Facts for Steel Buildings—Blast and Progressive Collapse"
- "Blast Safety of the Building Envelope" in the "Whole Building Design Guide"

In addition to the preceding standards, the U.S. Army Corps of Engineers and NIST continue to fund and conduct research on the issue of reducing progressive collapse as the result of blast and seismic events.

NIST's multiyear research initiative is working to develop and implement performance criteria for codes and standards, tools, and practical guidance for the prevention of progressive structural collapse. This project is considering four distinct but interrelated strategies to mitigate progressive collapse:

- Determine systems design concept—evaluate progressive collapse vulnerability of different structural system design concepts and develop new systems concepts that "are effective in mitigating progressive collapse under multiple threat scenarios."
- Retard collapse after triggering event—test and evaluate different connection details to ensure continuity of load-carrying capacity and provide strength and ductility following a localized failure to help assure that there is sufficient time and egress paths to evacuate a building.
- Build in redundancy via alternate load paths—look at ways in which redundancy can be built into a structure at minimal additional cost.
- Retrofit and design to harden a structure—look at different approaches to reduce progressive collapse risk from multiple sources through either structural retrofit or structural hardening by designing more massive structural elements.

As a part of the preceding work, NIST and the U.S. Army Corps of Engineers in mid-2006 conducted a large-scale test to demonstrate connection behavior. A report on the outcome of that testing and its relevance to preventing progressive collapse will be posted on the NIST Building and Fire Research Laboratory portion of the NIST Web site in the fall of 2006.

NIST currently also is reviewing progressive collapse prevention best practices from overseas. Great Britain's "Standards to Avoid Progressive Collapse—Large Panel Construction" standard has been out since 1968 and is being reviewed by NIST for possible application within the U.S. codes and standards. The Eurocode for building contains similar provisions.

The British Standard lists two methods for mitigating progressive collapse:

1. "Providing alternative load paths, assuming the removal of a critical section of the load bearing system."
2. "Providing stiffness and continuity to the structural system to ensure the stability of the building against forces liable to damage the load supporting members."

The British standard also "specifies an accidental static pressure of 5 psi and minimum tie forces for continuity."

The outcome of NIST's multiyear effort will be shared with the ASCE for consideration to update the current ASCE/SEI 7 standard. NIST anticipates that its final document will be made available for review and comment at the end of 2007, prior to its submission to ASCE.

Guidelines for Protecting the Interior of the Building from Other Blast Damage

Deaths and severe injuries in buildings result not only from progressive collapse but also from blast debris and localized collapses of walls and floors. For buildings with moderate to high risk from terrorism, the objective of the owner, designer, and construction

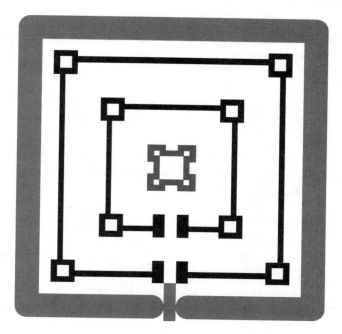

Figure 5-20
Original diagram, inner core, castle keep, by Andrew Corcoran

team is to limit the impact of that attack to something approaching "acceptable damage levels." The owner, be it a federal, state, or local government agency, or a private sector firm going through the risk-threat analysis methodology provided in Chapter 4 will need to define what that "acceptable level" is for them and their employees given a realistic assessment of the actual threats that are involved.

"Blast Safety of the Building Envelope" in the "Whole Building Design Guide" defines damage levels in the following three categories: minor, moderate, and severe and notes that it is a reasonable goal for new construction to experience only "moderate" damage from such an attack.

- "Minor: Nonstructural failure of building elements as windows, doors, and cladding. Injuries may be expected and fatalities are possible but unlikely."

- "Moderate: Structural damage is confined to a localized area and is usually repairable. Structural failure is limited to secondary structural members, such as beams, slabs, and non-load bearing walls. However, if the building has been designed for loss of primary members, localized loss of columns may be accommodated without initiating progressive collapse. Injuries and possible fatalities are expected."

- "Major: Loss of primary structural components such as columns or transfer girders precipitates loss of additional adjacent members that are adjacent or above the lost member. In this case, extensive fatalities are expected. Building is usually not repairable."

Having set what is an "acceptable level of damage," for his or her building, the owner and design and construction team then can select appropriate design criteria, building products, and materials above those required in the adopted building code and standards for the community in which the building is being sited.

In addition to those guidelines provided earlier to resist progressive collapse the following is a checklist of additional design criteria that should be considered to minimize localized structural failures and damage to the exterior of the building:

Guidelines to Reduce Blast Effects

For the building:

- Reduce or minimize exterior ornamentation (as this can become flying debris)
- Consider the use of bermed walls that can reduce blast impacts (and also increase energy efficiency)

For exterior walls:

- Resist the actual pressures and impulses acting on the building from the blast and be able to resist dynamic action of the windows from the event.
- Consider sheer walls that also function as exterior walls as primary structures where they are essential to lateral and vertical load-bearing systems.
- Give special consideration to construction types that reduce the potential for collapse where exterior walls are not designed for the full-load designs,.
- Ensure that requirements of the Army Technical Manual (5-853) standards for a medium protection level for exterior walls have the equivalent of 4 in. of concrete with # 5 reinforcing steel at 6-in. intervals each way or 8-in. CMU with # 4 reinforcing steel at 8-in. intervals.

For cladding and finishing

- Substitute strengthened building elements and systems where standoff distances cannot be adhered to.
- Use ductile materials that are capable of very large plastic deformations without complete failure.
- Provide blast-resistant walls when a high terrorist threat is possible.
- Consider use of sacrificial exterior wall panels to absorb the blast.
- Consider reinforced concrete wall systems in lieu of masonry or curtain walls to minimize flying debris.
- Consider using reinforced wall panels to protect columns and enable them to carry the load of a neighboring damaged column, thus assisting in the prevention of progressive collapse.

In addition to these guidelines, TSWG is working on making available to federal, state, and local governments and their contractors, information on blast-mitigating products and technologies that can be used to achieve the previously mentioned protection. Among the products studied not only by TSWG and other federal agencies are "blast wraps," a product that originally evolved to reduce the explosive force of small bombs being defused by bomb disposal squads in England. Addition information on blast wraps will be provided in Chapter 6.

Guidelines for Protecting Windows

Glass shards from bomb blasts have caused severe injuries and deaths in a number of bombings in the United States and overseas. There are varying degrees of shatter-resistant glazing that can be selected from depending upon the severity of the threat being mitigated. These can be selected from using a number of government-produced or sponsored software programs including WINGARD, WINLAC and SAFEVUE.

Glazing protection levels based on fragment impact locations have been set by GSA as follows:

- Protection level, safe: Glazing does not break, and there is no visible damage to either the glazing or the frame
- Protection level, very high: Glazing cracks but is retained in the frame. Dusting or very mall fragments near the sill or on the floor are acceptable
- Protection level, high: Glazing cracks. Fragments enter space and land on floor no further than 10 ft from the window.
- Protection level, medium: Glazing cracks. Fragments enter space and land on floor and impact a vertical witness panel at a distance of no more than 10 ft from the window and at a height no greater than 2 ft from the floor.
- Protection level, low: Glazing cracks and window system fails catastrophically. Fragments enter space impacting a vertical witness panel at a distance of no more than 10 ft from the window at a height greater than 2 ft above the floor.

Drawn from GSA's "Security Design" requirements (updated March 2005), the following guidelines and referenced standards can be followed to minimize such injuries for buildings that have been assessed to have moderate to high risk of attack or are located near such buildings and thus subject to potential collateral damage. The amount and type of safety glazing and blast resistance of mullions and frames will be determined by the owner based upon the level of risk. Once that has been determined the following guidelines can be considered.

- Window systems for exterior façade—designed to be in balance with the framing, anchorage, and supporting walls in order to minimize the hazard of flying glass in a blast event.
- Walls, anchorage of the window to the walls or floors, and the window framing—designed for the maximum capacity of the glass itself.
- Glazing hazard reduction products—all products for GSA use for the five protection levels require product-specific test results and engineering analysis performed by qualified independent agents who demonstrate and validate the performance of the product under specified blast loads. (GSA provides its contractors with a database that shows the performance of a wide variety of products that meet these requirements and that are available to the builder).
- Window fenestration—total fenestration openings are not limited, but a maximum of 40% per structural bay is GSA's preferred design goal.
- Window frames—should develop the full capacity of a chosen glazing up to 750 breaks per 1000 and provide the required level of protection without failure (shown either through calculations or testing methods).

- Anchorage—must remain attached to the wall of the facility during the blast event and not fail (shown either through design calculations or approved tests).

The following are the preferred systems of glazing:

- Thermally tempered glass with a security film installed on the interior surface and attached to frame.
- Laminated thermally tempered, laminated heat-strengthened, or laminated annealed glass and blast curtains.
- Monolithic thermally tempered glass with or without film, if the pane is designed to withstand the full design threat.

Unacceptable systems of glazing are as follows:

- Untreated monolithic annealed or heat-strengthened glass
- Wire glass
- Mullion design—frame members connecting adjoining windows must be designed in either a static approach where the breaking strength of the window is applied to the mullion or a dynamic load may be applied using the peak pressures and impulse values.
- Frame and anchorage design—the window frames need to retain the glass so that the entire pane does not become a single large piece of flying debris and also must resist the breaking stress of the glass.
- Supporting wall design—maximum strength must be equal to that of the windows.

In addition to these provisions, GSA has requirements for ballistic windows (must meet requirements of Underwriters Laboratories Standard 752, bullet-resistant glazing for a specified level [level set by agency] and security glazing, where requirement must meet ASTM standard F1233 or UL972 for burglary-resistant glazing material). The resistance of window assemblies to forced entry must meet ASTM F588 for a specified grade set by GSA.

Further guideline details are available from GSA and through the "Whole Building Design Guide." One important recommendation to building owners in this regard is that when putting in blast-resistant windows in a building, they make certain that the local fire department and other first responders are made aware of the exact type of windows used so that they have the tools necessary to break through those windows in a rescue emergency.

Protection of Other Areas Against Blast: Doors, Roof, and Other Parts of the Building

Blast impacts other areas of the building including doors, roofs, (especially in low structures) and air intakes (see next section where it is recommended that these be two stories above grade). The features that should be considered in designing these parts of the building to mitigate the hazards of blast are as follows:

Doors

Doorways pose another area of hazard from blast and, together with their frame and anchorage for high-risk buildings, must be designed to withstand the maximum dynamic pressure and duration of the load from the blast. Other design considerations include the following:

- Hollow steel doors or steel-clad doors with steel frames
- Blast-resistant steel doors for buildings with high threats and the need for high levels of protection
- One entry/egress for normal business access where possible
- Emergency egress accommodated, but the number of doors minimized due to higher vulnerability than solid walls.
- Exterior doors open outward and installation present a blank, flush surface to the outside to make them more resistant to attack. This includes locating hinges on the interior side of the building to make them tamperproof from the outside.
- Upright surfaces of door jambs strengthened and hardened.

Figure 5-21

Doors, California State Capitol, Sacramento

Figure 5-22

Roof-top security,
view of Boston

Roofs

- Roof load—blast places two loads on roofs: the primary loading is downward over-pressure and the secondary load may include upward pressure if any part of the building has been penetrated by the blast. It is conservative to do the calculations for these loads separately.

- Roof systems—two preferred systems (by GSA and FEMA) to withstand blast are poured-in-place reinforced concrete with beams in two directions and steel frames with a concrete and metal deck slab.

- Poured-in-place reinforced concrete system—the preferred design is for beams to have stirrups along the entire span spaced not greater than one half the beam's depth.

- Steel frame with concrete deck slab—the preferred design is a two-way system of reinforcing bars spaced not more than the total thickness of the slab.

- Puddle welds or other strong systems—these are needed along the perimeter to resist the sheer forces on the slab as it is deflected downward.

Louvers and Air Intakes

- Louver connections—these should be designed to withstand the louver's flexural capacity and where possible a catch system should be provided behind the louver.

- Air intakes—in general, they should be located at least two stories above grade (to reduce risk from a biochemical attack) and should have grates to keep explosive devices (or biochemical agents) from being tossed into them.

INTERNAL BUILDING SECURITY: PROTECTING THE BUILDING FROM INTERNAL AND EXTERNAL BIOCHEMICAL ATTACK

The Indoor Air Environment

The current building codes and national standards governing indoor air quality, heating and refrigerating, and cooling within buildings evolved from the post-World War II era onward. For buildings that in all likelihood will never be subject to a terrorist biochemical or radiological attack or even the accidental release of a chemical due to an industrial or transportation accident, the current editions of these codes and standards provide adequate safety for building tenants and visitors.

As energy prices continue to increase in the coming years, the effectiveness and efficiency of these mechanical systems and the importance of their proper maintenance will become an issue of growing concern to building owners and the members of their construction team. As noted in Chapter 7, "Homeland Security and the Issues of Energy, Sustainability, Environment, Accessibility, and New Products, Materials and Techniques," energy prices and environmental issues will result in the development of new technologies and further enhancements in the energy efficiency requirements for HVAC systems and more restrictive energy conservation provisions in future editions of building codes.

Both the terrorist attacks overseas (the Tokyo subway attack and release of sarin) and the anthrax attacks through the U.S. postal system in 2001 have added an entirely new area of concern regarding future safety inside the building envelope for building owners and managers. While most of the nation has focused over the past two decades on issues related to bombing and blast, considerable research and study of effective mitigation actions have been conducted by the public and private sector on the issue of biochemical or radiological attack. In Chapter 4, the work of the American Society of Heating Refrigerating and Air Conditioning Engineers (ASHRAE) to develop and encourage "Risk Management Guidance on Health, Safety and Environmental Security" was described along with information on their soon to be released guideline.

Since the anthrax attacks in 2001, ASHRAE, GSA and the DoD (including the Defense Advanced Research Projects Agency [DARPA]), Lawrence Berkley National Laboratory, the Centers for Disease Control (CDC), and National Institute of Occupational Health and Safety all have taken their research and contributed to guidelines on practices and technologies that at this stage appear to be the most effective approaches to either protect or mitigate the impact of either the internal or external release of biochemical agents.

Figure 5-23

Large public assembly/arena in Midwest

Prior to 2001, a significant level of effort went into joint work between the DoD, CDC, and the National Research Council's Committee on Toxicology to publish and release to the public health and first responder community a list of biochemical agents and their characteristics. (Two charts and a biochemical glossary providing that information is found Appendix C of FEMA 426 reference manual.)

The next section looks at the general guidelines developed by these agencies and associations and provides a synopsis of major actions that can be taken now in the design and construction of a new high-risk exposed building to address a number of the hazards currently associated with either a biochemical attack or the accidental release of these materials. Just as it was urged that owners include a licensed engineer with expertise in blast mitigation on their construction team to address structural issues, so too should owners include on their design team qualified mechanical engineers with expertise in the area of biochemical mitigation systems.

The following general guidelines provide an overview of the levels of complexity that are involved. Several notations on future directions in ongoing research in this field are provided at the end of this section. The core document covered in this section is the May 2002 CDC/National Institute of Occupational Safety and Health (NIOSH) report on "Guidance for Protecting Building Environments from Airborne, Chemical, Biological, or Radiological Attacks."

Design and Program Considerations for Protecting Buildings and Their Occupants from External and Internal Release of Biochemical Materials

Location of Fresh Air Intakes

- Fresh air intakes should be located at least two stories above ground to reduce the potential for hazardous materials (as well as vehicle exhaust). Many contaminates are heavier than the surrounding air and will remain close to the ground under calm conditions, therefore placing the intakes at the highest practical level on the building is beneficial.

- Intakes should be covered by screens that are sloped so contaminants cannot be tossed into them from ground level or from an adjacent building or structure.

- As covered in earlier sections, mechanical rooms should be secured and located away from public traffic areas or areas of the building that may be more vulnerable to attack such as mail rooms, loading docks, and building lobbies.

- There should be no public access to the roof of the building to eliminate possibility of attack via exhaust vents, HVAC units, or air intakes located there.

- Access to information on the buildings operating systems (including fire, smoke control, electrical, and other mechanical systems) and emergency procedures should be restricted and secured.

- HVAC systems should be isolated, well sealed, and maintained at negative pressure relative to the rest of the building to prevent widespread dispersion of any contaminates (e.g., anthrax) released within the building's mail room lobby or loading dock.

- Isolation of multiple HVAC zones in large buildings served by their own HVAC system minimizes the potential for the spread of an airborne contaminate within the building. This also reduces the potential number of building occupants exposed to such hazards. This requires a full height wall between each zone and its adjacent zone and the buildings hallways.

- In case of an outdoor release of a hazardous substance, the building should be designed to allow for occupants to "shelter in place" in rooms or locations where risk of outdoor air infiltration is low. These areas must have the following:
  - Doors that prevent airflow
  - Mechanisms and staff to operate them that are capable of reducing and then shutting down the indoor–outdoor air exchange rate prior to the arrival at the building

Figure 5-24

Evacuation and shelter-in-place instructions in Federal Building in National Capital Region

site of the contaminate plume. Depending on the design of the HVAC system this may include the closing of various dampers, especially those controlling the flow of outdoor air. Low leakage dampers should be considered to avoid the potential for outdoor air to migrate into the building because the internal air pressure inside the building remains below that of the air pressure outside even with the HVAC system shut down.

- In case of an indoor release, it is essential to have HVAC mechanisms that provide interior pressure and airflow control to vent the contaminate to the outside as rapidly as possible while isolating the contaminate from other portions of the building.

- The HVAC systems should be designed and tested in coordination with a qualified mechanical engineer as a member of the construction team. The actual nature of which operating procedures to follow will vary depending on the nature of the system in the building and of the indoor or outdoor contaminate to which the building is exposed.

- Ducted air returns reduce the access points in which a contaminate can be introduced. Placing return vents in high traffic areas reduces chances that a contaminate could be surreptitiously introduced into the return system.

- It may be a good idea to add a system of highly efficient filters to assure that a contaminate is not redistributed throughout a high-risk building with nonducted air return systems (that uses hallways or spaces above the suspended ceiling in a ceiling plenum return system) returns the air to the HVAC unit. (See discussion of filters later.)

- Sensors and Filters

- It may be a good idea to consider including biochemical sensors within the HVAC system in high-risk buildings. Considerable research is still ongoing in this field to eliminate false alarms that stimulate unnecessary evacuations from the building. GSA, DoD, and TSWG are working on further research into these systems and their results should be consulted.

- Filter systems likewise are still subject to ongoing research and testing by GSA, DoD, and TSWG and others. Current filter technology requires different filters for different types of biochemical agents.

Different types of filers currently available include particulate air filters designed to capture aerosols through one or more collection mechanisms (inertial impaction, interception, diffusion, or electrostatic) and are covered by two ASHRAE standards for rating: ASHRAE 52.1,1992, and ASHRAE 52.2,1999.

Particulate filters include low-efficiency dust filters, high-efficiency particulate air filters (HEPA) and ultra-low penetration air filters (ULPA).

Figure 5-25

National Governor's Association meeting and similar meetings of public officials today require added security

Chapter 5 of the FEMA 426 reference manual entitled, "Chemical, Biological, and Radiological Measures," provides the best overview of issues concerning filter availability and use. Federal, state, and local governments can again consult the TSWG Web site for additional information.

Other Useful Tools

DARPA Research: Toward Immune Buildings   DARPA is continuing its work with academic institutions, its colleagues in other federal agencies, and the construction and standards community to develop an unclassified version of a "Building Protection Tool Kit" that will enable future building owners and members of their design and construction team to consider a wide range of technologies, design, and construction practices that can be used to enhance levels of protection within new (and existing) buildings from biochemical and radiological attacks or accidental releases. Part of this effort involves the development of design software packages that contain options for different mitigation strategies and further development and availability of "smart" filters that detect and eliminate hazardous agents or facilitate the appropriate actions (including shutdown) by a building's HVAC system. Release of such a tool kit is still several years away.

HVAC Building Vulnerability Assessment Tool: Rhode Island   Covered in more detail in Chapter 6, "Existing Buildings: Inspections and Retrofitting," the "Building Vulnerability Assessment Tool" is another useful tool for the building owner and designer. Developed by the State of Rhode Island's Department of Health Office of Occupational and Radiological Health Indoor Air Quality Program in November 2004, this tool provides a checklist for owners of existing buildings to review their building's current HVAC system and note areas where its design and operation can be either enhanced or modified to provide better protection to building occupants from potential biochemical agents. Owners constructing new buildings will find this checklist to be an added resource as to the design features and systems they need to include (e.g., air-handling units; air intakes; recirculation modes and air returns, mechanical rooms, filtration specifications; and systems operation and maintenance).

Emergency Egress: Currently Available Codes

The current provisions of the ICC's IBC, the NFPA's Life Safety Code (NFPA 101) and NFPA Building Construction and Safety Code (NFPA 5000) all have emergency egress provisions that have repeatedly been proved to adequately handle emergency egress situations where those codes have been adopted and are effectively enforced by state and/or local governments. Provisions are based upon building use groups and occupancy loads. Among their provisions include those for lighting, exit signs, exit access travel distances (with and without sprinkler systems), emergency escape and rescue, width of exit stairs (calculated on minimum widths per occupant served), areas of refuge, and accessible means of egress.

The pertinent sections of the codes are as follows:

- ICC's 2003 IBC, Chapter 10
- NFPA's 2006 Life Safety Code, Chapter 7
- NFPA's 2006, Building Construction and Safety Code (NFPA-5000), Chapter 11

There are basic egress requirements in these model codes for mid-rise to high-rise structures. Both the ICC and NFPA codes have similar requirements for the number of exits: minimum of two exits for 1 to 500 people; 3 exits for 501 to 1000 and 4 exits for more than 1000 occupants. Under both the ICC and NFPA, exit access travel distances in buildings without sprinklers range from 200 to 300 ft and those with sprinklers range from 250 to 400 ft.

ICC and NFPA do not allow the use of elevators as a means of emergency egress, unless they meet special provisions (section 1007.4 IBC and section 7.2.13.1 in NFPA 101). The ICC's 2003 IBC requires that stair exit width minimums be 44 in. NFPA 101 2006 requires that exit widths range from 44 in. for less than 2000 occupants in a building and to as high as 56 in. for buildings with 2000 occupants or more.

Figure 5-26
Open stairway in smoke-proof portion of building in Washington, D.C.

EMERGENCY EGRESS: POST-9/11 ACTIONS AND ALTERNATIVE APPROACHES   The attack upon and ultimate fires and collapse of the WTC Towers, as noted in Chapters 1 to 3, stimulated significant research and discussion concerning possible needs to reassess existing code requirements and standards (including those for elevators) for high-rise structures, especially those that may be at risk from future terrorist attacks or natural disasters that may require rapid and full evacuations of those structures.

In addition to the research and recommendations cited by NIST in their WTC report, the nation's model building codes and standards development organizations, building owners, and federal agencies have been looking at cost-effective approaches that facilitate rapid and safe evacuation of individuals from high-rise structures. The disabled community in the United States in particular has led a national discussion of actions that can be taken to speed the safe evacuation of individuals with physical disabilities. The building owner may wish to consider some of the issues they identified in the design, construction, and operation of their buildings.

On October 13 to 14, 2004, the U.S. Department of Education Office of Special Education and Rehabilitative Services and the National Institute on Disability and Rehabilitation Research brought together leading representatives from the nation's code and standards and architectural accessibility community to establish a research and action agenda for "Emergency Evacuation of People with Disabilities from Buildings." Among their recommendations were the following:

- Find a safe way to use elevators in existing buildings by occupants during emergencies.
- Identify best strategies for keeping people with disabilities safe during an emergency event.
- Modify evacuation plans and codes to require effective ways to communicate emergency information to people with different types of disabilities.
- Do additional research on areas of refuge and safety of disabled individuals during full building evacuations (from high-rises).

As witnessed by the above the area of emergency evacuation devices and procedures for the disabled is in the need of greater research and development for safer evacuation devices, evacuation protocols, and training. Other issues relevant to architectural accessibility and public safety will be covered in Chapter 7.

Other Approaches

The level of current adopted codes and standards are generally at a minimum, which leaves building owners and their design and construction team free to consider including provisions that provide greater degrees of safety in emergency egress situations than those found in these codes. Two places that a current building owner may want to look for possible alternative design guidelines that address the issue of emergency egress are found at the end of this chapter. These involve changes made in the New York City building code for high-rise buildings (page 178 to 181) and proposed code changes submitted to the ICC in mid-March 2006 by members of the NIBS Multihazard Mitigation Council committee. The latter submission includes a proposed diagram for a special emergency elevator system for fire fighters that also could be used to evacuate disabled individuals from the building.

This chapter closes with a look at specific recommendations from the NIST report on the WTC collapse that have now been turned into proposed code changes that are currently before the ICC for possible inclusion in the 2007 edition of the IBC.

GUIDELINES, CODES, AND STANDARDS TO ENHANCE PROTECTION FROM NATURAL DISASTERS: SEISMIC, WIND, AND FLOOD

The all-hazard approach to disaster mitigation, be it terrorist threat or a natural disaster, is transforming the way the building construction team interacts with not only the owner but with the community in which their building is built. Few places in our nation are without violent storms of one form or another, and large portions of our nation are subject to high degrees of risk from seismic events. At some point in each structure's life, it indeed will be tested more than once to one or more of the minimum design criteria to which it was built, be it caused by snow, wind, water, fire, seismic activity, or the act of an individual.

Building codes and standards are developed by model codes and standards organizations and then adopted by elected officials and administered and enforced in our nation. They have evolved over the decades to incorporate lessons learned from natural disasters that impact that region of the nation where the code has been adopted.

As noted throughout this chapter, if elected officials keep their code adoptions current and provide direction and adequate funding to their building departments to assure that those codes indeed are effectively administered and enforced, then building owners and construction teams in adhering to those codes and standards will indeed provide adequate safety to their clients and building occupants.

From time to time, as witnessed by Katrina and numerous hurricanes before it and by seismic events that have struck other parts of the nation, some communities either do not adopt codes that contain safety provisions appropriate to the severity of natural hazards in their region, or have not assured the adequate enforcement of those codes.

Many times building owners want to incorporate design features in their buildings that may exceed the model code safety minimums. This next section briefly describes several currently available resources that provide guidance on steps building owners and their design team can take to add additional levels of safety to their new buildings. Building retrofit issues to mitigate natural disaster hazards are covered in Chapter 6.

What Level Do You Build to? What Features to Include?

If you have not already conducted your risk-threat assessment, here are reminders of some of the tools and databases that are available to the building owner and design team to make a determination as to just what realistic natural hazard threats are in their part of the nation.

The HAZUS tool available from FEMA (see Chapter 4) offer the owner, architect, and engineer the best single source for assessing the potential impact the hazards of wind, flood, and seismic activity will have on the building. In addition to the information contained within its database, the most current, up-to-date data, as well as historical data for a particular location, are available from multiple federal government sources including the following:

- U.S. Geological Survey for maps of the United States covering tornadoes, hurricanes, floods, earthquakes, volcanic eruptions, and landslides for areas that have "relatively high risk or relative frequent actual occurrences." These are available at hhttp://www.usgs.gov/themes/hazard.html.

- FEMA and their National Flood Insurance Program (NFIP) has the most current maps of the 100-year flood plain elevations for the nation, which are available from their Map Services Center at hhtp://www.msc.fema.gov.

- The National Weather Service also collects data on severe weather covering: snow, winter storm, cold, heat, wind, tornadoes, hurricanes and other tropical storms, and lightening, which are available at hhttp://www.nws.noaa.gov/om/hazstats.shtml.

Given the increased intensity and frequency of hurricanes and tornadoes over the past several years, building owners and designers may wish to review the latest data from these sources prior to determining exactly which codes and standards they specifically wish to follow that may be above the requirements for natural hazards contained in the mandatory building code in the jurisdiction where they are building.

High Levels of Risk from One or More Natural Disasters

Having conducted your risk-threat assessment and determined that you want to build above the minimum building code in your jurisdiction the following are resources that you can consult on building design and construction.

Figure 5-27
FEMA Disaster
Mitigation
Publications

Resources for Seismic Events: FEMA, NEHRP, Model Codes and "Whole Building Design Guide"

As noted earlier, one immediate action that a building owner can take is to construct his building to the provisions within the appropriate model building code for a seismic zone that is one level higher than that called for in the adopted building code in their jurisdiction. Building seismic safety codes adopted and enforced in California, Washington, and Oregon also can serve as models for construction guidance.

Not unlike the discussion earlier on blast mitigation, among the key provisions in seismic safety design are wall systems and glazing, roofing design and materials, sliding or ductile connections for heavy cladding systems, glass fiber reinforced concrete cladding systems, lightweight panel systems, building foundations, exterior skin envelope, and anchoring of mechanical equipment.

In addition to the following documents from the Applied Technology Council (ATC) and FEMA (developed in coordination with the National Earthquake Hazards Reduction Program, (NEHRP), NIST and a number of colleges and universities), the "Whole Building Design Guide" section on "Seismic Safety of the Building Envelope" is an invaluable resource.

- ATC 57 "The Missing Piece: Improving Seismic Design and Construction Practices"
- FEMA 389 "Communicating with Owners and Managers of New Buildings on Earthquake Risk: A Primer for Design Professionals"
- FEMA 424 "Design Guide for School Safety Against Earthquakes, Floods, and High Winds"
- FEMA 433, "Using HAZUS-MH for Risk Assessment"
- In addition, in late 2006 FEMA will issue publication 454, "Designing for Earthquakes: A Manual for Architects," and the ATC will be releasing ATC 58 "Guidelines for Performance Assessment" that converts structural analysis data into projected losses in the event of a certain earthquake loading.

Resources for Winds and Floods: Other Jurisdiction, Model Codes, and FEMA

Hurricanes and tornadoes are the two largest wind-related disasters that strike our nation. Weather experts announced that by 2006 we are in only year 5 of a potential 15- to 20-year severe hurricane cycle. This has many communities along the Gulf and Eastern Coasts of the nation not only reassessing their disaster preparedness plans for such events but also giving serious consideration to the wind and water penetration provisions within their adopted building codes and standards.

Building owners and their construction team may want to once again give serious consideration to marrying design and construction codes to meet higher wind speeds noted in the tables in the model building codes or may want to review the enhanced hurricane provisions adopted by the state of Florida in recent years. As will be noted later in this chapter, in 2005, Florida completed an upgrade of certain hurricane-related provisions within its statewide code and in 2006, implemented another round of proposed upgrade provisions. The provisions of the Florida Building Code are available online at www.florida.building.org/BC/old./c.

Figure 5-28

Seismograph and Seismic Display, Smithsonian Museum of Natural History, Washington, D.C.

Adding additional import to designing and building to higher wind standards are the findings in the NIST June, 2006 Reconnaissance Report, "Performance of Physical Structures in Hurricane Katrina and Hurricane Rita." Among those reports findings and recommendations were that builders and building departments need to pay greater attention to enforcement of building code provisions governing:

proper anchoring and reinforcing of masonry walls

roof shingle connections—using the proper number of fasteners and not installing fasteners in the wrong direction.

assuring that aggregate surface roofs are used in high wind zones (wind-borne gravel from roof tops did considerable damage on nearby structures).

proper installation of backup generators and electrical equipment, chillers, and other critical equipment above expected flood levels.

Figure 5-29
Aftermath of 2005
Hurricanes in Gulf
Region

The early portion of the 2006 tornado season brought several major outbreaks of devastating tornadoes to the mid-west and mid-south, which have taken dozens of lives despite advances in weather forecasting and early warning systems for communities.

FEMA later warned building owners in "tornado alley" that they may want to consider including, "Taking Shelter from the Storm—Building a Safe Room Inside Your House" in their building design. In addition, a safe room, hurricane, and tornado shelter standards is under development by a committee at the International Code Council. Additional information is available on the ICC web site www.iccsafe.org.

Figure 5-30
December 2005,
residents of some
New Orleans
neighborhoods still
lined up for ice,
water, and food

The following are a number of currently available design guides from www.fema.gov:

- FEMA 55, Coastal Construction Manual
- FEMA, How To Series: "Build with Flood Resistant Materials," "Dry Floodproofing Your Building," and "Raise Electrical System Components"
- FEMA with Texas Tech: "Taking Shelter from the Storm: Building a Safe Room Inside Your House"

RECENT CHANGES BY STATES AND MAJOR CITIES TO THEIR CODES, STATUTES, AND ORDINANCES

> Recommendations made by the task force must strike a balance between the physical impact of a catastrophic event, the assurance of life safety under normal everyday circumstances, and the livability, usability, and cost of buildings.
> —Excerpt from the Summary to the Final Report of the New York City Department of Buildings World Trade Center Building Code Task Force, February 2003

Having made the determination that a building needs to go beyond the minimum standards in the new construction requirements adopted and enforced in the jurisdiction where their building is erected, other sources for information are the amendments that some major jurisdictions have already made for added levels of safety.

Here are a few selected jurisdictions whose provisions may be considered.

New York City

In the aftermath of 9/11, the New York City Department of Buildings established a WTC Building Code Task Force and charged them with developing recommended changes to the New York City building code. In February 2003, the task force issued their final report to Mayor Michael Bloomberg and on June 24, 2004, the city had amended its building code to add the following provisions for new high-rise buildings throughout the city.

- Every high-rise structure must have a city approved "Office Building Emergency Action Plans." Staffing to fulfill that plan is spelled out in the ordinance and every building is mandated to conduct a "Full Building Drill" once every two years. Once a year every building occupant must participate in a stairwell familiarization evacuation drill.
- Every new building must have their air intakes located at least 20 ft above grade and away from exhaust discharges or off-street loading bays.
- All newly constructed high-rise buildings require controlled inspections of HVAC fire dampers.
- Every high-rise building owner must complete, file with the city, and maintain a building information card listing the building's vital features that first responders can use when they arrive at the building.

Figure 5-31
Ground Zero,
World Trade Center
reconstruction,
September 2003

- Made at applicant's option, fire towers are permitted in lieu of interior stairs or exterior stairs.
- New high-rise construction over 75 ft in height cannot use open web bar trusses pending the development of an appropriate standard recommended by NIST.
- High-rise commercial buildings with a floor plate of over 10,000 square ft cannot use scissors stairs.
- New construction must improve the markings of the egress path, doors, and stairs with photo-luminescent materials.

Chicago

The city of Chicago adopted a Life Safety and High-Rise Ordinance that "focuses on improving the life safety attributes of existing high-rise buildings." The ordinance addressed pre-1975 high-rise construction, which was the year that a major fire safety ordinance was passed for all new construction. Of 1700 existing high-rise buildings (buildings over 80 ft in height) in the city, 1300 were built prior to 1975. Of those 1300 structures, 200 buildings were commercial and 1100 were residential structures.

The rehabilitation portions of the ordinance will be covered in Chapter 7; the provisions in the Chicago ordinance that cover new structures are listed here.

Figure 5-32

High rises in downtown Los Angeles, California

All building owners of high rises (new and existing) must have an evacuation plan in place at the building and must file the plan with the city's Office of Emergency Communications. Buildings over 780 ft above grade must have a designated fire safety director, deputy fire safety director, building evacuation supervisor, fire wardens, and emergency evacuation teams. In addition, owners must run annual safety drills. Mandatory evacuation assistance for people with disabilities is also part of the ordinance.

Los Angeles

The city of Angels adopted evacuation drill requirements similar to that of Chicago's for high-rise structures. The Fire Department issued jointly with a disabilities rights group a set of "Emergency Evacuation Procedures for Disabled Individuals," which details the use of such techniques as office chair, two-person carry side-by-side, and others.

Pittsburgh

Like other cities with high-rise structures, in the wake of 9/11, Pittsburgh mandated that every owner "or other person responsible" for high-rise buildings in that city develop and submit for city review an "All Hazards Plan" for that structure and a copy of that plan must be given to every tenant.

Contents of the "All Hazards Plan" were mandated and included details for evacuation drills and for the posting of the building's floor plans. Each building is to exercise its plan twice a year.

Florida

The state of Florida in the wake of its experiences with the hurricanes of the 2003 and 2004 storm season researched and promulgated a number of changes in their 2005 amendments to the statewide building code regarding reducing water penetration in buildings. Among those amendments are changes governing the following:

- Design of exterior walls: "Drained wall assembly over mass wall assembly"
- Water-resistive barriers: "Exterior walls of frame construction receiving a veneer shall be provided with a water-resistive barrier"
- Testing and labeling of skylights and test methods for exterior windows and curtain walls
- Water penetration of roof assemblies
- Roofing in high-velocity hurricane zones

In addition to the preceding changes, Florida in 2005 to 2006 issued another round of proposed hurricane-related code changes (now out for comment). Among those changes were several governing attachment of HVAC equipment to roofs, use of mold-resistive construction materials, and several other design changes to reduce water penetration in buildings. The state also initiated a move to extend the hurricane provisions inside the statewide building code to include counties in the Florida panhandle that previously had been exempted from following those provisions that are in force in all of the other coastal counties within the state.

Figure 5-33

Residential construction Florida in post-Charlie Charlotte County

PROPOSALS AND PROVISIONS IN FUTURE EDITIONS OF BUILDING AND FIRE CODES FOR NEW CONSTRUCTION

Chapter 3, "Findings from the World Trade Center Towers Collapse and other Post-9/11 Disasters," provided a summary of each of the NIST 30 detailed recommendations for possible improvements in the nation's codes and standards, and building design and construction processes.

The NIBS panel (see Chapter 2, page 46) convened throughout the winter and early spring of 2005 to 2006 to develop proposed code changes from the WTC recommendations. Unfortunately, they did not complete the changes in time for the March 24 deadline for submission to the ICC for possible inclusion in the 2007 edition of the IBC.

A number of members of the NIBS committee, however, did take draft proposals that they were working on and on their own formally submitted 19 proposals to the ICC. These were largely submitted as "place holders" to allow committee members to further work through their development and proposal and make possible modifications to them when they come before the ICC membership for their consideration at the ICC annual meeting in Orlando, Florida, in September 2006. (See Appendix, "ICC Code Development Process.")

The proposals cover such areas as increased resistance to building collapse from fire and other incidents, use of spray-applied fire-resistive materials (fireproofing), performance and redundancy of fire protection systems (automatic sprinklers), elevators

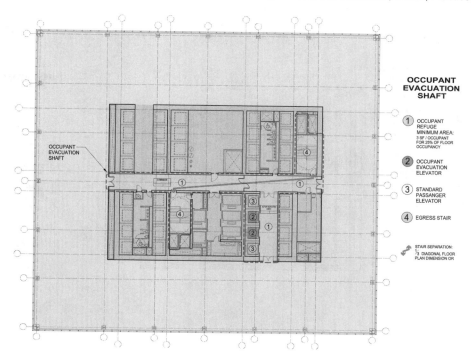

OCCUPANT
EVACUATION
SHAFT

1 OCCUPANT
REFUGE
MINIMUM AREA:
3 SF / OCCUPANT
FOR 25% OF FLOOR
OCCUPANCY

2 OCCUPANT
EVACUATION
ELEVATOR

3 STANDARD
PASSANGER
ELEVATOR

4 EGRESS STAIR

STAIR SEPARATION:
⅓ DIAGONAL FLOOR
PLAN DIMENSION OR

Figure 5-34

Diagram of proposed change to International Building Code in aftermath of 9/11 and NIST World Trade Center Report (Courtesy of International Code Council)

for use by first responders and evacuating occupants, the number and location of stairwells, exit path markings, and fuel oil storage/piping.

The proposals are available for viewing on the ICC Web site (www.iccsafe.org) and include several provisions that building owners may want to consider as possible approaches to enhancing safety in their high-rise construction. All changes that pass at the ICC's 2006 annual meeting and those which do not pass but do receive public comments will then be considered at the ICC spring 2007 meeting for inclusion in the IBC that will be issued later that year for possible adoption by state and local governments across the nation.

Figures 5-34, 5-35, and 5-36 are two of the diagrams submitted by the proponents of these changes and cover the design of a proposed occupant evacuation shaft to be used for emergency evacuations and a separate firefighting shaft. These designs are based upon structures already built in several buildings overseas.

In addition to these proposals two additional proposals call for an elevator strictly for fire department use in buildings over 420 ft in height. The elevator includes a shaft with a 2 hour fire-resistance rating. It will be the only elevator in this shaft, with doors and ventilation at the top of the shaft the only openings permitted. It will have standby power and its own communications and elevator equipment room.

Figure 5-35

Diagram of proposed change to International Building Code in aftermath of 9/11 and NIST World Trade Center Report (Courtesy of International Code Council.)

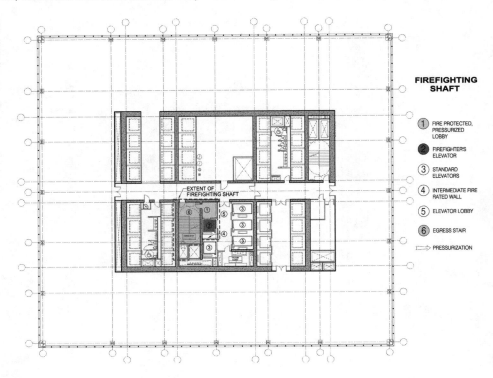

FIREFIGHTING SHAFT

1. FIRE PROTECTED, PRESSURIZED LOBBY
2. FIREFIGHTER'S ELEVATOR
3. STANDARD ELEVATORS
4. INTERMEDIATE FIRE RATED WALL
5. ELEVATOR LOBBY
6. EGRESS STAIR

⟹ PRESSURIZATION

THE CRITICAL ROLE OF THE CONSTRUCTION TEAM

The opening chapter of this book described the critical roles that each of the members of the construction team plays in helping to ensure that our buildings are designed, built, commissioned, and operated as safely and efficiently as possible. The owner, architect, engineers, contractors, building product manufacturers and suppliers, codes

Figure 5-36

Diagram of another design of a firefighting shaft for possible inclusion in International Building Code

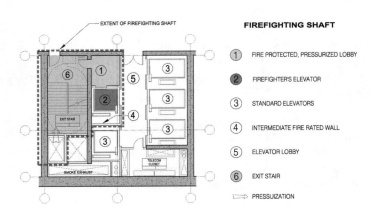

FIREFIGHTING SHAFT

1. FIRE PROTECTED, PRESSURIZED LOBBY
2. FIREFIGHTER'S ELEVATOR
3. STANDARD ELEVATORS
4. INTERMEDIATE FIRE RATED WALL
5. ELEVATOR LOBBY
6. EXIT STAIR

⟹ PRESSUIZATION

and standards community, and building officials and maintenance personnel have seen their responsibilities and the critical importance of their being able to work closely together as a team increase exponentially in the wake of the events of 9/11 and the large-scale natural disasters that have impacted our nation.

As noted by Knox and Ozolins in their quotation at the opening of this chapter, "our world is increasingly a smaller place, and people, ideas, and events are more connected." The guidelines, codes, and standards that are available to the building team for new construction are highly complex, and the interdependency of each of the members of the construction team is vital. This interdependency is more pronounced when in the next chapter we cover the renovation or rehabilitation of our nation's existing buildings to enhance safety from man-made and natural hazards.

6

Existing Buildings: Inspections and Retrofitting

To understand the critical importance of the disaster resiliency of our buildings and our communities it is important to realize that 80% of our small businesses go out of business if they are closed for more than two weeks.

> —Michael Chipley, Ph.D., Vice President of Strategic Development and Geospatial Solutions, Technology Associates at the February 15-17, 2006 TISP, CIR, ISBEE Conference

Yes, rebuilding to new codes will be more costly in some Louisiana parishes, especially those that had no codes prior to Hurricane Katrina. In the long run the upfront costs of rebuilding are an investment in the future.

We know that these types of investments pay off. For every dollar put into mitigation you can save $3 to $5 in future losses. Also these communities now have a starting point to ensure safer homes, schools, offices and other buildings.

> —James Lee Witt, President International Code Council in letter to the editor of *Engineering News Record*, January 16, 2006

SETTING THE STAGE: AN INTRODUCTION TO EXISTING BUILDINGS AND THE UNIQUE PROBLEMS AND HAZARDS THEY FACE

There currently are over 5 million nonresidential and nongovernmental buildings in the United States. These structures and our existing residential and government building stock constitute over 85% of the buildings that will be standing in this nation in 2020.

The majority of these buildings have already demonstrated their ability to perform well under the stresses of natural hazards such as wind, flood, fire and seismic events and, indeed, the owners of most of our building stock believe that with proper maintenance their buildings will be equal to the natural disaster challenges they will face over the remainder of their lifetime.

For our newer building stock and buildings that in some cities have already undergone disaster mitigating retrofits, this may well be true. Yet, given such events as the Murrah

Figure 6-1

Katrina damage
to high rises in
New Orleans

building in 1995, the attack on the World Trade Center (WTC), and the anthrax attacks in 2001 and the natural disasters of the past five years, a growing number of owners of our existing buildings are commissioning a risk assessment and mitigation plan and are voluntarily undertaking renovations to enhance the ability of their buildings to mitigate the impact of the next natural disaster or, for certain high-profile buildings, a terrorist attack.

As with new construction, there is no federal or model code that regulates building security in existing structures that owners can follow. Instead, each owner and the members of their construction team must draw upon a diverse array of resource documents from federal agencies and the construction industry and blend them with the building rehabilitation or retrofit requirements that their community has adopted.

In areas of our nation with a history of major earthquakes, floods, tornadoes, and hurricanes many of these local building codes include provisions that mandate an upgrade of

Figure 6-2
Lobby of the
Empire State
Building

construction design and materials strengthening the building's ability to withstand those forces when renovations on a significant portion of that structure are being undertaken or when there is a change in occupancy classification to a more hazardous use group. For example, California, which long encouraged its localities to adopt building codes with seismic safety provisions, enacted a law in 1986 requiring local governments in the highest risk seismic zones (Zone 4) to inventory all unreinforced masonry (URM) buildings and establish a URM loss reduction program.

In addition to those natural disaster related provisions in the aftermath of 9/11, a number of major cities from New York City to Chicago to Los Angeles have reviewed and, in some cases, revised their building codes that govern existing structures up to and including

Figure 6-3

Hanna Building,
Cleveland, Ohio

mandating retrofit of some life and even structural safety features to better protect the public against the next major man-made (or natural) disaster. These are provisions that go beyond the minimum health, welfare, and life-safety provisions found in the nation's model building codes and standards covering existing structures that jurisdictions adopt and enforce.

This chapter reviews each of the hazards covered in the previous chapter and provides guidelines and checklists that building owners and the members of their construction team can use in determining which technical provisions to consider applying to further enhance the ability of their existing building to withstand and mitigate the impact of these hazards.

Prior to that review, this chapter describes unique aspects of applying such upgrades to existing structures and also looks at the importance of two types of inspections in building rehabilitation. The first are the inspections by the building owner and their construction team to ascertain the exact conditions of the building prior to undertaking renovation or retrofitting to address identified security and safety vulnerabilities. The second are the inspections performed by the local building department to ascertain that the systems that are put in meet and do not conflict with the minimum safety requirements of the adopted building code enforced in that community.

As with Chapter 5, Chapter 6 closes with examples of changes in the building codes of a number of jurisdictions requiring renovation of different aspects of buildings – from exit lighting to structural upgrading.

AFTER 9/11: WHAT HAS REALLY CHANGED?

Chapters 1 to 3 traced the role of each of the members of the construction team and outlined the ways in which the events not only of 9/11 but our experience with large-scale natural disasters have changed the public's expectations of their levels of safety in the built environment and the design and construction of buildings. These forces are especially demanding on our existing building stock. As already noted, over 85% of the buildings that will be standing in this nation in 2020 are already here. In cities such as New York that have experienced terrorism firsthand there are over 1000 high-rise structures—most of which will never see another terrorist event in their lifetimes, others, the iconic structures and those next to them, live every day with the threat of another attack.

The following three sections address some of those unique factors that make the application of enhanced security and safety features a significant challenge to the owners of existing buildings: the sheer size of our existing building stock; the diversity of their construction materials and the codes and standards to which they were originally built; and the complexity of making changes to a building that address identified vulnerabilities and risks without negatively impacting the affordability of their building or their building's existing functionality.

THE SHEER SIZE OF OUR EXISTING INFRASTRUCTURE

The National Institute of Standards and Technology (NIST) in Appendix A, "A Nation At Risk," to their "Cost Effective Response to Terrorist Risks in Constructed Facilities" provided the charts shown in Tables 6-1 and 6-2 that describe the sheer size of our built infrastructure.

These two tables, produced originally by the White House for the report, "The National Strategy for the Physical Protection of Critical Infrastructures and Key Assets," and the Department of Energy for the annual report on energy conservation in buildings,

Table 6-1

NIST Table A-2, Critical Infrastructure and Assets in the United States, from "Best Practices for Project Security"

Infrastructure Type	Number	Units
Electricity	2,800	Power plants
	130 million	Households and institutions served
	3.6 trillion	kW consumed (2001)
Nuclear power plants	104	Commercial plants
	20%	U.S. electrical generation capacity
Oil and natural gas	300,000	Producing sites
	4,000	Off-shore platforms
	Over 600	Natural gas processing plants
	153	Refineries
	Over 1,400	Product terminals
	7,500	Bulk stations
Chemical industry and hazardous materials	66,000	Plants
Telecommunications	3.2 (2.0) billion	Kilometers (miles) of cable
	20,000	Physical facilities
Aviation	5,000	Public airports
Passenger rail and railroads	193,080 (120,000)	Kilometers (miles) of major railroads
	40%	Of inner city freight
	20 million	Inner city resident use annually
	45 million	Passengers on trains and subways operated by local transit authorities
Highways, trucking, and busing	590,000	Highway bridges
Pipelines	3.2 (2.0) million	Kilometers (miles) of pipelines
Maritime	300	Inland or coastal ports
Mass transit	500	Major urban public transit operators
Dams	80,000	Dams

Source: "The National Strategy for the Physical Protection of Critical Infrastructures and Key Assets," White House, February 2003.

demonstrate the sheer magnitude of our nation's existing built environment. Table 6-1 (NIST report Table A-2) provides a sense of the immense task that lies before federal, state, and local homeland security, the law enforcement community, and the private sector in protecting these critical infrastructures from being destroyed or disrupted by either man-made or natural disaster events.

Table 6-2

NIST Table A-3, Constructed Facilities at Risk: 1998–1999 from "Best Practices for Project Security"

Building Characteristics	Office	Education	Health Care	Mercantile/ Service	Industrial	Other	All
Number of buildings (thousands)	739	327	127	1,145	227	2,319	4,884
Building floor space (million m²)	1,119	804	271	1,281	1,193	2,781	7,449
Building floor space (million ft²)	12,044	8,651	2,918	13,786	12,836	29,939	80,174
Average building floor space (m²)	1,514	2,459	2,134	1,119	5,256	1,199	1,525
Average building floor space (ft²)	16,298	26,456	22,976	12,040	56,546	12,910	16,416

Source: U.S. Department of Energy's Commercial Buildings Energy Consumption Survey, 1999. Industrial building data from U.S. Department of Energy's Manufacturing Energy Consumption Survey, 1998.

Table 6-2 (NIST Table A-3) shows a breakout by building type of the over 4.9 million nonresidential private sector buildings in existence in the United States in 1998 to 1999. As these buildings age or owners change, they all at sometime undergo renovation or repair. Depending upon their age, location, and use, these buildings may be mandated by the state or local building codes or determined by their owners where they are sited to be subject to upgrades of their construction features to enhance their ability to mitigate damage from hurricanes, tornadoes, floods, seismic events, fire, or even a terrorist (domestic or foreign) attack.

Moreover as witnessed in the collapse of the roofs of public buildings in Poland and Russia in 2005, and as has been seen here in hurricanes which hit our nation in 2004–2005, lack of proper maintenance also plays a critical role in determining whether or not our buildings continue to safely shelter our citizens.

It is here that the critical role of the entire construction team comes into place: the owner, to continue to evaluate the soundness of their facility to withstand the forces for which it was designed and to pay for the renovation; the building facility manager and maintenance personnel, to assure both that the upgrade features operate properly and that the owner is made aware of the consequences of not meeting the basic maintenance requirements for the facility; the architect, engineer, contractor, product manufacturer, supplier, codes and standards community, and code enforcement personnel , to assure that the design, materials, and construction that go into the facility meet the applicable codes and standards governing renovation or rehabilitation.

Figure 6-4

Old Armory under renovation in Portland, Oregon

THE COMPLEXITY OF MITIGATING VULNERABILITIES AND RISKS TO NATURAL AND MAN-MADE HAZARDS AND THREATS

"Interventions stress in these guidance documents" (i.e., What to do to better protect the public after 9/11) "can be characterized as three types: 1) hardening of the building envelope, 2) filtration and air cleaning, and 3) emergency stop-start pressurization, and other control strategies. Each of these types of interventions has obviously benefits, but they are likely to pose significant cost and performance limitations unless system integration is assured that provides the desired performance and preparedness during normal operation."

—James Woods, Ph.D., P.E. Executive Director, The Building Diagnostics Research Institute, Inc., "What Changes are Occurring in Building Performance and Preparedness," in the February 2005 edition of *HVAC Engineering* Magazine

In addition to its sheer size, additional complexity in the issue of renovation of existing buildings stems from the fact that our existing building stock even within a single city have been built over the past 100 plus years to a wide array of construction codes and standards (or to no codes and standards at all) using an extremely diverse array of building products and materials. No one single set of construction renovation guidelines is going to fit all buildings. What works in making one commercial building in a city more resistant to a chemical spill in the area will not necessarily work in a commercial building immediately adjacent to it.

Indeed to borrow a metaphor from James Woods, retrofitting or rehabilitating a building to increase levels of protection is "a lot like medical diagnostics." In new construction you have a blank sheet of paper. The owner is free to determine asset values, threats, vulnerabilities, and risks and the cost to mitigate them; set a mitigation plan and then design those features that address the risks.

You do not have the luxury of a blank sheet of paper with existing construction any more than the doctor has with you when you go in for a physical. For existing buildings you first have to know everything you can about that existing structure from foundation to roof top. This includes having to look at the "health" (vulnerability) of neighboring structures. Then and only then can you do your analysis of threat, vulnerability, and risk and look at the economics to develop an affordable mitigation strategy that addresses what the owner determines will adequately mitigate those risks. And like a doctor, when you renovate the building and put in these feature to improve its ability to withstand the identified man-made or natural hazard risks, you must do so taking a form of a Hippocratic Oath—of first doing no harm to the ability of that building to perform its stated function or to put the occupants at risk. The owner also must commit to carrying out the doctor's prescription by assuring the proper maintenance of the enhanced security features for the life of the building.

HIPPOCRATIC OATH: FIRST DO NO HARM

As noted earlier, making an improvement within existing building structures, especially for high-rise buildings and large commercial and industrial structures can prove to be quite complex. Addressing one threat or area of building vulnerability can trigger the law of unintended consequences and create other problems regarding, for example, the building's functionality, emergency egress, or the productivity of its occupants. There were a number of examples of this in the news when in the immediate wake of the events of 9/11 building managers and maintenance personnel tried to immediately address issues of building security by locking emergency exit doors or exit doors into building stairwells, putting in fencing and bollards without taking into consideration the impact of these actions on emergency egress or even assuring that they were not damaging emergency vehicle access to the building.

While this chapter, like Chapter 5 will address risks and hazards from the outside ring inward into the buildings core, these "solutions" to the outcome of the owner's risk assessment cannot be taken as separate and distinct actions. The building (just as a doctor's patient) must be looked at as an entirety, not only as noted in conducting the risk assessment (see Chapter 4), but in assembling which combination of changes in various building systems and subsystems most effectively reduces those vulnerabilities, while at the same time assures that the building continues to effectively serve both its functions and the comfort, safety, and productivity of its occupants and those who visit the building. A watch phase for considering which modifications to make to reduce vulnerability should be to perhaps take and adhere to a Hippocratic Oath for the building— "First do no harm."

To be successfully added security features, such as those at the outer ring (where parking is located) or inner ring (structural hardening or modifications to the HVAC system) must be coordinated and balanced so as not to adversely affect or reduce the level of safety, comfort and productivity that existed within the building prior to upgrading one or more building system to address either man-made or natural disasters.

This, as noted in the close of Chapter 5, makes the close working relationship of all of the members of the construction team all that more important. The owner needs to make certain that licensed engineers in each of the technical areas that are being addressed have been engaged and are working cooperatively to assure that they have not inadvertently reduced the functionality, health, and life safety (including emergency egress) and, ultimately, productivity within the building.

What Do You Want the Building to Do?

This question is essential for the owner to answer before undertaking a renovation. With an eye toward the inspections about to be done on the existing structure and the development of the risk mitigation plan and design of upgrade features, the owner must set the parameters of what is called, "acceptable risk," for the occupants of the building and the building itself. To what levels of either a natural or man-made attack is his existing building going to protect its occupants and either suffer minor damage or protect people but suffer major damage from which it can later readily recover? The answer here will be unique to each owner, be they a private sector firm or a state or federal agency.

Most private sector firms, unlike their government counterparts, generally are not trying to provide the same levels of defense and have the structural hardness as an embassy or military base. Private sector owners, however, are concerned with two factors. The first is providing reasonable levels of protection against natural and man-made threats that have a high level of probability of occurring (for example, earthquakes in California and hurricanes in Florida) or by virtue of its location next to an iconic structure in Washington, D.C, protection against collateral damage from an attack on their neighbor.

The second is the issue of business continuity for the occupants as well as for the owner. How well must the building be able to withstand the disaster? Well enough so that the building stays operational throughout and after the event, or just well enough so that the building can be readily returned to working condition after the event.

Making changes to "harden" a building to withstand every possible threat is beyond the budgetary realities of nearly every owner. What many private sector owners are finding instead makes the most sense (and is much more affordable, especially from a life-cycle cost basis), is to make changes to the existing structure that address the unacceptable risks and also make the building "disaster resilient." A term that originally was used in Great Britain in conjunction with their terrorism experience, *disaster resiliency* is now being used by federal, state, and local governments to prepare for, respond to, and recover from disasters. The term, as defined by the Infrastructure Security Partnership introduced in Chapter 2, refers to the capability to prevent and protect against significant, all-hazards threats and incidents and to expeditiously recover and reconstitute critical services with minimum damage to public safety and health, economy, and national security. For the building owner, this means being able to provide a level of protection to the building and its occupants commensurate with its risk assessment and being able to put the building back into service as quickly as the owner and the occupants need it to be.

Life-Cycle Cost Perspective

Having determined what he or she wants the building to be able to do in response to the preceding assessment process, the owner then must deal realistically with the costs of making various security and safety improvements to meet that level of risk. To do that and to fulfill the Hippocratic Oath and the holistic view of the building, the owner also needs to consider not just the immediate costs of renovating their building to mitigate these risks but rather look at those costs over the ongoing life of the building—the life cycle cost basis. The categories of items that go into life cycle cost for retrofit include: doing the risk analysis, inspection, financing, redesign, specification, engineering, construction, restartup (perhaps even recommissioning), insuring, operation, maintenance, future retrofit, repurposing, disposal, demolition, and legal closure.

Over the future life of the building, what costs are affordable to ensure the ongoing function of the building and its ability to address future stresses (disasters) and readily recover from them? The potential loss of revenues from the building not being readily put back into use after a high-probability event, or the total loss of that structure (and worse, perhaps some of its occupants), helps owners think again about the long-term benefits and not just the immediate short-term costs of undertaking such a retrofit of their property. (For example, James Lee Witt's concept stated that for every $1 you put into strengthening a building you get $3 to $5 back from it later on.) "Cost-Effective Responses to Terrorist Risks in Constructed Facilities" from NIST described earlier in this book provides a good resource tool for building owners on the issue of life-cycle costs and the affordability of security and other building safety enhancements.

Figure 6-5

Richmond, Virginia building undergoing rehabilitation

The Critical Role of Inspections Commissioned by the Owner: Understanding the Existing Building Top to Bottom

Here is where the construction team is critical. Before developing any mitigation strategy for the building, the owner, like the doctor with his or her patient, needs to know what exists and how it works as a whole. The building needs a detailed evaluation of its structure, egress and accessibility, and its electrical, mechanical, and plumbing systems, including at a minimum what it will take to bring those features up to the provisions of the adopted building rehabilitation code within that jurisdiction. Armed with this information, the owner can then undertake and complete the threat, vulnerability, and risk analysis and develop the vulnerability mitigation strategy for that structure (following the steps noted on Figure 6-6) to finally determine what additional structural, mechanical, electrical, and HVAC system features are necessary to mitigate the vulnerabilities that emerge from this two-step process.

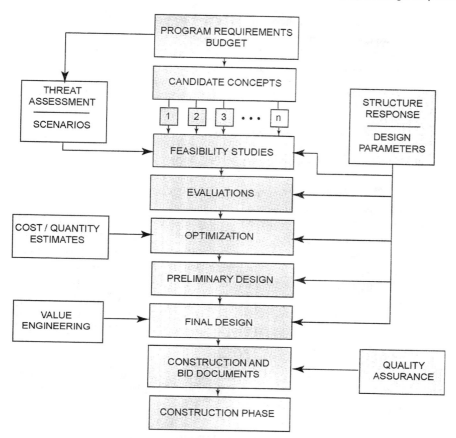

Figure 6-6
FEMA direct
design process
flow chart

Understanding the Base Construction Code Provisions that Underlie Renovation or Rehabilitation of Existing Structures

Rehabilitation Codes and Reducing the Costs of Renovation

Before addressing codes, guidelines, and standards that can be used to mitigate the vulnerabilities that emerged from the risk-threat analysis, it is worthwhile to briefly understand the building codes and standards that form the base level of requirements for repairs, renovations, or major rehabilitation projects of existing buildings. These codes and standards do not have special provisions for building security. They still, however, are important for the construction team to understand.

The code provisions in most states not only form the floor upon which a building owner will make general renovations to a structure, but when completed any additional security enhancements can exceed but cannot conflict with this code's minimum electrical, mechanical, plumbing, and structural provisions, including the requirements for emergency egress, fire protection, HVAC, and energy and architectural accessibility requirements that the jurisdiction has adopted.

Called by various names—rehabilitation codes, existing building codes and, in some states, "Smart Codes"—these codes in those states with high risks of natural disasters (e.g., California and Florida) will actually mandate that a building owner increases some hazard mitigating requirements as appropriate to that state for wind, flood, hurricane, and/or seismic events.

Rehab 101

In an increasing number of state and local jurisdictions today building renovation is covered under a different set of construction code provisions than what is used in the jurisdiction for new construction. That was not always so.

In the late 1970s and early 1980s, several states and a number of major cities began to look at strategies that could be adopted to promote the revitalization of their older inner cities. In these reviews, one of the barriers that were identified as inhibiting revitalization in many communities was the building codes. Up to that time, the construction code provisions adopted and enforced across the nation provided a mechanism known as the "25 to 50% rule," that was a ratio between the total cost of the alteration being done on the building and the total value of that building. When this ratio was between 25% and 49% only that portion of the building being renovated needed to comply with the building code provisions for new construction. When that ratio was 50%, then the entire building (and not just the portion being renovated) had to be brought into compliance with that jurisdiction's code for new construction. The net effect of this provision was to make it too costly for many owners and developers to undertake building renovations. While this provision was later dropped from the nation's model building codes, it was still generally applied across the nation in jurisdictions that had not adopted more current editions of the model codes.

Massachusetts and Early Model Rehabilitation Codes   The Commonwealth of Massachusetts in 1979 departed from that practice by linking any need to follow the current construction provisions for new construction when renovating a structure to those renovations that involved a change in occupancy that was for a more hazardous building use group than previously occupied that space. An example would be a warehouse renovated into apartment units. The successful application of that code by Massachusetts and its stimulation to urban revitalization spurred other communities to adopt similar provisions.

In 1985, the International Conference of Building Officials (ICBO) produced the "Uniform Building Code for Building Conservation" that went a step beyond the Massachusetts approach by recognizing that hazards in buildings are multidimensional and are best addressed by multiple hazard scales. Similar code provisions were later produced by the other two model code organizations at that time (Building Officials and Code Administrators International [BOCA], and the Southern Building Code Congress International, [SBCCI])

New Jersey Rehabilitation Subcode   In 1996, the state of New Jersey developed and, in January 1998, released the "New Jersey Uniform Construction Code: Rehabilitation Subcode" to stimulate urban revitalization there. Addressing concerns of the need for timeliness of code processing and enforcement, predictability, and reasonableness, New Jersey took a new approach toward developing a code specifically for existing buildings.

Code provisions were set up recognizing that you cannot just arbitrarily apply the provisions for new construction to an existing building code. New Jersey considered and brought common sense to the logic of the building renovation process. The state balanced the need to both stimulate renovation and rehabilitation of existing buildings within New Jersey and also to avoid anything that reduced or lessened the degree of health and life safety of the occupants of those buildings once the renovation had been completed.

The New Jersey Subcode notes that there are three types of projects: rehabilitation, change of use, and additions. The subcode further notes that there are four categories of rehabilitation all relating to the extent of the work being undertaken: repair, renovation, alteration, and reconstruction.

Based upon which category of rehabilitation a person was undertaking, the building owner and his or her contractors would have to adhere to different portions of five sets of requirements within the subcode—those covering products and practices, materials and methods, new building elements, basic requirements, and supplemental requirements that apply to categories of work. The subcode then applies all of this to the work areas in the building (work areas being defined as just that, the places where the work is being done).

Now in place over eight years, the New Jersey Subcode has significantly increased building rehabilitation and revitalization of many communities within the state. Moreover, the subcode has become a model that other states have considered in updating their rehabilitation regulations. (A copy of the New Jersey Rehabilitation Subcode can be downloaded from the following site: http:// www.state.nj.us/dca/codes/rehab/rehabguide.shtml).

HUD NARRP and International Existing Building Code and State Adoptions
U.S. Department of Housing and Urban Development (HUD) from 1996 to 1997 funded the development of "Nationally Applicable Recommended Rehabilitation Provisions" (NARRP) to stimulate the adoption of building rehabilitation codes elsewhere in the nation. NARRP borrowed some concepts from New Jersey and established four work categories: repair, alternation, addition, and change of occupancy. Based upon successful innovations in New Jersey and the release of the NARRP by HUD, a number of other states including Maryland and Maine and cities such as Wilmington, Delaware, and Louisville, Kentucky, have adopted similar rehabilitation codes.

In addition, some of the modifications made in the preceding codes were incorporated by the International Code Council (ICC) in the 2003 edition of the International Existing Building Code (IEBC), which has been widely adopted elsewhere in the United States. Tables and charts within the IEBC cover such issues as retrofit for seismic and wind zones. California, for example, urges the adoption and enforcement of the

Figure 6-7

International
Existing Building
Code and state
rehabilitation
codes

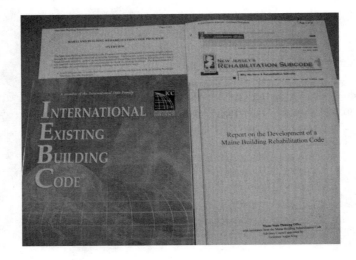

IEBC for communities as a means to bring about seismic upgrade of older building stock when those structures go under renovation or rehabilitation.

In addition to the preceding rehabilitation and existing building codes, owners of existing buildings may also have to take into consideration following locally adopted historic preservation requirements that may impose specific limitations on the nature of visible security features and materials used in building renovation.

Having reviewed the previous elements of complexity in building renovation and the underlying base building rehabilitation codes that an owner may encounter, the next section initiates a review of the actual building security principles that should be followed.

OVERVIEW OF THE BASIC SECURITY PRINCIPLES FOR EXISTING STRUCTURES

Rings Of Defense: The Challenges for Existing Buildings

It's always the best to attack and counter attack the source (of terrorism), do something at the source, prevent the source from doing what it wants to do. It helps in biowarfare, helps everywhere. Stop the source, you stop the attack. And therefore I would actually like to see what's happening in London, what's happening in Singapore-wherever you want to go in a building, if you want to go to Canary Wharf or you want to go to the Consulary in Paris, for example, you have to enter the building through security. You have to give your name. You have to say who you want to visit. If you want to go to the parking lot, you have to say who you're going to visit. You're on record before you even enter the place.

—Johannes de Jong, Kone Corportation, Finland, at the October 15, 2001
Council on Tall Buildings and Urban Habitat Task Force meeting
on "The Future" held in Chicago, Illinois

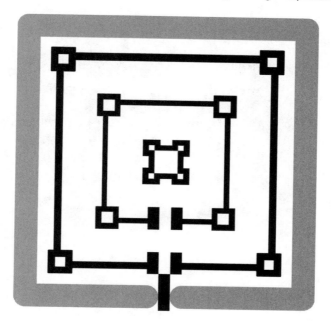

Figure 6-8

Outer rings of defense

The basic principles of rings of defense, or layering security, certainly apply to existing structures, but the ability of the building owner and their construction team to control those rings and change or modify the footprint of their existing building and its relationship to the buildings that surround it are significantly more restricted when compared to new construction. Nevertheless, the principles of CPTED (crime prevention through environmental design) and the federal security guidelines developed after the bombing of the Alfred P. Murrah building in Oklahoma still can be applied here for existing buildings. The FEMA risk management series publication 427, "Primer for Design of Commercial Buildings to Mitigate Terrorist Attacks," and its basic three principles to prevent, delay, and mitigate the effects of the attack all still apply for existing construction as they did for new buildings.

Preventing the Attack with Intelligence and Deception: Beyond the Outer Ring

Where possible, this basic concept calls for the building owner and architect to make modifications to the exterior perimeter and façade of the building to make it more difficult for obvious attack by burglary or car or truck bomb. Developing and maintaining close contact with the public safety community and state and/or local homeland security personnel can provide the owner with valuable intelligence not only in the renovation of the structure but in its ongoing operation.

Delaying the Attack with Operational Protection: The Outer Rings

To the degree that the existing building's sight and configuration allow, owners should create and maintain a "buffer zone" between the public and vital areas of the building. This may delay the attack and give security forces more time to respond to the event. This includes some of the security features that de Jong refers to when citing how difficult other nations, prior to 9/11, were making it to access and move within buildings that

Figure 6-9

Security patrol
checking parked
vehicles,
Washington, D.C.

they have deemed at risk. As with new construction, outer ring protection includes building setbacks, parking, physical barriers (landscaping, fences, bollards, security gates), protective lighting, cameras with closed-circuit television, and guard posts with clear lines of sight.

Mitigate the Effects of the Attack: Structural and Other Hardening in the Inner Rings of Defense

This third approach is by far the most expensive. Here is where extensive inspection of the building by the owner and the construction team and the subsequent use of the threat, vulnerability, and risk-mitigation assessment covered in Chapter 4 will provide an understanding of what the relative costs will be. In addition, it will also show where it is necessary to actually harden the building's exterior and interior design to reduce the loss of life and physical or injury consequences of any attack (criminal or terrorist) that breaches the outer rings of the building's defense.

Examples of the inner ring defenses include limitations on public access to portions of the building, shipping and receiving areas, high security locks, internal gates and guard stations, magnetometers, blast-resistant windows, mullions and doors, blast-resistant building structural features, and features in the HVAC system (possibly including filters) to protect the building from internal and external releases of bio-chemical agents.

Applying Risk-Threat Analysis and Mitigation Plan to Existing Buildings

All effective security depends on the following: Thoroughness of the initial security assessment prior to and through building construction (renovation); development of a policy: what will the security be designed to secure; who will be in charge of it; what are the protocols before technology is purchased.

Making an assessment of the available technology and then the appropriate selection of the technology; integration of physical and electronic technology with other building systems.

—Richard Chase, Executive Director, Security Industry Association at October 15, 2001 Council on Tall Buildings Council and Urban Habitat Task Force meeting on the "Future" held in Chicago, Illinois

As a result of conducting the detailed inspection of the building and using one of the risk analysis methodologies covered in Chapter 4, the owner of the existing building and his or her construction team determine the level of acceptable risk for their new structure. They also develop a budget and mitigation strategy that will be incorporated into the building's renovation or rehabilitation to address one or more of the following threats:

- Criminal threats that are being mitigated may include: assault, vandalism, threat of property, threat of information, workplace violence, kidnapping and hostage taking, and demonstrations

- Terrorist (domestic and foreign) threats that are being mitigated may include: surveillance, hostage taking, blast, biochemical-radiological events (both internal and external to the structure) and ballistic and aerial attack (9/11)

As with new construction, regardless of the level of risk from criminal activity or terrorism, the guidelines and standards referred to in this chapter afford the building owner and the design and construction team a range of options from which to select in providing for the relative safety and security of the occupants of their structure. The General Services Administration's (GSA) five building classifications provided on pages 98 and 99 in Chapter 4 and Tables 4-1 through 4-4 also offer the owner of an existing building a point of departure for determining what security features they may wish to include within their structure for each of the rings of defense:

- External (GSA Perimeter Security; see Table 4-1)
- Internal (GSA's Entry and Interior Security; see Tables 4-2 and 4-3).

In addition, Table 4-4, "Recommended Minimum Security Standards, Security Planning," gets into the operational and a few of the building maintenance issues that the building owner and designer must be cognizant of and include within their life-cycle cost calculations in selecting different security elements to include within their building's renovation.

Selecting the Best Approach or a Blend of Guidelines, Standards, and Codes for Existing Buildings

The level of determined threat, vulnerability, and acceptable risk and the owner's mitigation plan lead the owner and the construction team to a range of guidelines, standards, products, and services from which to select that work best for them both with cost as well as with the purpose and function of the building. Here are three examples for existing structures:

Example 1

The owner of an existing shopping center in a small midwestern town may want to add CPTED guidelines for heightened security and several tornado shelters in the aftermath of the tornadoes of 2004 to 2006 in "Tornado Alley" to minimize potential injuries to shoppers and workers.

Figure 6-10

World Trade Center Ground Zero reconstruction September 2003

Example 2

The owner of an existing high-rise structure, located next to a new high rise that will be an iconic structure in that city, may want to look at a number of items: the GSA's level 5 security features, FEMA's "Reference Manual," and "Primer for Design of Commercial Buildings to Mitigate Terrorist Attacks" (FEMA 426 and 427), the enhanced structural provisions of the International Building Code, and, perhaps where such renovation is possible, even some of the egress-related recommendations from the NIST report on the WTC disaster.

Example 3

The owner of an existing building decides that he or she wants to attract as tenants one or more federal agencies. Depending in part on its location and on the federal agencies involved, that owner and his or her construction team may want to select relevant provisions from GSA's construction guidelines.

A variation on this last example is a situation where the owner recognizes that while the building and its location may have at this time a low-risk profile, some higher levels of security features may be incorporated into the building as a marketing advantage, given either the climate of the times, potential higher risk buildings, and tenants coming into the area or just wanting the flexibility to one day have a federal, state, or local government agency as a tenant.

In addition to the earlier examples, before selecting which codes, standards, and guidelines to use in their building above those that are mandated by the state or local building code in their jurisdiction, it is useful for owners to make certain that they have gone through the following screening checklist, which has been modified from Chapter 5, to address existing structures.

Screening Checklist: Rechecking What Level of Security and Security Retrofit, Materials and, Operation Features You Want in Your Existing Building

Do these more stringent codes, standards, and guidelines interfere with the overall function of the building?

Are these additional features sustainable? Do they require significant education and training of personnel to provide them or service them? Are such skilled personnel available? Were these costs included in the cost-benefit analysis that was conducted before selecting these provisions?

Will putting these security features in (under the jurisdiction's existing building code) trigger other building upgrades (e.g., architectural accessibility provisions, renovated to standards for new construction as opposed to following the provisions of the rehabilitation code)?

How readily upgradeable are these security features? At what cost? Will such an upgrade require retraining?

If the level of vulnerability and risk were to suddenly increase and the owner were to want or need to further upgrade security in his or her building, how expensive would it be to upgrade these features that are now being selected? Given what the owner and his construction team now know, how likely is it that an event (terrorism or building an iconic or high-risk structure next door) will occur causing the owner to consider upgrading elements of this building's security features?

How big a market does the owner have from which to select these products, materials, or services? Are these products and materials likely to be available in the future when they need to be serviced or replaced?

What retrofit and rehabilitation guidelines, standards, and codes are available to apply to different types of buildings with different levels of risk in each of the three rings of security areas?

Figure 6-11
Bollards, security barriers, U.S. Department of Housing and Urban Development

What resources are available to determine the costs of incorporating these design features into an existing structure?

Starting first with the outer ring of security and moving into the inner ring, the guidelines, standards, and codes that are currently available from the federal government and from the codes, standards, and construction community for use in existing buildings have the following varying degrees of risk from criminal and terrorist events:

- Building group 1: Buildings with varying levels of risk from crime but low levels of risk from terrorism
- Building group 2: Buildings with a varying risks from crime and moderate to high levels of risk from terrorism

GUIDELINES FOR EXTERNAL PROTECTION OF EXISTING BUILDINGS: THE OUTER RING OF DEFENSE

Perimeter Security to Prevent or Delay Attack

Building Group 1: Buildings with Varying Levels of Risk from Crime but Low Levels of Risk from Terrorism

As with new construction, if all existing buildings in the United States today were first checked by a risk-threat analysis, the vast majority of them would fall into this security category—low risks from terrorism but low to moderate risks from crime. Where owners have conducted a risk assessment and determined that while not at a moderate or high risk from terrorism they do want to include features that enhance the safety and security of the occupants and visitors to their buildings. They will want to look first at any design guidance that the principles of CPTED offer for enhancing public safety.

Drawn from the same range of resources covered under this section in Chapter 5 for new construction, the following publications and guidelines from FEMA, GSA, the American Planning Association's "Policy Guide on Security" and the previously mentioned works of Barbara Nedel and Joseph Demkin, here are the basic principles of CPTED that owners may find adequate to address the added level of security they have determined that they need to include in their existing building.

Crime Prevention Through Environmental Design for Existing Structures

Better lighting of neighborhoods, improved lines of sight, setbacks from roadways, even the growth of gated communities all enhanced public safety through the application of the CPTED principles. The following guidelines, based upon CPTED's three strategies of territoriality, surveillance, and access control and its 3D process of designation, definition, and design provide the owner of an existing structure with an overview of security provisions that might be suited for their building.

Provisions for Consideration of Incorporation into Building Renovation to Reduce Threat of Criminal Activity

Layering of Security

- Does the building's current configuration and location on its site contribute to making use of layering of security in several of the following areas?
- Can changes be made given the way the building is oriented or located on its site to maximize natural surveillance with clear direct lines of sight for occupants of the building or a guard station?
- Can changes be made given the way the building is located or oriented to take greater advantage of natural lighting to help surveillance and, where necessary, should more artificial light be provided?
- Can changes be made given the building's location on the site to make greater use of natural plantings providing the neighborhood watch (if one is available), police, and the general public with clear direct lines of sight of the entrances and exits to the building?
- Can natural (trees and berms) and man-made barriers (fences, bollards, gates) be added to the site to provide obstacles limiting access to the structure?
- Can changes be made given the building's location on the site to use features, such as low bushes or garden edging to the sidewalks, that give people "psychological ownership" of the space and thus discourage vandalism, or other criminal activity?

Building Design

SECURITY ZONING

- Can modifications be made to the building to reduce the potential for criminal activity thus enabling building occupants and visitors to enter, leave, and move within the building to their various destinations without fear of attack?
- Can the building be modified to either include or increase the amount of physical barriers that enable building tenants to control access to certain portions of the building (security desk, keyed entry systems, metal detectors, and so on)?
- Can the building be modified to include or increase features that clearly separate zones for public access and unrestricted use, such as lobbies, public restaurants, or public meeting rooms, from those areas that require restricted access?
- Can the building be modified to provide or increase limits to access to fire control, HVAC equipment and controls, loading docks, mail rooms, and other sensitive areas from anyone other than appropriate authorized personnel?

As noted in Chapter 5, a growing number of communities have adopted CPTED standards into their zoning, land use, and site development standards. The owner should consult their zoning, land use department to see if CPTED or the American Planning Association's "SafeScapes" provisions are being used.

Figure 6-12

New York City and a major rehabilitation project near Penn station

The Inner Ring for the Low-Risk Building

Provisions in Model Codes and Standards

In addition to CPTED, provisions in some of the jurisdiction's adopted codes and standards for existing buildings may also offer protection from criminal activities and some degree of protection from low levels of perceived threat from terrorism. While these provisions regarding the outer ring of safety for buildings are not contained in the provisions of either the ICC's IEBC or in the provisions of the National Fire Protection Association's "Building Construction and Safety Code" NFPA 5000 and "Life Safety Code" NFPA 101 regarding inner ring defenses, and NFPA 730, "Guide for Premises Security" and NFPA 731, "Standard for the Installation of Electronic Premises Security Systems" offer the owner some guidance in retrofit situations. (See Chapter 5, pages 133 to 135 for details on the content of these two NFPA documents.)

Building Group 2: Existing Buildings with Varying Levels of Risk from Crime and Moderate to High Risk from Terrorism

As noted for new construction in Chapter 5, critical deficiencies identified by the federal government regarding building security in the wake of the 1995 Oklahoma City bombing included site access, standoff distances, setback requirements, anti-ram barriers, glazing and hardening of the buildings from blast, and ultimately progressive collapse. Owners of existing structures can draw from the Department of Defense's (DoD) unclassified version of their May 2002, "Unified Facilities Criteria—DoD Minimum Antiterrorism Standards for Buildings," and from the GSA's updated March 2005 "Security Design" requirements. (See Appendix for Web site links to these documents.)

Beginning with the outer ring of defense, this section looks at each of these layers of security for existing buildings that are deemed at high levels of risk from terrorism.

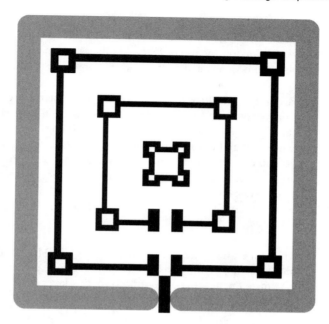

Figure 6-13
The Outer ring
of defense

Outer Ring Security for Buildings with Moderate to High Risks from Terrorism

As noted in Chapter 5 with approximately 80% of terrorist attacks relying on explosive devices (truck and car bombs), the orientation of a building on its site can be an important strategy to mitigate risk. Wherever possible in conducting the risk assessment and developing the appropriate mitigation strategies for existing structures, it is critical to start first by looking at the building's orientation on its existing site and its relationship to its neighbors.

Characteristics of the Surrounding Area Whether the building that is being renovated is to become a secure government facility or private sector commercial structure with a high-risk level, there are a range of security redesign considerations and guidelines for the owner to choose from to provide adequate levels of protection for the occupants of that building. Pages 137 to 139 of Chapter 5 provided a checklist that a building owner can use to assess potential vulnerabilities based on the characteristics of the area surrounding their new building. That list is equally applicable for use by the owner of an existing structure and should be reviewed.

After Reviewing the Site and Risks Having carefully reviewed the nature of the neighborhood that surrounds their existing building, the owner should determine if they have any latitude in reorienting the building to reduce some of its identified vulnerabilities. For instance, if the existing location of the primary entrance is extremely vulnerable, can the location of the primary entrance be changed? Can loading docks be relocated? Or are the owner and construction team locked into the existing orientation and functional use activities of the building?

Where the owner has some latitude in the functional orientation of the building on that site, basic principles of standoff security (including those from CPTED) can be applied. These also involve the use of fences, bollards, and natural barriers to provide maximum setbacks from streets and alleys that may border the property.

The section on blast (pages 153 to 163) of Chapter 5 provided in Figure 5-18 details information on how far back from roadways a building needs to be to minimize the effects of various-sized explosions. In general, however, with a given existing building an owner does not have the ability to change the existing standoff distances other than possibly to relocate the entrance to provide some of the benefits of setback. For a very high-risk property, this may not eliminate the need for structural hardening of the building, but it may reduce risk of threat from blast to those who enter and exit the building, enabling the owner to fulfill the basic minimum standoff distances recommended by federal agencies.

Drawn from earlier referenced publications of FEMA, DoD and American Institute of Architects, the following two basic checklists offer a useful starting point in helping owners maximize the benefits of security from this layer that lies "beyond" the outer ring.

Guidelines for Considering Reorientation of Building Functions on the Existing Site

The owner and his/her construction team should look at the building as a whole and consider both from a functional and a safety perspective, if the location of highly vulnerable portions of the building can be mitigated by relocating or reorienting certain portions of the building such as moving the location of the lobby, loading dock, utilities, and parking structures. In that regard, the following screening questions form a checklist that can help the owner make such a determination:

Would a reorientation of the existing building and some of its functional elements impact the business and financial requirements of the owner? If so, how does it?

Does the reorientation of the building on its site increase or decrease secure access to needed, available transportation (roads, rail, airport, waterway, and so on), and are any of these critical transportation lines themselves subject to high degrees of risk from natural or man-made disasters?

Does the nature of the building, or of the site, require that any special security features need to be in place during the renovation process?

Can the reorientation of certain building functions on its existing site afford either maximum or at least greater standoff distances from streets, alleys, or other potential access points for a car or truck bomb for key portions of the building (e.g., entrance, primary exits, loading docks, mechanical equipment rooms)?

What uses and kinds of buildings are on properties bordering or in immediate area of the property? Are any of these hazardous use facilities? Do any of these have potential high risk for terrorist activity? (Available from fire, police, and possibly from local homeland security agency) Does the location of that high hazard neighboring structure necessitate the benefits of reorienting a functional part of the existing building away from that neighboring structure? (e.g., move the primary entrance and exit to another side of the building, more out of the way of potential collateral damage should the neighbor be attacked)

Are there any plans before the jurisdiction to change the zoning for an adjacent area to the existing building and thus increase the potential hazard level within this area?

What has been the crime rate in this area? (Police departments can supply this information.)

Are there natural security barriers that can be taken better advantage of by virtue of reorienting different building functions within that structure (e.g., better lines of sight for observation of potential criminal activity; trees or other landscaping features that set site apart from other properties)?

Can the entrance to the building and location of utilities be relocated to reduce their current level of vulnerability to natural or man-made hazards?

How expensive will any of the preceding reorientations of one or more of the building's functions be? What is the cost/benefit for doing one or more of these reorientations of function to reduce potential risks?

What are the relative costs of mitigating those risks not by reorienting a function but instead by increasing the use of hazard mitigation design features, including security guards and guard stations, locked gates, anti-ram barriers, or blast-proofing? Putting in place restricted access to the street adjacent to the building? Putting in security cameras and blast-resistant fencing around the facility?

Does putting any of these special security features into the building provide increased value to the owner in terms of tenants? Future resale of the building?

Does placing any of these features into this building and the building's orientation on its site reduce the expense of perhaps upgrading that level of security at a later date as hazard conditions warrant?

As mentioned in Chapter 5, the NIST 2004, "Best Practices for Project Security" and the soon to be issued (fall of 2006) "Primer for Incorporating Building Security Components in Architectural Design" can aid the owner in completing the preceding checklist. These publications are useful tools in making decisions concerning site selection, building renovation, and possible reorientation. The first NIST publication provides additional cost-analysis information for choosing different risk-reduction designs and the new FEMA primer offers additional detailed guidance on building orientation and design features.

Guidelines for Protection: The Outer Ring of an Existing Building

Armed with the outcome of their risk assessment and mitigation strategy and having reviewed the possible benefits and costs from reorienting different building functions within the existing site, the owner and his construction team have a large number of final decisions to make concerning various security options. Drawn once again from FEMA, DoD, GSA, NIST, American Society for Industrial Security and other publications, the following are a series of construction and design guide checklists that owners can use to make their final determination as to which provisions work best for providing outer ring security to the new building.

Features to Include to Provide Outer Ring Security: Perimeter Control

Use of Natural Features for Perimeter Control   As noted for low-risk structures covered earlier in this chapter, the CPTED principle of making use of natural topography or landscaping features afford some levels of security for buildings, especially from bomb attacks or in some cases biochemical-radiological attacks. These include the possible adding of a natural berm around the building that offers shelter protection from blast or provides additional standoff distance for the ground floor of the building and planting of trees or shrubs to form a natural barricade or lines of demarcation between public areas and areas that the owner wants kept secure from general public traffic.

Figure 6-14
Construction
of security
planter/barricade
at Hall of
the States,
Washington, D.C.

Figure 6-15

Completed security planter/barricade at Hall of the States, Washington, D.C.

Use of Built Physical Barriers for Perimeter Control: Bollards, Fencing, and Gates
Where natural barriers do not exist or cannot be put in place to provide safe setback distances for the building to form a secure outer defense ring, man-made structures can be provided. These features include bollards, planters, fences or walls, gates, benches or decorative art that act as bollards or barricades, other vehicle anti-ram devices; structures that preclude a high-speed direct approach at the building, closed-circuit television and lighting.

Anti-Ram Bollards   As noted in Chapter 5, overseas moving vehicular bombing attacks have been a major taker of lives in Lebanon, Israel, Saudi Arabia, and Iraq. Anti-ram bollards such as those in Figure 5-9 are designed to be anchored into the ground and at street corners or T intersections to withstand the impact of cars and trucks striking them at speeds of 50 mph. The weight of these vehicles may vary between 4000 lb to 15000 lb.

Figure 6-16

Anti-ram street
security devices,
Capitol Hill
Washington, D.C.

Anti-ram bollards protecting portions of buildings that are parallel to adjacent streets are designed to withstand impacts from vehicles of similar size but at lesser speed—30 mph.

A reminder, in addition to these resources, federal, state, and local government agencies can obtain from the joint Department of State/DoD Technical Support Working Group (TSWG) a classified software tool, "BIRM3D" for use by their physical security staff to test the vulnerability of different types of vehicular security barriers against a wide range of vehicular bomb threats. (Visit the TSWG Web site at www.tswg.gov for more details).

Use of Special Design Features and Location of Access Point Considerations for Perimeter Control Since car and truck bombs have been the most common form of terrorist attack in the United States and Europe, in addition to using the natural and man-made barriers to separate the building from vehicles, the relocation and operation of parking structures, the location of roadways, passenger dropoff, and truck delivery areas (loading docks) and pedestrian traffic flow all are of critical importance to building security for an existing structure. Pages 145 to 147 of Chapter 5 provide a detailed set of checklists of design considerations that have been drawn from FEMA publication 426, "Reference Manual to Mitigate Terrorist Attacks Against Facilities," that can likewise be followed by existing buildings.

Upgrade Physical Security Lighting If it is not already available, security lighting should be provided or upgraded for the entire site including the building perimeter, entrances, pedestrian walkway, and parking and loading dock areas to assure maximum surveillance by security personnel. Lighting systems should have backup power systems, which should be located away from loading docks or other places with vehicular traffic. The provisions for lighting in rehabilitation situations should follow the same guidelines for lighting provided in Chapter 5 (pages 147 to 148).

Site Utilities A building can only be as secure as its access to the utility services that support its operation, that is, power and water (potable and sewer) services. These services can be particularly vulnerable to the effects of blast and (as with the WTC) their being severed can adversely impact the life safety of the building occupants in the aftermath of a terrorist attack. Unfortunately this fact has often been overlooked in strengthening the security of existing buildings.

Because of their critical importance, this checklist, also provided in Chapter 5, has been modified slightly for existing structures and repeated here.

Wherever possible, utilities should be protected, concealed and placed underground. Places where utility lines pass through the outer perimeter (fences, and the like) should be sealed to assure no one passes through that security barrier.

Redundant utility systems entering the building from different directions should be provided to support security, life safety, and rescue functions. (This may have equal importance in mitigating against adverse effects from large scale natural disasters, such as with a major earthquake).

Where possible, provide quick connects for portable utility backup systems if redundant systems are not functioning or available. (This also is useful following natural disasters such as a seismic event that may take down a portion of or the entire power grid and water system.) Emergency backup power systems may include the use of fuel cell technology.

Prepare a vulnerability assessment of all utility services to the site—including power lines, storm sewers, water lines, gas lines, and other utilities that the building is dependant upon and/or which cross the site perimeter.

Secure manholes and underground utility conduits that enter the building grounds and building itself. This includes protecting water treatment plants and storage facilities from waterborne contaminates.

Conceal incoming utility systems as much as possible and minimize signs marking them; do, however, provide fire emergency personnel with diagrams of utility feed locations and connections for use in response to emergency situations.

Relocate utility systems 50 ft or more from loading docks, front entrances and parking areas and consider blast-resistant construction to harden utility rooms.

Relocate petroleum, oil, lubricant, or chemical storage tanks and operate buildings downslope from all other buildings. Where possible, site fuel tanks at lower elevation than operational buildings or utility plants. Fuel storage tanks should be a minimum of 100 ft from other buildings and away from loading docks, entrances, and parking.

Provide utility systems with redundant loop service (especially electrical system).

Decentralize a site's communications resources. When possible, use multiple communication networks that will strengthen the communication system's ability to work during a disaster. Network control centers should be protected and if possible concealed.

Reroute critical or fragile utilities so that they are not on exterior walls or on walls shared with lobby or mailroom (or loading docks).

Fixtures and all overhead utilities weighing 31 lb or more should be mounted to reduce likelihood that they will fall during blast (or seismic event) and cause injuries. (Follow appropriate provisions for seismic portions of local building code.)

Other Resources for Defending the Outer Ring

As cited in Chapter 5, the following resources from the DoD also can be useful in making decisions on providing greater outer ring protection for existing structures: unified facilities criteria: UFGS-02821A, Fencing, published February 2002; UFGS-02840A, Active Vehicle Barriers, February 2002; and UFGS-02841N, Traffic Barriers, August 2001.

Codes and Standards and the Outer Ring

With the exception of NFPA Guide 730 and Standard 731, the nation's model building codes for either new or existing structures do not have specific security provisions governing perimeter access. Building owners should consider following these two NFPA documents and other procedures/systems described in FEMA-426, design guidance for premises security and the installation of electronic premises security systems.

NFPA Standards 730, "Guide for Premises Security," 2006 edition, and 731, "Standard for the Installation of Electronic Premises Security Systems," 2006, are found on pages 133 to 135 of Chapter 5.

The Inner Ring

Security Inside the Outer Ring: Protection from Blast and Progressive Collapse

Thanks to the declassification of earlier work by federal agencies, a building owner and the construction team have available to them a growing number of design approaches and building materials to use when faced with a building site that either does not allow adequate standoff distances to mitigate the effects of a bomb blast or whose risk assessment and mitigation strategy have led them to consider providing varying degrees of protection from similar attacks on a neighboring structure.

Figure 6-17

Inner ring of defense

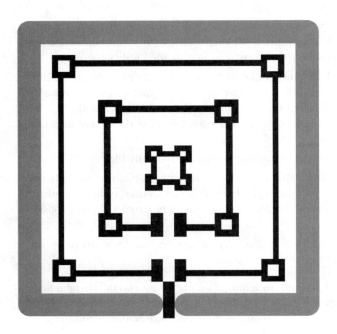

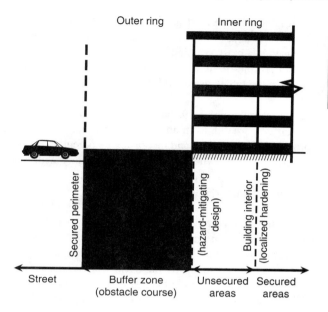

Figure 6-18
FEMA schematic showing lines of defense against blast, from FEMA, Figure 5-2

Figure 6-18 denotes the proper standoff distances to be used in building design and, where possible, in building renovation to minimize the impact of blast on structures. This FEMA diagram has come from out of the experiences of both the U.S. Departments of State and DoD between 1970 and 1990, researching and developing classified guidelines and practices addressing the issue of protecting buildings from blast.

Together with the work of the GSA and FEMA, the following blast-related documents have been produced that owners and their construction team can refer to in developing approaches to mitigate the impact of blast on their existing building: "Primer for Design of Commercial Buildings to Mitigate Terrorist Attacks," its companion document from the risk management series, FEMA 426, "Reference Manual to Mitigate Potential Terrorist Attacks Against Buildings," and the American Institute of Steel Construction's (AISC) "Facts for Steel Buildings: Blast and Progressive Collapse." Released in December 2003, the FEMA documents build upon the bombings in Oklahoma City, Khobar Towers and 1993 WTC. (As noted earlier, the AISC document, released in April 2005, adds information compiled from terrorist bombings in Iraq.) The "Whole Building Design Guide for Building Retrofit from Blast" (www.wbdg.org), developed and maintained by the National Institute of Building Sciences, is neither a building code nor a standard and does not contain mandatory criteria.

In addition to these unclassified resources, governmental agencies at the federal, state, and local levels also have available to them classified blast-protection information, including details on blast-mitigating products, from the earlier mentioned TSWG. Federal, state, and local government officials have access to this information via a secure section of the TSWG Web site.

Blast 101: Revisited for Existing Buildings

As described in Chapter 5, pages 153 to 165, the supersonic expansion of energy released in a blast, coupled with the shockwave reflections off the ground and any object within its line of sight are devastating to buildings located inside of the setback clearances in the tables provided by FEMA, GSA, and the DoD in their publications.

As noted in Figure 6-19, buildings with such features as overhangs or internal corners (reentrant corners), as in an l- or t-shaped building, will trap the shockwave for a while, prolonging its duration and increasing its potential damage to that portion of the building. Where possible, owners of an existing building with a high risk from a blast event may want to consider making changes to the building to either eliminate the reentrant corners or at a minimum reinforce them from blast.

Blast and Exterior Building Damage   As noted in Figure 5-19 in Chapter 5, different building shapes and different standoff distances have a significant effect on the relative impact of an explosive device. Shapes that dissipate air blast perform better than those that trap or accentuate the air blast. Impacts may range from shattered windows and cracked walls to the kind of catastrophic structural failures witnessed in Khobar Towers, the Murrah Building, the American Embassy, and Marine Barracks in Beirut.

The largest losses of life have been from progressive structural collapses caused by the spread of any initial localized collapse of a column, exterior wall, roof, or floor system to other parts of the structure that may have received lesser damage but are unable to sustain the building load that has been transferred to them by the destruction of those localized columns, walls, or floor. The close proximity of a powerful bomb to critical load-bearing columns produces progressive collapse, by propagating forces vertically upward or downward from the explosion's source and laterally from bay to bay.

Guidelines for Protecting Existing Structures from Progressive Collapse

The guidelines for protecting existing structures from progressive collapse are the same as those for new construction, with one major difference. The retrofitting of an existing structure, where standoff distances are not available, is generally more expensive to

Figure 6-19
Reentrant corners
in a floor plan,
from FEMA

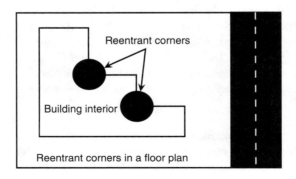

Reentrant corners

Building interior

Reentrant corners in a floor plan

Source: *U.S. air force, installation force protection guide*

undertake than designing the blast resistance into the building when it is new. The owner must be careful when making the columns and other features "more robust" not to do so in a manner that may actually weaken the structure.

As previously noted, the DoD, GSA, Department of State, and FEMA at the federal government level and from the private sector, the American Society of Civil Engineers, AISC, and the Concrete Masonry Institute, all have worked on and produced either construction guidelines or standards addressing technical issues regarding the design of new (and retrofit of existing) buildings to prevent or reduce the risk of progressive collapse from explosive devices. The guidelines provided in Chapter 5 for blast mitigation are equally true here. Drawn from the risk mitigation series, FEMA 426, "Reference Manual to Mitigate Potential Terrorist Attacks Against Buildings" and GSA's "Progressive Collapse Analysis and Design Guidelines for New Federal Office Buildings," here are retrofit design features that will provide a more robust structure and decrease the potential for progressive collapse:

Redundancy

- Use ductile structural elements and detailing.
- Provide capacity for resisting load reversals.
- Provide capacity for resisting sheer failure.

Determine the appropriateness for considering using one or more of the following engineering practices:

- Consider retrofitting to incorporate internal damping into the structural system to absorb the blast impact.
- Use symmetric reinforcement that can increase the ultimate load capacity of the structure.
- Consider wire mesh in plaster to reduce the incidence of flying fragments.
- In retrofit applications, wherever possible, avoid the use of masonry when blast is a threat, avoiding a potential problem experienced with masonry walls breaking up and becoming secondary fragments during the blast.
- Use multiple barrier materials and construction techniques that can sometimes accomplish the same goal with less expense than a single material or technique.
- Lap splices should fully develop the capacity of the reinforcement.
- Deflections around certain members, such as windows, should be controlled to prevent premature failure. Additional reinforcement is generally required.
- In general, column spacing should be minimized so that reasonably sized members can be designed to resist the design loads and increase the redundancy of the system.
- It is a general principle in blast mitigation that floor-to-floor heights should be minimized less than or equal to 16 ft. In retrofit situations this will quite often be impossible given the building's original construction.
- When the existing building is made of CMU (concrete masonry unit) construction, the designer should use fully grouted and reinforced CMUs.

- The designer coordinates structural requirements for blast with other disciplines in the project, including architectural and mechanical.
- The use of one-way wall elements spanning from floor-to-floor is generally a preferred method to minimize blast loads imparted to columns.
- Carefully study design approaches that are being used to make sure that they are not in conflict. This may be true in use of ductile detailing requirements for seismic design and alternate load paths provided by progressive collapse design.
- Use architectural and structural features that deny contact with exposed primary vertical load members. A minimum standoff of at least 6 in. from these members is required.

Building materials that are acceptable in the adopted rehabilitation building codes from the jurisdiction in which the building is being constructed are allowed, however, "special consideration should be given to materials that have inherent flexibility and that are better able to handle load reversals (i.e., cast in place reinforced concrete and steel construction)." "The construction type selected must meet all performance criteria of the specified level of protection."

The FEMA and GSA documents also note that all building components "requiring blast resistance should be designed using established methods and approaches for determining dynamic loads, structural detailing, and dynamic structural response." Working with a licensed structural engineer with expertise in blast design and construction, owners and architects should consult and, where applicable, abide by the following design criteria and standards:

- American Society of Civil Engineers, "Minimum Design Loads for Buildings and Other Structures," ASCE 7
- GSA's "Security Design Criteria"
- The AISC's "Facts for Steel Buildings: Blast and Progressive Collapse"
- The "Whole Building Design Guide's" section on "Retrofitting Existing Buildings to Resist Explosive Threats"

In addition to the aforementioned, the U.S Army Corps of Engineers and NIST continue to fund and conduct research on the issue of reducing progressive collapse as the result of blast and seismic events.

Guidelines for Protecting the Interior of the Building from Other Blast Damage

As noted in Chapter 5, deaths and severe injuries in buildings come not only from progressive collapse but also from blast debris and localized collapse of walls and floors. The objective of the building owner, designer, and construction team is to renovate their building to limit the impact of that attack to something approaching "acceptable damage levels." The owner, be it a federal, state, or local government agency, or a private sector firm going through the risk-threat analysis methodology provided in Chapter 4 will need to define what that acceptable level is for them and their employees, given a realistic assessment of the actual threats that are involved.

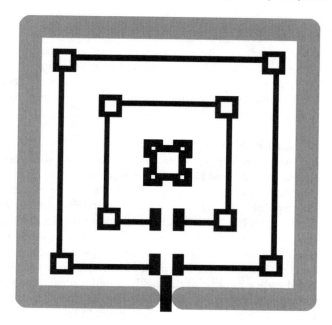

Figure 6-20
Rings of defense—
the inner core

The retrofit provisions for mitigating the effects of blast on windows, doors, roofs, and other internal and external structures are the same for existing buildings as they are for new construction. Pages 161 to 165 of Chapter 5 should be reviewed and applied by the owner of an existing structure.

In addition to the preceding actions, blast wraps, which first emerged in Europe, are now being studied by the DoD and other agencies for possible use not only in emergency situations, but also as a low-cost retrofit method for adding additional protection to columns and other structural members that may be subject to blast. Some wraps include using Kevlar fibers and others use a combination of compressible materials and flame-retarding chemicals. The technology is still far off from being applied to building renovations, but it may afford building owners with a lower cost alternative to existing methods of reducing risk from blast.

INTERNAL BUILDING SECURITY: PROTECTING AN EXISTING BUILDING FROM INTERNAL AND EXTERNAL BIOCHEMICAL ATTACK

The Indoor Air Environment

As noted by Woods, knowing just what actions to take to effectively retrofit the existing HVAC system for a building is an extremely complex task. Especially where there is such a wide range of potential contaminants to try and with which to protect the building from.

The continued rise in energy prices now projected for the foreseeable future, will bring more and more building owners to consider making modifications to their existing HVAC systems just to increase the efficiency of these systems and reduce as much as possible the costs of heating and cooling the building. The effectiveness and efficiency of these mechanical systems and the importance of their proper maintenance will become an issue of growing concern to building owners and members of their construction team.

Rhode Island's "HVAC Building Vulnerability Assessment Tool" can be useful to building owners wondering where to start in trying to determine whether their existing HVAC system should be upgraded to address potential biochemical threats. This section then looks again at the general guidelines developed by the American Society of Heating Refrigerating and Air Conditioning Engineers (ASHRAE; "Risk Management Guidance on Health, Safety, and Environmental Security" and their soon to be released guideline) and other associations to provide a synopsis of major actions that can be taken now in the retrofit of a high-risk exposed building to address a number of the hazards currently associated with a biochemical event (attack or accidental release). As noted earlier, because of the highly complex nature of trying to develop the best possible mitigation strategy for a widely diverse array of biochemical agents, owners should include on their building retrofit team qualified mechanical engineers with expertise in the area of biochemical mitigation systems.

Begin with an Evaluation of Existing Systems: The Rhode Island Guide

Rhode Island's "HVAC Building Vulnerability Assessment Tool" provides a checklist for owners of existing buildings to review their building's current HVAC system and note areas where its design and operation can be either enhanced or modified to provide better protection to building occupants from potential biochemical agents. While a complete copy of the "HVAC Building Vulnerability Assessment Tool" has been provided in the Appendix of this book, its main features are listed later. The assessment tool asks the building owners and managers in conjunction with an HVAC professional to go through their building assessing the following aspects of its system:

1. Review of type of air ventilation/conditioning system in building.
   A. What type of air ventilation/conditioning system exists in the building?
      1. Natural (functional windows)
      2. Individual (wall, window, or unit vents)
      3. Air handling units with ducts (AHU)

2. AHU
   A. How many AHUs service the building?
   B. Are any of these features on separate (dedicated) AHU?
      1. The lobby?
      2. Mail rooms, delivery areas, and publicly accessible areas?
      3. Stairways?
   C. Can the AHU system be placed under positive pressure?
   D. How are AHUs controlled?
      1. ___Computer ___ Manual ___ Other

E. Is there an emergency AHU shutdown plan?
F. How is shutdown initiated?
G. Is there a manual override switch? If yes, where is it located?

3. Air intakes
   A. How many air intakes service the building?
   B. Are any on the ground level? If yes, are they secured? How?
   C. If not secured, can they be elevated or secured?
   D. If they can be elevated or secured, are they angled or grated?
   E. Are any on the roof top level? If yes, who has access? Authorized people only?
   F. If not secured, can they be?

4. Recirculation modes/return air
   A. Is return air ducted or open plenum?
   B. Is return air from different zones mixed?
   C. Are return air grills secure? If no, can they be secured?

5. Mechanical rooms
   A. Are mechanical rooms/areas kept locked with controlled access?
   B. If not, can they be?

6. Filtration specifications
   A. What is the maximum filtration capacity?
   B. Where is the filtration media?

7. System of operation/maintenance
   A. Is the system maintained by in-house personnel?
   B. Is the maintenance contracted to an outside entity?
   C. Are filters changed regularly?
   D. Is there a schedule for cleaning?
   E. Is there a schedule for period balancing?

8. Other considerations
   A. Is there an area that can be used as "shelter in place?"
   B. Does the building have exhaust fans/systems? How many, and where are they located? Where are their switches located?
   C. Does the building have smoke purge fans? How many and where are they located? Where are their switches located?

The Rhode Island assessment tool concludes with a place to record a summary of findings and a place to list actions required.

Redesign and Program Considerations for Protecting Buildings and Their Occupants from External and Internal Release of Biochemical Agents

In addition to the Rhode Island tool, the following general guidelines provide an overview of the levels of complexity that are involved. Several notations on future directions in ongoing research in this field are provided at the end of this section. The core document covered in this section is the Centers for Disease Control/National Institute for Occupational Safety and Health, May 2002, "Guidance for Protecting Building Environments from Airborne, Chemical, Biological, or Radiological Attacks."

Figure 6-21
Seattle,
Washington

Relocation of Outdoor Air Intakes

- Outdoor air intakes should be relocated at least two stories above ground to reduce the potential for hazardous materials (as well as vehicle exhaust). Many contaminates are heavier than the surrounding air and will remain close to the ground under calm conditions and placing the intakes at the highest practical level on the building is beneficial.

- Intakes should be covered by screens that are slopped so contaminants can not be tossed into them from ground level or from an adjacent building or structure.

- As covered in earlier sections, mechanical rooms should be secured and located away from public traffic areas or areas of the building that may be more vulnerable to attack, such as mail rooms, loading docks, and building lobbies.

- There should be no public access to the roof of the building to eliminate possibility of attack via exhaust vents, HVAC units, or air intakes located there.

- Access to information on the building's operating systems (including fire, smoke control, and electrical and other mechanical systems) and emergency procedures should be restricted and secured.

- HVAC systems should be isolated, well sealed, and maintained at negative pressure relative to the rest of the building to prevent widespread dispersion of any contaminates released within the building's mail room (e.g., anthrax), lobby, or loading dock.

- In large buildings with multiple HVAC zones served by their own HVAC system, the isolation of those zones minimizes the potential for the spread of an airborne contaminate within the building. This also reduces the potential number of building occupants exposed to such hazards and requires a full height wall between each zone and its adjacent zone and the buildings' hallways.

In case of an outdoor release of a hazardous substance, the building should be designed to allow for occupants to "shelter in place" in rooms or locations where risk of outdoor air infiltration is low. These places must have the following:

- Doors that prevent air flow.

- Mechanisms and staff to operate them that are capable of reducing and then shutting down the indoor-outdoor air exchange rate prior to the arrival at the building site of the contaminate plume. Depending on the design of the HVAC system, this may include the closing of various dampers, especially those controlling the flow of outdoor air. Low-leakage dampers should be considered to avoid the potential for outdoor air to migrate into the building because the internal air pressure inside the building remains below that of the air pressure outside even with the HVAC system shut down.

- In case of an indoor release, HVAC mechanisms must provide interior pressure and airflow control to vent the contaminant to the outside as rapidly as possible while isolating the contaminant from other portions of the building.

- The preceding systems should be designed and tested in coordination with a qualified mechanical engineer as a member of the construction team. The actual nature of which operating procedures to follow will vary depending on the nature of the system in the building and of the indoor or outdoor contaminant to which the building is exposed.

- Ducted air returns reduce the access points in which a contaminant can be introduced. Placing return vents in high traffic areas reduces chances that a contaminant could be surreptitiously introduced into the return system.

- Buildings at high risk with nonducted air return systems that use hallways or spaces above the suspended ceiling in a ceiling plenum return system that replace the air to the HVAC unit may need to add a system of highly efficient filters to assure that the contaminant is not redistributed throughout the building.

- Sensors and filters

- Buildings at high risk may want to consider including biochemical sensors within their HVAC system. Considerable research is still ongoing in this field to eliminate false alarms that stimulate unnecessary evacuations from the building. GSA, DoD, and TSWG are working on further research into these systems, and their results should be consulted.

- Filter systems likewise are still subject to ongoing research and testing by GSA, DoD, and TSWG and others. Current filter technology requires different filters for different types of biochemical agents.

Different types of filers currently available include the following:

Particulate Air Filters—designed to capture aerosols through one or more collection mechanisms (inertial impaction, interception, diffusion, or electrostatic) and are covered by two ASHRAE standards for rating, ASHRAE 52.1-1992 and ASHRAE 52.2-1999. Particulate filters include low-efficiency dust filters, high-efficiency particulate air filters (HEPA) and ultra-low-penetration air filters (ULPA).

Chapter 5 of FEMA's reference manual, "Chemical, Biological, and Radiological Measures," FEMA 426, provides the best overview of issues concerning filter availability and use. Federal, state, and local governments here again can consult the TSWG Web site for additional information.

Other Useful Tools and a Brief Look at Retrofit Costs

DARPA Research: Toward Immune Buildings   Chapter 5 briefly described the work that the Defense Advanced Research Projects Agency (DARPA) is doing with academic institutions, other federal agencies, and the construction and standards community to develop an unclassified version of a "Building Protection Tool Kit." The tool kit will enable future building owners and members of their design and construction team to consider a wide range of technologies, design, and construction practices that can be used to enhance levels of protection within new and existing buildings from biochemical and radiological attacks or accidental releases.

At their May 4, 2005, Immune Building Conference, DARPA discussed with their colleagues steps that need to be taken to develop the tool kit. The meeting also reviewed the need for building owners to address the issue of mitigating the potential impact of biochemical attacks by taking a life-cycle cost view of making changes to the building to improve its ability to meet that challenge.

In discussions on renovation costs, based upon then available technologies and construction costs, the installation of a military-grade filtration system for a 30,000 sq ft building would run in the neighborhood of $1,400,000 assuming that the building was unoccupied during renovation. This is a sizeable financial commitment for any owner who needs such a high level of security for their building.

Emergency Egress: Currently Available Codes and Future Trends

The building codes adopted by state and local governments carry provisions for emergency egress that have been generally drawn from either the ICC's family of codes (the IEBC or the International Building Code) or the NFPA's Life Safety Code (NFPA 101) and include provisions from the state's architectural accessibility code for people with disabilities. The general outline of these provisions were covered in Chapter 5 and do not generally change for building retrofit, other than the issue of what features and what amount of the building that is being renovated may trigger renovation of larger portions of the building to provide for accessible access throughout the structure. As will be covered later on, emergency egress provisions, however, are being modified in some jurisdictions for high-rise structures, especially those that are not yet sprinklered and require the owner's attention.

A new resource for owners of existing high-rise structures is the Council on Tall Buildings and Urban Habitat's "Emergency Evacuation: Elevator Systems Guideline." This publication is the result of a 14-month study by a 16-member task force from experts within the elevator, life safety, engineering, and building owner community. The guide includes key issues that design teams should consider in developing emergency evacuation plans for high-rise structures (new and existing) and three design approaches to elevator evacuation systems. Also available from the Tall Buildings Council is "The Building Safety Enhancement Guidebook," which was written in the aftermath of 9/11 specifically for building owners and managers. These publications are available on the Tall Buildings and Urban Habitat Council's Web site: www.ctbuh.org.

Figure 6-22
FEMA Manual 426

Owners of existing buildings will want to keep track of the research agenda of the U.S. Architectural and Transportation Barriers Compliance Board and its progress toward the proposed emergency egress and evacuation code changes that are now before the ICC. While the proposed code changes apply to new construction, they may point to future retrofit requirements.

GUIDELINES, CODES, AND STANDARDS TO ENHANCE PROTECTION FROM NATURAL DISASTERS: SEISMIC, WIND, AND FLOOD

Between 1990 and 2002 over $19 billion was spent in that state on earthquake loss reduction. Despite those efforts, in January 2006, the Governor's Office of Emergency Services, together with the Earthquake Engineering Research Institute and the Seismological Society of America, released their study ("When the Big One Strikes Again.") of what the impact would be today on losses of life and property if the 1906 San Francisco earthquake were to happen again. The findings are sobering.

"As many as 10,000 commercial buildings would sustain major structural damage and between 160,000 and 250,000 households would be displaced from damaged residences."

Figure 6-23

Katrina damage,
New Orleans

Half of this damage and the projected between 800 and 3400 deaths (depending upon the time of day the quake struck) would come from the collapse of old concrete, unreinforced masonry and other vulnerable buildings that have not yet undergone seismic retrofit.

—"Managing Risk in Earthquake Country," April 17, 2006,
report issued at the 100th Anniversary Conference
of the 1906 San Francisco Earthquake and Fire
by the conference sponsors, which include
California Office of Emergency Services,
Earthquake Engineering Research
Institute, Disaster Resilient California,
and Seismic Safety Association.

Reports such as the previous one and the headlines from Hurricanes Katrina and Rita have made our nation more aware of the catastrophic impact of large-scale natural disasters upon the built environment. As a result, more jurisdictions are considering either including in their building rehabilitation codes or mandating retrofit statutes to enhance the ability of structures—from residences to commercial office buildings—to better withstand the next round of intense hurricanes, wind storms, seismic events, or floods.

The all-hazard approach to disaster mitigation, be it terrorist threat or a natural disaster, indeed is transforming the way the building construction team interacts with not only the owner but also with the community in which their building exists. The HAZUS tool described in Chapter 4 and again in Chapter 5 affords building owners an excellent guide for considering what upgrades to their existing structure they may wish to add to further reduce the building's and its occupant's vulnerabilities to natural disasters beyond those mitigating provisions in the adopted codes and standards in their community.

In addition to the information contained within its database, the most current, up-to-date data as well as historical data for a particular location, are available from multiple federal government sources including the following:

- U.S. Geological Survey for maps of the United States covering for six natural hazards (tornadoes, hurricanes, floods, earthquakes, volcanic eruptions, and landslides) for areas that have, "relatively high risk or relative frequent actual occurrences." These are available at http://www.usgs.gov/themes/hazard.html.
- FEMA and their National Flood Insurance Program (NFIP) have the most current maps of the 100-year flood plain elevations for the nation, which are available from their Map Services Center at: http://www.msc.fema.gov.
- The National Weather Service also collects data on severe weather covering snow, winter storm, cold, heat, wind, lightening, tornadoes, hurricanes, and other tropical storms, which are available at http://www.nws.noaa.gov/om/hazstats.shtml.

High Levels of Risk from One or More Natural Disasters

Having used the HAZUS or other tool and conducted a risk assessment and determined that he or she wants to indeed build above the minimum building code in their jurisdiction, here by natural hazard area are resources that owners can consult on building retrofit.

Seismic Resources

National Earthquake Hazards Reduction Program, Model Codes, "Whole Building Design Guide" and Retrofit Provisions in State and Local Codes   As noted earlier, one immediate action that building owners can take is to renovate their building to the provisions within the appropriate model building code for a seismic zone that is one level higher than that called for in the adopted building code in their jurisdiction. Retrofit provisions within the seismic safety portions of building codes adopted and enforced in California, Washington, and Oregon also can serve as models for construction guidance.

Not unlike the discussion earlier on blast mitigation, among the key retrofit issues in seismic safety design are wall systems and glazing, roofing design and materials, sliding or ductile connections for heavy cladding systems, glass-fiber-reinforced concrete cladding systems, lightweight panel systems, building foundations, exterior skin envelope, and anchoring of mechanical equipment.

In addition to the following documents from the Applied Technology Council and FEMA (developed in coordination with the National Earthquake Hazards Reduction Program, NIST and a number of colleges and universities), the "Whole Building Design Guide" section on "Seismic Safety of the Building Envelope" is an invaluable resource.

- ATC 57, "The Missing Piece: Improving Seismic Design and Construction Practices"
- FEMA 389, "Communicating with Owners and Managers of New Buildings on Earthquake Risk: A Primer for Design Professionals"
- FEMA 395, "Incremental Seismic Rehabilitation for School Buildings (K-12)"
- FEMA 396, "Incremental Seismic Rehabilitation of Hospital Buildings"
- FEMA 397, "Incremental Seismic Rehabilitation of Office Buildings"
- FEMA 398, "Incremental Seismic Rehabilitation of Multi-family Apartment Buildings"
- FEMA 399, "Incremental Seismic Rehabilitation of Retail Buildings"
- FEMA 424, "Design Guide for School Safety Against Earthquakes, Floods, and High Winds"
- FEMA 433, "Using HAZUS-MH for Risk Assessment"

In addition, by late 2006, FEMA will issue the following additional Incremental Seismic Rehabilitation documents:

- FEMA 400, "Hotel and Motel Buildings"
- FEMA 401, "Storage Building"
- FEMA 402, "Emergency Building"
- FEMA 454, "Designing for Earthquakes: A Manual for Architects" and the Applied Technology Council will be releasing ATC-58, "Guidelines for Performance Assessment," which converts structural analysis data into projected losses in the event of a certain earthquake loading.

As noted in the opening quote from the 100th Anniversary Conference of the San Francisco Earthquake and Fire—even in California that has had building codes with seismic safety provisions on the books for over 50 years and a law promoting the mitigation of hazards from unreinforced masonry construction since 1986—there still are a lot of hazardous buildings to mitigate within the state to reduce the kinds of casualties that that report describes.

A building owner in a region of the country prone to seismic events, but whose jurisdiction has not adopted or upgraded its seismic safety provisions to address the threat from a major future quake, can look to building codes adopted in California, Oregon, and Washington for guidance. Listed in the Appendix are Web sites for state building codes and several local governments and also a copy of the California Unreinforced Masonry Building Law and the unreinforced masonry construction requirements for San Francisco.

Wind and Flood: Resources: Other Jurisdictions, Model Codes, and FEMA

Hurricanes and tornadoes are the two largest wind-related disasters that strike our nation. As noted earlier, the analysis by weather experts that by 2006 the United States was only in year 5 of a potential 15- to 20-year severe hurricane cycle has many communities along the Gulf and Eastern Coasts of the nation not only reassessing their disaster preparedness plans for such events but also giving serious consideration to the structural, wind, and water penetration provisions within their adopted building codes and standards.

Building owners and their construction team may want to once again give serious consideration to including in their building retrofit upgrades the ability to meet higher wind speeds from the tables in the model building codes or to review the enhanced hurricane provisions adopted by the state of Florida in recent years.

Among the following FEMA publications that building owners in Tornado Alley may want to peruse when considering their building design is "Taking Shelter from the Storm: Building a Safe Room Inside Your House." In addition to a safe room, a hurricane and tornado shelter standard is under development by a committee at the ICC. Additional information is available on the ICC Web site: www.iccsafe.org.

Here are a number of currently available design guides from www.fema.gov:

- FEMA 55, "Coastal Construction Manual"
- FEMA's How To Series, "Build with Flood Resistant Materials," "Dry Floodproofing Your Building," and "Raise Electrical System Components"
- FEMA with Texas Tech, "Taking Shelter from the Storm: Building A Safe Room Inside Your House"

Figure 6-24
Portland, Oregon skyline

RECENT CHANGES BY STATES AND MAJOR CITIES TO THEIR CODES, STATUTES, AND ORDINANCES FOR EXISTING BUILDINGS

As noted in the previous section, having made the determination that a building needs to go beyond the minimum code in the building rehabilitation or renovation requirements adopted and enforced in the jurisdiction where their building is located, building owners can turn to the amendments that some major jurisdictions have already made to address the need for added levels of safety in existing buildings. Following up on the discussion in Chapter 5 of changes that several jurisdictions made in the wake of 9/11 to their codes and standards for new construction, here are changes which New York City and Chicago made to their statutes regarding existing buildings.

New York City

The New York City Department of Building's World Trade Center Building Code Task Force developed and submitted recommended changes to the New York City building code that were warranted out of the WTC disaster. On June 24, 2004, amendments were made to the building code to add the following provisions for existing high-rise buildings throughout the city.

Figure 6-25

Midtown New York City residential and commercial high rises

1. Every high-rise structure must have a city-approved "Office Building Emergency Action Plans." Staffing to fulfill that plan is spelled out in the ordinance and every building is mandated to conduct a "Full Building Drill" once every two years. Once a year every building occupant shall participate in a stairwell familiarization evacuation drill.

2. In existing construction, these retroactive provisions are to be made for buildings 100 ft in height or more:
   A. By July 1, 2019, buildings shall have installed a sprinkler system within the building.
   B. No building 100 ft or more in height can be converted into an office building or high-hazard classification without installation of a sprinkler system.
   C. Elevator enclosures installed under renovations after July 1, 2006, shall be constructed to new minimum impact resistance standards.
   D. Every high rise is required to complete, file with the city, and maintain a Building Information Card listing the building's vital features that first responders can use when they arrive at the building.
   E. Improve marking of the egress path, doors, and stairs with photo-luminescent materials.

Chicago

In the summary of key provisions in "Life Safety and High Rise Ordinance," the city of Chicago noted, "The wide variety of ways Chicago buildings were built, renovated, and used during the past 100 years is the reason that every building must be looked at individually and evaluated for its potential to protect its inhabitants in case of an event such as a fire. Our new requirement of a Life Safety Evaluation concerns buildings that (1) were built prior to 1975, (2) are more than 80 feet in height, (3) are without sprinklers throughout, and (4) are occupied for non-transient users."

As noted in Chapter 5, of Chicago's 1700 existing high-rise buildings (buildings over 80 ft in height), 1300 were built prior to1975, and of those 1300 structures, 200 buildings were commercial and 1100 were residential structures. In those structures that currently do not have sprinkler systems, the following retrofit requirements were established in addition to the mandatory designation for each building of a fire safety director, deputy fire safety director, building evacuation supervisor, fire wardens, and emergency evacuation teams and owners who must run annual safety drills. In addition, mandatory evacuation assistance for people with disabilities were required.

1. Complete a life safety evaluation of the building and establish a commitment to repair any deficiencies over a seven-year period (2005 to 2012).

2. All pre-1975 high rises must have both a one-way and a two-way voice communication system. Residential buildings less than 15 stories and 60 units only require a one-way voice communication system. Residential building owners must complete the installation of that system by 2012.

3. By 2012, one-hour fire-rated stairway doors and frames must be installed in residential buildings in order to protect the path of egress in case of fire.

4. All existing high-rise buildings were required to provide basic information to the fire department regarding the building's standpipe and sprinkler system as well as the building's use, ownership, and management.

Figure 6-26

High-rise buildings in Los Angeles

5. Any building over 80 ft that is altered or repaired, the cost of which in any consecutive 30 months exceeds 50% of the reproduction cost of the building, shall comply with the requirements for new high-rise construction and stair, elevator, and shaft enclosure requirements of the city of Chicago Building Code.

THE CRITICAL ROLE OF THE CONSTRUCTION TEAM REVISITED

This chapter has demonstrated the vital importance to the building owner of having a fully involved, competent team of architects, engineers, contractors, and product suppliers to help them through the challenges of threat, vulnerability, and risk assessment and developing and implementing a risk mitigation plan for their existing building and then renovating that building to that plan.

Figure 6-27
Euclid Avenue,
Cleveland, Ohio

It is of critical importance to the owner to have the construction team conduct a full inspection of the building to determine what areas within the building need improvements to meet the risks and threats that that structure will face. It is also important to have the renovation fully inspected at several stages by the local building department or, when necessary, by a qualified outside third party. The degree of complexity of renovating a building to address the vulnerabilities and risks posed by natural and man-made disasters described in the opening chapters of this book requires a competent check of the finished renovation to help assure that the holistic approach toward improving the security, health, and life safety of the occupants of that structure indeed has succeeded. The members of the construction team, from owner through to the codes and standards put in place in that structure, are critical to improving our nation's ability to adequately respond to the hazards posed by Mother Nature and those individuals or groups of individuals who would do us harm.

Figure 6-28

Small town, New England

Competent professional upgrades to the security and safety features of our existing structures, whether they be voluntarily undertaken by building owners as a result of conducting their own risk assessments or triggered by the provisions of the adopted rehabilitation provisions of the local building code, go a long way toward both helping to keep our small businesses running and helping our communities recover more quickly from the next disaster Mother Nature or mankind throw at us. The guidelines and checklists provided in this chapter help guide the building owner toward making the critical decisions for how best to enhance the protection of their individual building and its occupants.

Chapter 7 places everything that has been covered thus far into the broader context of their relationship to other major forces that are impacting construction in this nation besides those we normally associate with homeland security. The next chapter addresses the interconnection between natural and man-made disasters and construction and the issues of energy, sustainability, environment, accessibility, and the new products, materials, and techniques that are transforming not only the construction industry but our society as well, regardless of where we live, whether it be a small rural community or a major city.

Part III   Addressing New Issues: Viewing the Building as a Complete Life-Cycle System

OVERVIEW

The nature of the built environment and the construction industry in the United States are changing. Part I of this book (Chapters 1 to 3) explored how the man-made and natural disasters of 2001 to 2006 have begun to transform the construction industry and the roles, relationships, and responsibilities of the members of the construction team, that is, building owners, architects, engineers, contractors, building product manufacturers and suppliers, codes and standards developers, and building officials and building managers.

Part II (Chapters 4 to 6) reviewed the resources, guidelines, codes and standards, and best practices that currently are available to the building owner, designer, and members of the construction team to provide enhanced levels of protection to the public from man-made and natural disasters. Beginning with a look at the need to conduct threat, vulnerability, and risk assessments for new and existing buildings, the previous section of this book ended with the introduction of several key concepts that will be explored further in Part III, that is, treating the building in a holistic fashion, life-cycle cost, and the concepts of acceptable risk and disaster resilience.

Building upon the earlier sections, Part III turns to a more comprehensive view of both the life cycle of buildings and of a diverse array of forces that are impacting the future of construction in the United States. This section looks at one possible vision of where those forces are taking us. Chapter 7 introduces these forces, starting first with a broad look at homeland security issues and then the issues of energy, sustainability, environment, accessibility, and the new products, materials, and techniques that are transforming this industry.

Figure 7-1

This innovatively designed state office building built in the 1990's in Sacramento, CA is one of many early state government efforts to promote energy efficient and green building technologies

Chapter 8 provides a vision of what the construction industry may look like in the year 2025, a quarter of the way into the 21st century. This final chapter revisits the issue of architectural security codes and the role that the construction team can play to help shape the future of construction and public safety in this nation.

7 Homeland Security and the Issues of Energy, Sustainability, Environment, Accessibility and New Products, Materials and Techniques

The events of 9/ll opened the eyes of many American's to the fact that the world indeed is a dangerous place. The triumph of the United States and the Western allies in the cold war with communism did not make the world the safer, saner place that most Americans assumed or at least hoped it would become.

Not only were we engaged in a new war with a demonstratively effective enemy attacking our shores, but in the "game" of global economic competition, there were no guarantees that the United States would remain on top as the most productive and world's largest and strongest economy. Indeed in 2006, the national news media was running cover stories and week-long evening news features asking "Can America Compete?" and noting that by 2030 economists predict that China will replace the United States as the world's largest economy.

In statements similar to the preceding opening lines, the definition of homeland security has been broadened significantly since it first came into use in 2001 to 2002. What once referred originally to protecting our nation from future attacks by Al Qaeda, was expanded with the absorption of the Federal Emergency Management Agency (FEMA) into the then "new" Department of Homeland Security (DHS) in 2002, and the arrival of Michael Chertoff as its new director, into an all-hazards approach, incorporating the full range of accidental man-made and natural disasters described earlier in this book. In early 2006, this included preparations for the potential onset of the next projected global pandemic—the avian flu.

Indeed, homeland security, as a concept has expanded from its original narrow concern of how does our nation (or any nation) protect itself from attack by foreigners out to do us harm, to what makes America stronger, more defensible from external (and internal) vulnerabilities that can adversely impact the health, welfare, and life safety of our citizens? How do we make sure we remain competitive in the global economy? To be competitive, how do we keep down components of our overhead costs? Not just health care or energy or transportation, but the costs of our aging infrastructure including the costs

Figure 7-2

To enhance public safety, the state of Pennsylvania adopted a statewide code in 2000 State Capitol Harrisburg, Pennsylvania

of building new or renovating existing structures? How do we become more energy efficient and less dependent upon foreign oil? How do we reduce production of greenhouse gases that threaten our environment?

Homeland security has a major impact on how building owners, managers, architects, engineers, and their colleagues on the construction team think about the design, construction, and operation of our buildings. Under this broader more complex definition, we now need to incorporate not only the concepts of physical security (protection against crime, biochemical–radiological weapons and explosives) covered in the first two-thirds of this book, but also take into consideration these other risks to our security in our building's design, construction, and operation of buildings.

Increasingly, owners and their construction team are asking themselves how do we design and operate buildings to be more energy efficient, environmentally "friendly," and better able to be modified for different future uses? Last, some owners too are beginning to ask how do we design or renovate our buildings to be more readily used by the fastest growing age demographic group in our nation—the aging baby boomers?

Figure 7-3

Even smaller jurisdictions like Richmond Heights, Ohio are applying information technology to make their regulatory systems more effective and efficient

These are the topics that are focused upon in Chapter 7. We start out by looking first at the creation of DHS and the growing federal, state, and local political and economic infrastructure that support it and then turn to the impact these other forces have on the design, construction, and operation of buildings—writing the concept of "Architectural Security Codes" into this much broader context.

THE DEPARTMENT OF HOMELAND SECURITY: ITS STRUCTURE, PROGRAMS, AND RELATIONSHIP TO THE BUILT ENVIRONMENT

Twenty-one different governmental agencies and programs (and cultures) had to be assembled and subsequently absorbed into the U.S. Department of Homeland Security, while at the same time this department had to watch, develop, and administer projects that assured the safety of the American public from terrorism and natural disasters. In the aftermath of Hurricanes Katrina and Rita, reports from the White House and Congress called for changes in policy and structure to increase the effectiveness and efficiency of this, the second largest federal agency (after the Department of Defense, DoD).

While it is too early to tell whether or not FEMA will be either restructured within or removed from the DHS, it is important to the construction team to understand how the DHS is currently constituted and the relationship of that structure, DHS policies, and homeland security directives to the built environment.

Department of Homeland Security Structure

The Department of Homeland Security is comprised of over 170,000 employees who work within the following directorates, offices, or programs (which include former federal agencies):

Figure 7-4

White House and Senate Reports on Hurricane Katrina which includes discussions on the future of FEMA

- Directorates for Preparedness, Science and Technology, and Management
- Offices of: Intelligence and Analysis, Operations Coordination, Policy, and Domestic Nuclear Detection.
- The Federal Emergency Management Agency
- The Transportation Security Administration
- Customs and Board Protection
- Immigration and Customs Enforcement (ICE)
- Federal Law Enforcement Training Center
- Citizenship and Immigration Services
- The U.S. Coast Guard
- The U.S. Secret Service

In addition, DHS is provided public and private sector input through two advisory councils: (1) The Homeland Security Advisory Council, which provides advice and recommendations to DHS secretary on matters related to homeland security. It is comprised of state and local government officials, first-responder community representatives, the private sector, and academia. (2) The National Infrastructure Advisory Council, which provides both the President and DHS secretary with advice on security of information systems and private institutions that are a part of the nation's "critical infrastructure." In addition, the secretary of DHS receives input from the Interagency Coordinating Council on Emergency Preparedness and Individuals with Disabilities to assure that the federal government "appropriately supports safety and security for individuals with disabilities in disaster situations."

The primary documents governing the work of DHS and establishing its basic policies are its 2002 enabling legislation and several Homeland Security Presidential Directives (HSPDs), the latter of which are described later.

POLICIES THAT IMPACT THE CONSTRUCTION INDUSTRY AND BUILT ENVIRONMENT

In the wake of 9/11, President George W. Bush issued a series of Homeland Security Presidential Directives. The first few helped immediately establish the Homeland Security Council (the Office of Homeland Security, the forerunner of DHS), whose mission was to secure our borders and to combat weapons of mass destruction. Subsequent directives provided initial direction to the homeland security structure he established within the White House, with former Pennsylvania Governor Tom Ridge as its head.

Two later directives issued in December 2003, HSPD-7, "Critical Infrastructure Identification, Prioritization and Protection" and HSPD-8, "National Preparedness," provided the framework for the following policy and program documents, respectively.

National Preparedness Goal: Under HSPD-8, the secretary of the new DHS was tasked to coordinate with other federal agency heads and develop a national domestic all-hazards preparedness goal. State, local, and tribal governments were invited by the White House to work with the secretary in the development of that goal and submit the draft goal to the President for his approval through the Homeland Security Council. The National Preparedness Goal is supported by six national basic components:

- NIMS, The National Incident Management System
- NRP, The National Response Plan
- NIPP, The National Infrastructure Protection Program
- CBRNE, Chemical, biological, radiological and explosive detection capabilities program
- Interoperable Communications capabilities
- Medical surge capabilities

Figure 7-5

Department of Homeland Security documents including the Draft National Preparedness Goal

Three of the preceding components—NIMS, NRP and NIPP—have direct relevance to the all of the members of the construction team: building owners, architects, engineers, contractors, materials and product manufacturers, suppliers, model codes and standards organizations, building officials, and building managers.

National Incident Management System: According to DHS, NIMS "provides a consistent national template to enable federal, state, local, and tribal governments and the private sector and nongovernmental organizations to work together effectively and efficiently to prepare for, prevent, respond to, and recover from domestic incidents, regardless of cause, size, or complexity, including acts of catastrophic terrorism."

Designed as a replacement to the previous Federal Incident Command System, NIMS provides a general overview of, "who does what at what level of government" in response to a disaster of national significance. Those roles, relationships, and responsibilities to prepare for, mitigate, respond to, and recover from different types of natural and man-made disasters are spelled out in greater detail in two supporting documents—the Universal Task List (UTL), and the Target Capabilities List (TCL). Developed with input from state and local governments and tribal councils, the UTL includes over 1800 tasks that need to be performed by both the public and private sectors. This includes specific tasks performed by local building officials, police, fire, and emergency medical service personnel and tasks and services provided by the private sector. In the wake of a disaster, the latter includes everything from finding and using heavy earth-moving equipment to setting up mobile communications systems. In 2005, DHS mandated that all state and local governments, in order to continue to be eligible to receive DHS funds after the end of 2006, had to have certain key staff go through NIMS training and become "NIMS certified."

There are two areas in which NIMS is relevant to the construction team. The first is that NIMS and its UTL have identified some specific roles and responsibilities for some of the construction team members, much of it with very little input being provided to DHS from those members, be they owners, architects, engineers, or contractors. NIMS, for instance, notes situations where local officials may be issuing requests to architects, engineers, or contractors for use of professional services or equipment in disaster response and recovery operations.

Second, while nothing within NIMS specifically modifies building design and construction codes and standards, it does require that jurisdictions adopt and have in place modern building codes and standards and impose potential restrictions on communities being able to apply for and receive future DHS funds for disaster mitigation and recovery should those communities not "become NIMS certified." Having in place a modern building code with disaster mitigation provisions appropriate to that region of the country is a condition of NIMS certification for a community.

NATIONAL INFRASTRUCTURE PROTECTION PLAN AND 17 DIFFERENT CRITICAL INFRASTRUCTURES

The National Infrastructure Protection Plan (NIPP) was mandated by HSPD-7 "Critical Infrastructure Identification, Prioritization, and Protection," under which federal departments and agencies have identified and prioritized critical infrastructure and key resources in the United States to protect them from terrorist attacks. Since 85% of the nation's critical infrastructure (which includes iconic buildings) is owned by the private sector, this includes properties owned and serviced by the members of the construction team.

Adding an additional level of complexity to the NIPP and to the role of the construction team is the way the federal government looks at buildings. Buildings are not treated in anything resembling a cohesive or holistic manner, but rather are looked at within their context as to which one of the following 17 different critical infrastructures sectors they serve:

- Agriculture and food
- Water
- Public health and health care
- Emergency services
- Defense industrial base
- Information technology
- Telecommunications
- Energy
- Transportation
- Banking and finance
- Chemical
- Postal and shipping
- National monuments and icons
- Dams
- Government facilities
- Commercial facilities
- Nuclear reactors, materials, and waste

Figure 7-6

Nonnuclear Power Plants fit within the DHS Energy Critical Infrastructure Category

Buildings are involved in all 17 of critical infrastructure areas. This includes dams that have buildings on site that support the operation and maintenance of the dam. With 85% of all these infrastructure facilities owned by the private and not the public sector, there is a huge role for the construction team to play in infrastructure protection, whether it is adding the physical security of "gates, guards, and guns," or looking at actions that may need to be taken to "harden" that structure.

DHS, under its Plan for National Critical Infrastructure Protection Research and Development (NCIP R & D), has undertaken projects that support the basic homeland security goals of preventing terrorist attacks, reducing America's vulnerability to terrorism, and minimizing the damage and speed of recovery from attacks that may occur.

The critical infrastructure research and development plan also is working in coordination with other national research and development plans that are designed to:

- Focus on countering weapons of mass destruction (including the development and use of highly sensitive detectors)
- Provide protective clothing and specialized equipment to first responders
- Develop, with the standards community, requirements and certification processes needed to implement research advances (as in new products for use in buildings)

These projects supplement the work of the DoD, General Services Administration, (GSA) and FEMA in the area of supporting federal research that will make additional guidelines and other information available to the construction community on blast resistance and protecting HVAC systems from biochemical attacks. DHS under this program also is looking into protection from cyber attacks and to the interrelationship and interdependencies between the 17 critical infrastructures and between cyber and physical attacks.

DHS in executing their research and development plan is aware of how important "efforts to reduce vulnerability can be more effective if they are linked to and inserted into the normal design process, so that all these goals (of critical infrastructure protection) can support each other." This may result in the issuance in coming years of more design guidelines that owners and architects can draw upon to enhance security.

Shift in Focus within DHS and Critical Infrastructure Community

With over 2800 power plants, over 750 oil and natural gas processing plants, 66,000 chemical industry and hazardous materials production facilities, 20,000 telecommunications facilities, 5000 public airports, 127,000 health care facilities, 227,000 industrial plants, 327,000 educational facilities and 739,000 office buildings identified as a part of our critical infrastructure in this nation (see Tables 6-1 and 6-2 in Chapter 6), how do you provide adequate protection to all of them from natural and man-made disasters under any critical infrastructure program?

In the summer of 2005 and through into the winter of 2005 to 2006, a gradual shift has been occurring within the DHS leadership, as well as within the critical infrastructure community, which when complete will have an impact on the construction team. Initial policy adopted by the White House and put in place within the DHS when it was "stood up," was that everything is important, and since terrorists can strike anywhere you must design programs to protect everything.

As budgets were appropriated and spent trying to carry out the national directives to implement that policy, it became abundantly clear—especially once the war in Afghanistan and Iraq began to place its demands on Congressional funding—that it was going to be virtually impossible to protect everything. In 2004, Michael Chertoff as the incoming DHS secretary began to address this problem by talking about risk assessments and risk-based planning.

Enter the British. In response to domestic and foreign terrorist attacks on London, Great Britain in the 1990s established networks of government, public utilities and private sector into what they called the London Resilience Group. Their objective was not to protect everything 100% of the time, but to provide a level of security and durability that meant that when a system and its services were attacked—be it the subways, buses, bridges, office buildings, government ministries—those services could either be provided by other means or be readily returned to service with minimal disruption and certainly with minimal losses of lives. That concept the British call resilience (and is one they originated and demonstrated brilliantly during the Blitz in World War II).

As was noted earlier, terrorists want our nation to spend incredible sums of public and private resources for building, turning our buildings into the modern equivalent of the medieval fortress. Doing so, our nation (and others that are the targets of terrorism) will reduce our productivity and squander funds that need to go into public health, education, research and development of new products and services, and other key contributions to national health, economic productivity, and ability of the nation to successfully compete in the global economy. To protect everything 100% of the time against every eventuality is too brittle a national policy to work.

Instead, as Ruth David, head of Adaptive Network Solutions Research, Inc. (ANSR), told members of The Infrastructure Security Partnership in March 2006 in her remarks on disaster resilience, "We need to be able to take a licking and keep on ticking." This same philosophy also is beginning to be applied to large-scale natural disasters.

Hurricanes Katrina and Rita demonstrated how large-scale disasters can bring about massive losses of life and property and paralyze the economic viability of regions of our nation. These disasters also emphasize the importance of building disaster resilience into a community.

BLUE CASCADES III AND THE NEED FOR DISASTER RESILIENCY

Lessons from these two hurricanes were applied to a major disaster exercise, Blue Cascades III, held in the Pacific Northwest. It included two Canadian provinces (British Columbia and Alberta), one Territory (Yukon), and five U.S. states (Alaska, Washington, Idaho, Montana and Oregon), which have been working cooperatively since the early 1990s through a government-sanctioned entity called the Pacific NorthWest Economic Region (PNWER).

In the wake of the events of 9/11, PNWER identified, designed, and conducted a series of exercises to explore regional preparedness and response to common disasters. In June 2002, Blue Cascades I, held in Portland, Oregon, focused on a terrorist attack on the power system infrastructure; in September 2004, Blue Cascades II, held in Seattle, explored preparedness and response to an attack on the region's cyber infrastructure.

With funding from the DHS and several of its members, PNWER on March 1 and 2, 2006, brought together over 300 representatives from public utilities, major employers, health care, emergency managers, other government officials, and personnel from five states and three provinces and the national governments of Canada and the United States in Bellevue, Washington, to discuss the impact a level 9 earthquake along the Pacific North West Subduction Zone had on the region. It also considered an action agenda for strengthening the region's response to, recovery and reconstruction from such a large scale disaster.

The March 1 and 2 program focused on long-term disruptions of critical infrastructure within the region, as well as large losses of life and property from collapsing bridges, highways, and buildings, and fires from ruptured gas lines caused by both the quake and its subsequent aftershocks and tsunamis.

Among the major objectives of the Blue Cascades III exercise were the following:

- Illuminate reconstruction and business continuity challenges
- Increase understanding of interdependency issues
- Validate mutual value of public–private sector cross-function and multidiscipline coordination to deal with the large-scale and prolonged duration event
- Highlight the extent of existing cooperation, increase the level of collaboration, and explore the development of plans for setting restoration priorities
- Highlight the existing extent of cooperation and understanding of roles, responsibilities, and authorities of local, county, state, and federal jurisdictions and private sector organizations during such an event
- Highlight existing laws (regulations) and gaps that may impede restoration or recovery efforts
- Further explore cross-border physical and cyber U.S. and Canadian interdependencies
- Examine and begin to better understand how to deal with the welfare of citizens in such a large-scale event
- Assemble input on these items to begin to develop an action agenda to strengthen regional disaster resilience

Figure 7-7

Blue Cascades III
Exercise, Bellevue,
Washington,
March 1 and 2,
2006

The two day exercise exposed both the importance of disaster resilience and the critical role that the construction community and owners of our buildings play in disaster preparedness, mitigation, response, and recovery. The exercise documented that while many segments of the public and private sector indeed had developed plans for responding to and recovering from the level 9 earthquake, because of the interdependencies and complexity of that event, those plans required greater coordination with each other and greater detail to make them successful should they need to be implemented. This was found to be especially true of recovery plans.

Blue Cascades III also provided a template for successful regional disaster preparedness initiatives in other parts of the nation. The exercise not only firmly documented the critical role that the construction and building regulatory community plays in disaster preparedness, response, and recovery, but it also generated a list of actions that should be taken to strengthen the ability of the community to successfully fulfill their role including the following:

• The need for owners of existing buildings to conduct risk assessments to determine the vulnerabilities of their structures to a large-scale disaster and implement mitigation programs to reduce those vulnerabilities and business continuity plans to assure that the functions and services provided from those buildings can continue there, be put back online as rapidly as possible or moved to another location.

• Look at the interrelationship between the facility and the critical infrastructures that serve it (issues such as the multiple feed to a building of power discussed in Chapters 5 and 6).

• The construction team members need to assess and, if possible, make contingency plans to provide continuity of operations by perhaps relocating the business activities to another section of the city or region that was not damaged by the man-made or natural event in order to provide services critical to response and recovery: engineering and design services, construction equipment and manpower, building materials and products, damage assessment and inspection services, and building maintenance expertise.

- Consider where they are going to draw professional design, engineering, contractors, and construction materials from outside the region to aid in disaster rescue and recovery and establish a system to preapprove or precertify those professionals (and their equipment) to move into the region after the disaster.

- Work in advance of a future disaster to identify and eliminate areas of regulatory overlap and duplication in the construction process that may slow down reconstruction so that buildings can come back online faster.

- Take a serious look at the adopted building codes and standards in their region and the staffing and professional capabilities of the building departments to enforce those codes and also fulfill their role in disaster mitigation, training, and response and recovery.

RESOURCES AND BEST PRACTICES: TISP AND THE GUIDE TO REGIONAL DISASTER RESILIENCE

In Chapter 2, "Challenges Facing the Construction Team: Revising Codes and Standards, Redefining Roles and Responsibilities," the work of The Infrastructure Security Partnership (TISP) was introduced. Established in response to the events of 9/11, the 100 organizations that are partners in that organization and the 1.5 million individuals and firms they represent have worked to share expertise and best practices between all of the public and private sector segments of our infrastructure to enhance our nation's resilience against the adverse impacts of natural and man-made disasters.

TISP's "Guide for an Action Plan to Develop Regional Disaster Resilience" provides building owners, architects, engineers, contractors, suppliers, codes and standards community, building officials, and building managers with a template to use in their community to improve disaster preparedness, response, and recovery. It also provides the construction team with a mechanism to better understand the concept of resilience and the complexity of the interrelationship between their roles and responsibilities and those of all the other organizations, companies, and governmental agencies that serve their community.

The guide is as comprehensive as possible in offering a range of activities which organizations, government agencies, and companies can collectively and individually take, based upon perceived needs, to achieve regional disaster resilience. "The focus is on multihazards, with the goal of sensibly and cost-effectively securing independent cyber and physical infrastructures. Toward this end, the Guide provides recommendations for activities and projects to be undertaken by stakeholders to address resilience needs, as well as examples of best practices and solutions employed by organizations and jurisdictions across the nation." The guide addresses the following needs:

- Awareness and understanding of interdependencies
- Appreciation of cyber threats, incidents, and restoration needs
- Risk assessment and mitigation

- Cooperation and coordination
- Information sharing and alert and warning
- Reliable/interoperable/compatible communications and information systems
- Roles and responsibilities/incident management
- Recovery and reconstitution
- Business continuity and continuity of operations
- Logistics and supply chain management
- Public information/risk communications
- Exercises, training, and education

The guide incorporates a number of lessons learned from 9/11 (from both the World Trade Center and the Pentagon), Hurricanes Katrina and Rita, and the Blue Cascades III exercise mentioned earlier in this chapter. The guide can be downloaded directly from the TISP Web site: www.tisp.org.

Homeland Security and Our Nation's Resilience Written Large: What Is It That Keeps Us Safe and Secure?

As defined in the TISP guide, "disaster resilience refers to the capability to prevent or protect against significant, all-hazards threats and incidents, including terrorist attacks, and to expeditiously recover and reconstitute critical services with minimum damage to public safety and health, the economy, and national security."

Chapter 5 and 6 noted that the average life span of new construction is between 50 and 100 years during which time, a building owner can expect their building several times to be placed under some form of stress (a natural disaster, fire, and so on) that will test the building to the maximum of some level of its design capacity. This includes those stressors that can come from radical increases in energy prices testing the limits of the building's capacity to conserve energy, or increases in their number of occupants with disabilities stressing under a fire or other emergency situation, or the emergency evacuation and/or sheltering-in-place capacities of these structures.

Writ large, homeland security and the concept of disaster resilience refers not just to physical protection of our people and buildings from terrorists and natural disasters, but to economic protection from the threats of other destabilizing forces that can stress our nation, damage public safety, and our economic viability. As noted at the opening of this chapter these forces include the ever-rising energy prices due to increased international demand for oil; global warming, including its suspected impact on causing more intense natural disasters (tornadoes, floods, hurricanes and draughts); demographic shifts in our nation's population, which by the year 2020 will have 25% of our people over 65 years of age; and the impact of new technologies and products.

Each of these areas—energy, environment, demographics, and the advent of new products and technologies—also place new demands on our nation's construction industry, on the roles, relationships, and responsibilities of each of the members of the construction team and on the buildings which they build or renovate.

A review of "Architectural Security Codes and Guidelines: Best Practices for Today's Construction Challenges" would not be complete without looking past what we have traditionally viewed as homeland security and survey the impact of these additional forces on building design, construction, maintenance, operation and renovation, and the codes, standards, and guidelines to which the construction team builds.

ISSUES IMPACTING THE CONSTRUCTION TEAM AND BUILT ENVIRONMENT

Energy and Environmental Quality as Part of Homeland Security

The secretary (of the Department of Energy, DOE) shall support the ongoing activities of the National Center for Energy Management and Building Technologies, NCEMBT, to carry out research, education, and training activities to facilitate the improvement of energy efficiency, indoor environmental quality, and security (emphasis added) of industrial, commercial, residential, and public buildings.

—Energy Policy Act of 2005, Section 1104

Energy Conservation

Buildings consume over 40% of the energy used in the United States today. It goes to heat and cool our buildings, run our domestic appliances, operate lighting and elevators, and power computer networks and other building systems.

The energy crisis caused by Organization of the Petroleum Exporting Countries (OPEC) and the long lines at gasoline stations in the mid-1970s led to serious changes in energy use in the United States. The forces that caused the price of oil in early 2006 to reach $70 a barrel will reoccur in 2007 and beyond, thus stimulate a second wave of changes in our nation's energy consumption that will impact building design, construction, and retrofit.

Figure 7-8
U.S. Congress

The first wave of major changes in American energy consumption came with OPEC boycott's stimulation of the development by the American Society of Heating, Refrigerating and Air-Conditioning Engineers (ASHRAE) in the late 1970s of the nation's first energy conservation standards for buildings. Under the DOE funding, those standards were turned into the nation's first model energy codes in the early 1980s by a consortium comprised of the National Conference of States on Building Codes and Standards and the nation's three model building code organizations (Building Officials and Code Administrators, International Conference of Building Officials, and the Southern Building Code Congress International, and their coordinating body, the Council of American Building Officials, CABO).

Subsequent federal and state legislation brought about the adoption and enforcement of energy conservation codes for buildings by state and local governments across the nation by the early 1990s. Those efforts also led to the development and launching of a number of energy conservation support initiatives for the entire construction industry including the following:

- Industry's appliance energy efficiency standards and DOE's efficiency requirements.
- DOE's Energy Efficiency and Renewable Energy Programs, Building Technologies Program that works with the private sector, state and local governments, and colleges and universities to research, develop, and implement designs, products, and services that improve building energy efficiency. Including the development of software tools that can be used by designers to improve energy efficiency (REScheck, COMcheck, and MECcheck)
- The joint Housing and Urban Development/DOE Partnership to Advance Technology in Housing (PATH) project to improve the quality, durability, energy efficiency, and environmental performance and affordability of housing.
- The National Association of State Energy Efficiency Officers to support state (and local) building energy efficiency programs including the effective enforcement of energy efficiency codes.
- The Environmental Protection Agency's (EPA) and DOE's, Energy Star Program to encourage builders and consumers to purchase and use more energy efficient and environmentally friendly products (see section on Green for additional details on Energy Star).

The preceding programs and others that target either energy conservation and/or the development and use of alternative nonfossil fuels (hydro, photovoltaic, nuclear, geothermal, hydrogen and wind) or the development of cleaner and more efficient burning of coal and use of domestic sources of natural gas, all have received a significant boost in their importance to consumers and the construction industry in this first decade of the twenty-first century. For the reasons noted later, funding for these programs, and perhaps our energy conservation requirements for buildings, in all likelihood will be raised in the years that lie immediately ahead as the nation enters a second wave of change. In particular, two major areas that will receive added attention are energy displacement and energy efficiency.

Energy displacement is the use of energy sources such as the sun to displace energy used in buildings (and in building materials) produced from fossil fuel resources. Displacement sources include day lighting, solar ventilation preheat, solar hot water

Figure 7-9

New Delhi, India in 1972 pictured here, largely moved on human power, today New Delhi moves by car, bus, and subway

heaters, photovoltaics, natural/mixed-mode ventilation, thermal mass/ambient cooling, and evaporative cooling.

Energy efficiency is making better use of current and future energy resources by such programs as improved efficiency of building design, components such as insulation, reduced air infiltration, improved glazing, and better maintenance; improved HVAC systems, and improved energy efficiency in equipment such as lighting, office equipment, energy-saving controls, and low-energy personal computers.

The continued growth in American dependence (today at 60% up from 35% in 1974) upon foreign and increasingly less politically stable sources of oil and gas (Middle East, West Africa, and Venezuela) and the rapid expansion of China and India's consumption of oil and gas from these same sources, led oil to reach $70 a barrel in early 2006. While those prices fell in the late summer of 2006, projections for oil prices through the end of this decade and out into the middle of this century are just as bad if not worse. The growing demand for oil and natural gas from the 2.3 billion consumers in China and India as their economies continue to grow at rates of 7 to 8% per year and the potential continued (or worse) political instability of or hostility toward the United States from governments who sell the U.S. oil pose a serious threat to the productivity and economic competitiveness of our nation and much of the developed world.

As projected at a minimum, these trends will mean that the costs of heating and cooling the buildings designed and built or retrofitted today will only increase in the years to come. At their worst, these trends will impact both the affordability and profitability of our buildings and the costs of the products and services we produce, making us less competitive in the global marketplace and making the nation not only less wealthy but less disaster-resilient and more vulnerable to significant all-hazard threats be they another OPEC oil embargo or hurricanes striking our oil and gas production facilities in the Gulf Coast. Unless new, less-expensive energy sources are developed and come online, or significant enhancements are made in the energy efficiency in our transportation, industrial processes, and buildings, the American economy and its ability to compete in the global marketplace, expanding and even retraining jobs here for Americans, are going to become increasingly more vulnerable.

In the opening quote to this section taken from the 2005 Energy Policy Act, the U.S. Congress and the White House have already made this important link between our nation's energy policy, programs, resources, and use and homeland security.

Established in 2002 with federal funds, the referenced National Center for Energy Management and Building Technologies (NCEMBT) is charged with "providing education and training to those who are responsible and accountable for building assurance," building operators and managers. The mission of NCEMBT is "to provide 'certified technicians' and 'authorized professionals,' who can assure that public and private buildings are adequately prepared to protect occupants from external and internal releases of chemical and biological agents caused by natural, accidental, and intentional events, while achieving improved energy efficiency, indoor environmental quality, and productivity during normal operations."

Going back to the definition of disaster resilience, given the preceding realities, in the coming years building owners and the members of the construction team indeed will have an increasingly more important role to play in assuring that the buildings they build are energy efficient in their design and operations. A building owner today designing or renovating an existing structure can increase the energy efficiency of the structure by exceeding the minimums in the adopted energy code in that jurisdiction and considering building to meet the Energy Star and Green Building (LEED) provisions noted in the next section. Indeed as energy prices resume and then continue their projected rise, there will be more pressure brought by the public on elected officials to even mandate that new homes be built to Energy Star and Green Building requirements. In 2005, the city of Frisco just outside of Dallas, Texas became the first in the nation to adopt ordinances mandating that all new homes meet Energy Star requirements.

Green as a Part of Homeland Security

"7 World Trade Center and Hearst Building: New York's Test Cases for Environmentally Aware Office Towers."

A decade ago, office towers guzzled energy as fast as they could and "sick building syndrome" was dismissed as a hypochondriac's all-purpose excuse. Since then, however, the rise of "green" architecture has encouraged architects, developers, and construction managers to consider the effect their buildings have on the health of their occupants and the environment.

New York now has two important test cases, as workers prepare to occupy the city's first officially green office towers, Seven World Trade Center, a 52-story, $7 million replacement for the building that fell at that address on 9/11, was certified by the U.S. Green Buildings Council last month. The 46-story Hearst Tower, on 57th Street near Eighth Avenue, is expected to follow suit after completion next month.

—Robin Pogrebin, Architecture Columnist for the *New York Times*
in the April 16, 2006, edition of the *New York Times*.

Green building and sustainability trends in the construction industry are a fact of life. The building industry needs to embrace green building technology in order to stay competitive."

—Norbert Young, FAIA, President McGraw-Hill Construction,
from an interview reported in the February 21, 2006 issue
of *LANDonline, Landscape Architecture News Digest.*

Looking back on this century, the central design concept in the practice of architecture will be green.

—Christopher Hawthorne, *Los Angeles Times* Staff Writer for Architecture, at the May 17, 2006, opening of "The Green House: New Directions in Sustainable Architecture and Design" held at the National Building Museum, Washington, D.C.

Dating back to the first Earth Day on March 21, 1970, and stretching through to the more recent findings on greenhouse gases and global warming, the issues of energy conservation and environmental quality have been inextricably linked and as such have relevance to both disaster resilience and the future of building design, construction, and operation.

First, they have been linked by the interrelationship between tightening buildings up to support energy conservation needs and indoor air quality, the "sick building syndrome" (which includes the issue of mold). The second, and older, link has been the issue of reducing stresses on our environment, the production of greenhouse gases, carbon footprints, and alternate transportation and fuel efficient vehicles.

Building Green from Market Niche to Mainstream

Where it was initially seen as a market niche issue, a design concept to meet the specific needs of only a handful of clients, environmentally friendly green building design and construction, as witnessed by the opening quotes in this section, have entered the mainstream of building design, construction, and operation. The movement into the mainstream has come in two waves, starting with the EPA's Energy Star Program launched in 1992 and proceeding through the establishment of the U.S. Green Buildings Council in 1993 and their creation of the LEED program, Leadership in Energy and Environmental Design and in the past few years entering the second wave of new and enhanced green programs.

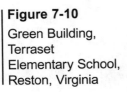

Figure 7-10

Green Building, Terraset Elementary School, Reston, Virginia

Energy Star

In 1992, the U.S. EPA introduced Energy Star as a voluntary labeling program. The program was designed to encourage consumers and builders to use energy-efficient products that reduced greenhouse gas emissions and initially only labeled computers and monitors. Within four years, the program had been expanded to label residential heating and cooling equipment and office equipment products and had been joined by the DOE in applying labels to major appliances and lighting. Presaging the LEED program, EPA/DOE extended the Energy Star Label to also cover new homes and commercial and industrial buildings.

The program now provides labels and support information for over 40 different product categories (covering thousands of models) and in 2005 alone was credited with saving consumers, organizations, and businesses over $12 billion in energy costs. Over 2000 homebuilders currently partner with EPA in the Energy Star Program. EPA notes that using Energy Star products save the average consumer over $400 each year over the use of nonprogram complying products. The Energy Star program can be accessed at www.energystar.gov.

U.S. Green Building Council and LEED Program

The U.S. Green Building Council was established in 1993 from a coalition of leaders from the building industry working to promote buildings that are environmentally responsible and healthy places to work and live. To support that mission, the council developed a series of rating systems for different types of construction with three different levels of excellence: silver, gold, and platinum based upon a score that was given for a building's environmental responsibility for six different features:

- Sustainable sites, water efficiency, energy and atmosphere, materials and resources used in construction, indoor air environmental quality, and innovation and design processes.
- LEEDS rating systems currently cover: New construction and major renovations (LEED-NC), existing buildings (LEED-EB), and commercial interiors (LEED-CI).
- Core and shell (LEED-CS), homes (LEED-H), and neighborhood development (LEED-ND).
- Currently under development are LEED Application Guides for retail, multiple buildings/campuses, schools, healthcare, laboratories, and lodging.

An example of the points that are given under the LEED certification system are the following three of six areas covered under the LEED certification program for new construction:

- Sustainable sites
  —Construction and pollution prevention
  —Site selection
  —Development density and community connectivity
  —Brownfield redevelopment
  —Alternative transportation (four different types)
  —Site development (two types: protect or restore habitat, maximize open space)

Figure 7-11

LEED Program documents

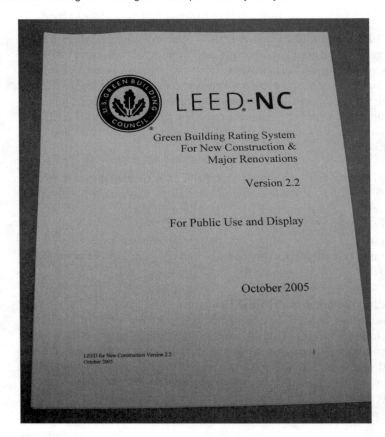

—Storm water design (two types: quantity or quality control)
—Heat island effect (two types: nonroof and roof)
—Light pollution reduction
- Water efficiency
—Water-efficient landscaping (two types: reduce by 50%; no potable or irrigation use)
—Innovative water technologies
—Water use reduction (two types: 20% or 30% reduction)
- Indoor environmental quality
—Minimum IAQ performance
—Environmental tobacco smoke control
—Outdoor air delivery monitoring
—Increased ventilation
—Construction IAQ management plan (two types: during construction, before occupancy)
—Low-emitting materials (four types: adhesives and sealants, paints and coatings, carpet systems, composite wood and agrifiber products)

—Indoor chemical and pollutant source control

—Controllability of systems

—Thermal comfort (two types: design, verification)

—Daylight and views (two types: daylight 75% of spaces, views for 90% of spaces)

These requirements also address the amount of wastage of construction materials on a building site, an area that involves on an average at least 25%, and in some cases as much as 40%, of all of the construction materials being used in a project. Recognizing that no two buildings are the same, the LEED rating system takes a holistic view of each structure and its siting, construction, and operating systems.

Kicking off the second green wave at the start of the new century a number of state and local governments began supporting the green building initiative and LEED program by providing tax incentives for LEED buildings and zoning enhancements. Some have even constructed their government facilities to obtain LEED certifications. The city of Seattle, Washington, in 2000 became the first city to formally adopt a sustainable buildings policy that calls for new and renovated city projects with more than 5000 sq ft of occupied space to have a LEED silver rating. States with such programs include Pennsylvania and Arizona, while Arkansas is considering similar requirements for state-owned construction.

As more state and local governments address the pressing issues of environmental quality, the number and nature of these incentives and perhaps too disincentives for constructing nonenvironmentally responsible buildings will increase. In addition to the preceding program, U.S. Green Building Council, ASHRAE, and the Illuminating Engineering Society of North America announced in March 2006 that they were developing for release in 2007 a new minimum standard for high-performance green buildings. Called Standard 189 P, "Standard for the Design of High Performance Green Buildings Except Low-Rise Residential Buildings," the standard will be American National Standards Institute (ANSI) accredited for potential incorporation into state and/or local building codes. Additional information on LEED, including downloads of the LEED certification requirements can be obtained from the U.S. Green Building Web site www.usgbc.org.

And the cost of building green under the LEED rating system? The April 2006 of www.Buildings.com's publication "Buildings," noted in a feature story "True Costs of Building Green," that the end result of research regarding the costs to build green taken over the life of the building is anywhere from "nothing more to nominal amount to build green over the budget for a traditionally designed building." One of the major barriers to getting more owners to consider building green has been the disconnect that most owners have between initial construction cost and the year-to-year operating costs of the building which generally are not linked.

National Association of Home Builders Green Program

A third initiative in this area was announced at the National Association of Home Builders (NAHB) International Builders Show in January 2006 with a set of "Model Green Home Building Guidelines." Developed by the NAHB Research Center in Maryland in conjunction with 60 stakeholder groups, the guide provides homebuilders with voluntary national guidelines to facilitate their adoption of green building practices and the formation of local green building programs not currently served by such programs. Provisions within the guide include lot preparation and design, resource efficiency, energy efficiency, water efficiency and conservation and occupancy comfort, and indoor air quality.

NAHB, together with McGraw-Hill, in May 2006 released preliminary findings from a national survey that documented an increase in the number of the nation's homebuilders following green building practices. The survey projected that between 2005 and 2010 the market for new green residential structures would grow from $7.4 billion (or 2% of new home starts) to between $19 billion and $38 billion new green homes (5 to 10% of the market). For more information visit the NAHB Web site at www.nahb.org.

Sustainable Building Industry Council's Programs

Originally formed in 1980 as the "Passive Solar Industries Council," the evolution of that industry and the growth of the concept of sustainability broadened that group's horizons, causing them to expand their purpose and membership to embrace a number of environmentally responsible design practices and technologies. Providing guidance on solar and photovoltaic technologies, the council expanded to embrace high-performance windows, lighting systems, mechanical equipment, natural ventilation, day lighting, and well-insulated building envelopes. The council produces the software, "Energy-10," which analyzes and illustrates energy and cost savings that can be achieved by applying the preceding sustainable design strategies. More information can be found on their Web site at www.sbicouncil.org.

SICK AND HEALTHY BUILDINGS

The second major interface area between energy conservation and environmental quality comes with the issue of sick buildings, including the issue of mold in buildings. This is an example of the law of unintended consequences that was discussed earlier in this book.

With an emphasis on tightening up the building envelope born out of the energy conservation movement of the 1970s and 1980s, a number of designers reduced the amount of outdoor air being brought into the building through gaps and leaks and operable windows common in most construction prior to the energy crisis and the development and enforcement of energy conservation codes.

In addition, owners and their building maintenance staff quite frequently found themselves either not following building maintenance cycles for their HVAC equipment or not understanding the proper operation of those systems. The result of both of these factors was the growth in the 1980s and 1990s of the sick building syndrome, where occupants complained of eye, nose, and throat irritations; breathing problems; headaches; fatigue; and rashes and also complained of chemical pollutants and other physical factors, including uncomfortable temperatures, low humidity, too much humidity, (hence the growth of mold) and poor lighting—all factors that contribute to reduced productivity as well as to potential serious hazards to worker health. The LEED program and recent modifications in energy codes and energy-conservation-related products (including installation instructions), all are working to address these issues and increase the number of healthy buildings.

Related to the sick and healthy buildings issue and to homeland security is the need to adequately balance in building design and construction provisions regarding indoor air and protection of the building from accidental and intentional external and internal releases of biochemical agents. This is another area where, as mentioned in Chapters 5 and 6, building owners will want to include a qualified engineer on their construction team to address this issue in building design, selection of HVAC equipment, and their operation and maintenance plans and assure that their staff are properly trained in the emergency features of their HVAC and related systems. This also is an area where the concept of 'building commissioning,' the actual testing, and operation of all building, electrical, mechanical, HVAC, and emergency evacuation systems prior to the acceptance by the owner of the completed building, will play an increasingly more important and common role in the construction cycle.

In the coming years the construction team will become more involved in the programs that have been highlighted here in the areas of energy conservation, and environmental responsibility and sustainability. Where building owners and their construction team today are relatively unfamiliar with these programs in the coming years, the ASHRAE Standards and energy conservation codes adopted and enforced in this nation and the Energy Star and LEED programs are going to become more important and integral tools in the nation's disaster resilience from man-made and natural events.

CHANGING DEMOGRAPHICS AND ACCESSIBILITY (EMERGENCY EGRESS)

By 2020, nearly a quarter of the nation's population will be 65 or older and nearly 40% will be 50 or older. These population projections by the Department of Health and Human Services (HHS) and the U.S. Administration on Aging will put added demand on the construction industry in three areas: scarcity of skilled construction workers as many in the construction trades and industry retire, changes in housing, and the related issues of architectural accessibility for people with disabilities, including such issues of areas of refuge and emergency evacuation.

In the manpower area, federal government projections done within the White House Office of Science and Technology Policy in 2003 noted that approximately 40% of the current senior positions in the construction industry and in the government agencies that regulate construction will be retiring in the next 10 years. The construction professions and trades, ranging from architects and engineers to construction supervisors and journeymen electricians and plumbers, all are focusing resources on addressing this issue, attempting to both attract into their professions younger workers and to identify, train, and promote middle-aged employees to replace their senior level skilled retirees.

These changing demographics also will impact the nature of our residential building stock and architectural accessibility. This will not just mean greater demands for retirement communities, hospitals and health care facilities, but it also is projected that a larger percentage of those over 65 will continue to be a part of the American workforce into perhaps their seventies, which will put added demands on adequate accessibility and emergency egress in office buildings. In 2004, HHS statistics showed that nearly 63% of "noninstitutionalized" persons over 65 had one or more chronic conditions (heart disease, cancer, arthritis), most of which could be a factor in building access or egress (especially in high-rise structures).

As the "baby boomer" generation retires, the front edge of this large generation wave is beginning to ripple through our nation. As some boomers retire they are going through the process of downsizing, selling the larger homes that they raised their families in and looking for smaller homes or perhaps townhouses, which incorporate adaptable design concepts that will enable them to remain in their homes longer by including such features as wider doorways and bathrooms to accommodate a wheelchair, or adjustable kitchen sinks, countertops, and shelves.

In a number of communities in Illinois, including Naperville, Bollingbrook and Urbana, "Visitability" standards have been adopted that mandate that new homes must be designed to facilitate the ability of people with disabilities to visit those homes. The requirements include at least one accessible "zero step" entrance, all doorways on the main floor have a minimum of 32 in. of clear passage space and at least one wheelchair accessible bathroom on that floor. A bill supporting this movement was introduced in the U.S. Congress by Illinois Representative Jan Schakowsky, but has not been moved beyond its assigned committee.

In addition to the added pressure on architectural accessibility, this demographic wave will place greater demands both on the construction of retirement communities and the

Figure 7-12

Construction of retirement community

need to find retrofit solutions that enable more Americans to remain in their existing residences longer and "age in place." The Center for Aging Services and Technologies already is working to support research and development and testing of a number of new technologies that will enable older Americans to add safety monitoring systems, including motion sensors, range hood fire extinguishers, and direct voice communication links with either security services or even their children located elsewhere in the neighborhood or across the nation. The changing demographics from the aging of Americans also is putting renewed research and development dollars both into devices for the mobility impaired that may aid in the emergency evacuation via stairwells of those who are unable to walk down by themselves and into better provisions for areas of refuge and use of elevators for emergency evacuation (see end of Chapter 5).

INFORMATION TECHNOLOGY AND ITS IMPACT ON INDUSTRY

The capability of the computer to create holistic simulations of complex systems changes the nature of design, virtually reintegrating the design process with the craft of building. Sophisticated simulation allows the designer to once again work as a craftsman, building virtual buildings while retaining the capacity to represent ideas for analysis, evaluation, and communication. The simulation enhances human capacity to understand and manipulate complex systems. The computer can manipulate complex details far better than the human mind, freeing the designer to focus on judgment, something that computers do not do well at all.

—Richard Nordhaus, Professor, School of Architecture and Planning,
University of New Mexico in *Professional Practice 101:
A Compendium of Business and Management Strategies
in Architecture*, John Wiley & Sons, 1997.

Three years ago when the first Virtual Design and Construction meeting was held at CIFE (Center for Integrated Facility Engineering at Stanford University), none of our members had done projects using virtual design. Now, eight out of ten members of our Board have.

—John Kunz, Executive Director, Center for Integrated Facility Engineering
at the December 12, 2005, Virtual Builders Roundtable held
at the General Services Administration, Washington, D.C.

The streamlining of building department regulatory processes and the application of information technology to those processes has been able to reduce the regulatory portions of the cost of construction by as much as 60% in a number of jurisdictions from across this nation.

—*The Guide to More Effective and Efficient Building Regulatory Processes
Through Information Technology*, Produced by the National Partnership
to Streamline Government for the U.S. Department of Housing
and Urban Development, September, 2006.

As witnessed by the preceding quotes, the advent of computers and computer technologies are radically transforming the way the owner, architect, engineer, contractors, suppliers, codes and standards community, code enforcement personnel, and building managers all interact. Computer technology, including three- and four-dimensional design, interoperable hardware and software for use in the building design and construction,

Figure 7-13

Stanford University is the home of the Center for Integrated Facility Engineering, CIFE

and regulatory processes have a major role to play in increasing construction productivity and reducing the regulatory cost of construction.

In an article released in December 2004, Preston H. Haskell, the Chairman of Haskell, Inc., documented the lagging of productivity of the construction sector within the American economy, noting that its 33% increase in productivity over a 37-year period (1966 to 2004) was substantially below that of the rest of U.S. industry. Citing the relatively small size of individual construction firms and the disaggregated nature of the industry, Haskell noted five areas in which construction industry productivity could be significantly increased.

Among those five areas, two referred directly to the use of information technology and included automation and the use of visualization and four-dimensional immersion technology and radio frequency identification (RFID) technologies, which are described later in this chapter.

Figure 7-14
Greater use of information technology by design community and construction industry, photo from exhibits hall at International Builders Show, January 2006

Building Information Modeling and Three- and Four-Dimensional Virtual Design

The use of computers with three- and four-dimensional design capabilities is being pioneered by a number of large arts and entertainment firms across the nation and by the GSA. Moving from simple two-dimensional drawings and paper flow of data has reduced design times and construction costs for a large number of firms. At the December 12, 2005, Virtual Builders Roundtable meeting hosted at GSA headquarters in Washington, D.C., one presenter noted that he spent $58,000 developing a three-dimensional construction model for a large medical center project and through it achieved over $500,000 in savings in time and materials in his project.

Other presenters at the same conference, noted that their firms were able to use their three-dimensional model and share it with all of their construction material and building product suppliers, link the suppliers directly to the model, and minimize time delays and waste and have no change orders whatsoever during their project.

Three- and four-dimensional design building information modeling (BIM) that links all of the members of the construction team and extends the use of the same data across the design, engineering, construction material specification, delivery of materials, and construction, commissioning, and operation of buildings is a radical new tool and is proving especially useful in reducing time delays and construction costs in complex structures. Some of the benefits of BIM include the following:

- Visualization and the ability to view different parts of the building and its components from an infinite number of viewpoints all without having to produce drawings.
- Enables the designer, engineer, and each of the building systems (structural, electrical, mechanical, plumbing, and accessibility) to inside the computer (and not on site) identify and avoid areas of conflict, interference, or collision.
- Enables the builder to look at different scheduling and phasing options as well as sequencing, workflow safety, and site logistics.

- Speeds and simplifies estimating and quantity extraction and helps clarify scope and trade coordination.
- Aids in building commissioning and provides "as-builts" that facilitate facility management and maintenance cycles.

Moreover, given the level of complexity discussed in Chapters 5 and 6 in planning, designing, and constructing buildings to mitigate against multihazard threats and the greater degrees of diverse engineering expertise now brought into projects, BIM and three- and four-dimensional modeling enable building owners to design, build, commission, and operate a building within a computer and subject that building to a diverse array of stresses and disaster scenarios.

Besides GSA and the Virtual Design Roundtable, other groups supporting BIM include an impressive array of colleges and universities, the American Institute of Architects, Associated General Contractors, the Sustainable Buildings Industry Council, Construction Users Roundtable, Construction Industry Institute, the National Institute of Building Sciences, National Institute of Standards and Technology (NIST), Fully Integrated Advanced TECHnology (FIATECH) and the National Partnership to Streamline Government.

Interoperability

In a study commissioned by NIST in 2003, LMI Government Consulting and RTI International documented that lack of adequate interoperability, the ability to enter data once into a system, and have it migrate across to other systems was costing the nation's capital facilities industry alone over $15.8 billion per year in avoidance, mitigation, and delay costs, with the vast majority of those costs being born by owners and managers. A key to successful growth of BIM will be the degree to which hardware and software used by each of the members of the construction team, all are interoperable—that they can transfer data across different software functions without having to just use one software supplier's suite of products.

Figure 7-15

CAVE: Computer-Assisted Virtual Environment, at Parsons Brinkerhoff in New York City

The International Alliance for Interoperability (IAI), an international consortium of construction industry and software firms, was formed in the 1990s and since then has been working on technologies that enable data to be exchanged between distinct systems and supports interoperability based upon open global standards. Under the banner of "buildingSMART," IAI North America is using its Industry Foundation Classes (IFC) system to develop common open interoperability standards that all software used in the construction process can interface with. Several national organizations including the International Code Council and GSA have joined in this initiative.

More information on IAI's "buildingSMART" project can be obtained by visiting the IAI International Web site www.iai.international.org or by contacting the National Institute of Building Sciences (NIBS), which provides secretariat services to IAI North America through the Web site www.nibs.org.

Information Technology Applied to Regulatory Processes

While some segments of the nation's construction industry are rapidly embracing BIM and three- and four-dimensional design, nearly 90% of the 40,000 jurisdictions that adopt and/or enforce building codes throughout the nation do not use information technology for anything more than word processing. Led by the National Conference of States on Building Codes and Standards, a national project was begun in 1996 to identify best practices in the building regulatory process that help reduce the regulatory cost of construction and improve the effectiveness and efficiency of code administration and enforcement.

In June 2001 that effort brought together representatives from the nation's construction, building regulatory, and information technology community and formed the Alliance for Building Regulatory Reform in the Digital Age, which identified barriers to greater use of information technology in the building regulatory process and developed a number of products and materials to assist in removing those barriers. In addition to associations representing the construction industry, members of the Alliance included the National

Figure 7-16

Licensing section, city of Los Angeles, Department of Building Safety

Figure 7-17

Mapping the Building Regulatory Process Environment, June 1, 2001, at the opening work session for the creation of the Alliance for Building Regulatory Reform in the Digital Age

Governors Association, U.S. Conference of Mayors, National Association of Counties, National Association of State Chief Information Officers, National Fire Protection Association, NIBS, NIST, GSA, DOE, FEMA, the National Science Foundation, and Department of Agriculture.

These initial efforts helped over 40 jurisdictions take steps first to streamline their building regulatory processes and then determine which types of information technology best fit their program and the needs of their customers. Early work products helped several jurisdictions reduce by 60% the amount of time that buildings were within the building regulatory process and provided model procurement guidelines for state and local governments.

Faced with the devastating impact of Hurricanes Rita and Katrina and looking at the need both to promote greater disaster resilience and to establish a closer link to construction industry BIM and interoperability work, the Alliance in March 2006 took steps

Figure 7-18

Pile of debris in New Orleans during Hurricane Katrina clean up, November 2005

to restructure itself. The group established a working committee to take steps to establish a new body, tentatively called the National Partnership to Streamline Government, to more effectively focus on actions that can be taken to both reduce the regulatory cost of construction and improve the ability of state and local governments to prepare for, respond to, and recover from disasters.

Among the first work products of the new body were the release in the summer of 2006, to the nation's governors, mayors, and county administrators of a CDROM annual report and an 8-page streamlining Guide for Elected officials and the opening of a new streamlining website: www.natlpartnerstreamline.org.

In the fall of 2006, under funding from the U.S. Department of Housing and Urban Development, a detailed step by step "Guide to More Effective and Efficient Building Regulatory Processes Through Information Technology" will be made available for use by state and local governments and the construction community. The HUD Guide can be downloaded from the HUD Users Web site by going to www.huduser.gov. Among the features of the guide is how to involve all of the members of the construction team

Figure 7-19

"Guide to More Effective and Efficient Building Regulatory Processes Through Information Technology," funded by U.S. Department of Housing and Urban Development and produced by the Alliance/National Partnership and Robert Wible and Associates

within a community's efforts to assess whether or not barriers exist to effective and efficient code enforcement and to develop programs and where appropriate apply information technology to improve that vital program.

CRITICAL ROLE OF NEW PRODUCTS AND MATERIALS AND METHODS AND TECHNIQUES

The 100th anniversary issue of *Building* magazine (now online at www.Buildings.com) in January 2006 published their list of the "100 Influences That Have Shaped the Buildings Market." Within that list were the following technologies and products. Technologies:

- Air conditioning, 1921
- The Internet, 1970
- Glazing technologies, 1980s
- CD and three-dimensional modeling, 1990s
- Systems integration, 2000

Products:

- Drywall, 1926
- Fire and smoke detectors, 1970s
- Lighting controls, 1980
- Closed circuit television, 1980s
- Window film, 1990s
- Construction-related software, 1990s
- Personal computers, personal digital assistants, 1990s

Figure 7-20

The importance of the advent of personal computers also is memorialized by this display at the Smithsonian Institution's American History Museum

In addition to these technologies are those covered in Chapters 5 and 6, new filters and sensors for detecting biochemical and radiological hazards and new materials such as Kevlar being used for blast protection. Looking ahead, the following technologies and products are either under development or are projected to be available in the next 10 years and will strongly impact building design, construction, and operations.

New Technologies in Existence or Under Development

Firefighter Lifts and Use of Elevators for Emergency Evacuation of the Disabled

These already have been put in place in high-rise buildings in Europe and Asia and are among the code changes that have been recommended out of the final NIST report on the World Trade Center Collapse (see Chapter 5). Hardened, smoke evacuated towers would be constructed with the dedicated use for fire service and emergency rescue personnel. The elevator committee for the American Society for Testing and Materials is reviewing possible changes to that standard for possible application in the next five years. Those changes to the ASTM standard coupled with studies and protocols to assure adequate and public response to the safe use of elevators during an emergency evacuation situation may change the nature of emergency evacuation in high-rise structures.

Flame-Retardant Polymers

NIST currently is working on finding alternatives to existing brominated fire-retardant materials. If successful, this technology could significantly reduce the flammability of foam furnishings that are common in residential and commercial structures.

Technologies for Building Operations in Biochemical and Radiological Attacks

NIST also is working in conjunction with other federal laboratories and with several universities to better predict where CBR materials will move within a building and develop different mitigation and/or evacuation strategies. This also involves work on new sensors and filters.

Fire-Resistive Steel and Coatings for Steel

This is another set of research being conducted at NIST in conjunction with their findings from their World Trade Center disaster. This research includes new coatings that are more resistant to shock and methods to ascertain how fire-resistive coatings will perform 20 years into the life of the building.

Interoperable Hardware and Software for Building Construction, Operation, and Building Construction Regulation

Well under development by the International Alliance for Interoperability and an information technology industry committee working with the National Partnership to Streamline Government, truly interoperable software will reduce the constant reentry of building-related data and facilitate greater use of information technologies noted earlier in this chapter, which will speed construction and reduce its regulatory costs.

Low-Power Wireless Sensor Networks

Already under development by the DoD and Massachusetts Institute of Technology, these small remote wireless sensor networks are, in the words of University of California at Berkeley computer scientist, "spearheading what the future of computing is going to look like." Uses in construction include monitoring indoor air quality, mechanical systems, outdoor environment, and communicating potentially hazardous conditions to HVAC control systems that either shut down and seal off the building from the outside air or evacuate indoor contaminates to the outside.

Nanoscale Technology

Nanoscale construction building small machines and sensors using chemical building blocks that can form either singly or in combination features in the 1 to 100 nanometer-size range will make possible a whole range of new building sensors such as those discussed at the end of the section "When Buildings Talk." Nanoscale technology also may assist in the development of new building products and materials.

New Products Existing or Under Development

Nano Solar Cells

Work is underway in the U.S. at the University of California at Berkeley and Santa Barbara and overseas at Cambridge in the United Kingdom and Swiss Federal Institute of Technology, to research the development of photovoltaic material that can be spread like plastic wrap or paint and be integrated into building materials to power sensors and to generate power for the building itself.

Electronic Plans Review Software Packages

The International Code Council (ICC) has already begun a multiyear project to establish a software package for building departments and design and engineering firms to use to review building plans for compliance with the ICC family of construction codes. This technology and their related products will speed code compliance and also be useful for field inspectors. It is anticipated that other groups producing codes and standards will follow suit in coming years.

Another effort currently underway is a project between the National Partnership to Streamline Government and the U.S. Department of Energy and Pacific Northwest National Laboratories to provide interoperability to the DOE/Pacific Northwest National Laboratory REScheck and COMCheck energy conservation software tools, already in use helping architects design energy-complying residential and commercial buildings.

New Green Recyclable Construction Materials

The Michael Kauffman prefabricated Glidehouse, which was displayed at the National Building Museum in Washington, D.C., in early May 2006, contains a number of low-cost recyclable construction materials in its countertops, wall insulation, and siding. A number of colleges and universities are conducting research along with industry partners in this area.

Fuel Cells

Already used more widely as a source of long-lasting backup power after a natural disaster, fuel cell technology powers energy in homes and businesses by converting natural gas into hydrogen and water and generating power. The technology, developed in the late 1980s and early 1990s, has been applied successfully to emergency backup generators provided by the state of Florida to some local jurisdictions to serve as emergency backup power generation units that will run for several weeks without refueling.

Figure 7-21
New residential construction in Midwest retirement community. Some builders are considering offering fuel cells as backup power supplies for multi-family structures in disaster prone areas

Sensors in Buildings: When Buildings Talk Back

In the mid-1990s the NAHB developed and marketed "Smart House" technologies, which basically enabled the homeowner to control lighting, heating, and air conditioning and home appliances through a centralized data processing center usually located in the kitchen. Since that event a number of firms have marketed similar systems and/or have developed small sensors that monitor and track the whereabouts within a building of people or status of various appliances.

The advent of RFID technology has made it possible for architects and contractors to keep track of construction materials on site by providing those materials with inexpensive RFID chips. It also has made several new applications possible that could significantly change building code inspections and disaster response and rescue, including emergency egress from buildings during an "event."

Expensive RFID chips can be placed on certain building components to make it easier for building inspectors to "query the building to make certain those components indeed are in place. Hurricane clips to make sure that roofs are properly attached and wall anchoring for hot water heater tanks in seismic areas are two simple applications that have been discussed.

RFIDs, coupled with other inexpensive sensors such as those that measure flow through a HVAC system, CO_2, and temperatures, could be used to assure indoor air quality within a building. Centrally connected such sensors could tell building managers, occupants, and first responders if there is a fire in a certain portion of the building or smoke in a stairwell and monitor the progress of a fire within the building if it has not otherwise been contained or extinguished.

Structural collapse indicators also have great future potential for buildings in high-risk seismic zones or buildings that may have high potential of risk from blast (or collateral damage from a neighboring structure that has been subjected to a blast event). NIST is currently doing research with structural sensors used on dams to see if they can be applied to buildings. This kind of sensor would need to be more sophisticated that those detecting heat or smoke and would need to relay real data. Ideally, first responders could connect to the sensors when they first arrived at the building—before they go in so they know what they are facing and, for example in a seismic event, whether or not there is a good chance the building will not withstand the next aftershock.

The benefits here to building occupants, first responders, and building officials, who later must do damage assessments on buildings, are tremendous. In the first instance there perhaps will be benefit in helping direct people out of a damaged structure through exits that suffered less serious damage. In the second instance first responders not only know what they are facing but perhaps the safest ways into and out of the structure. In the third, such sensors could significantly improve the quality and speed up the conducting of damage assessments by building officials. They also would aid the owner and building maintenance personnel in knowing just what the real condition of that structure is and whether it is a good candidate for repair or should be demolished. Similar structural reporting benefits would occur in areas with structural damage caused by winds, hurricanes, and tornadoes.

The advent of low-cost, accurate sensors such as the previously mentioned could ultimately find their way into the provisions of building codes for structures in areas that are subject to such potential disaster events.

IMPACT ON THE CONSTRUCTION TEAM

The impact of all of the forces described in this chapter on the members of the construction team are immense. Reflecting that fact, associations representing each segment of the construction team have held forums, conducted studies, and issued articles dealing in one form or another with the preceding forces and their significance to their industry members.

Owners, for example, have participated in such sessions at meetings of their associations, which include Building Owners and Managers Association, National Association of Realtors, Construction Users Roundtable, The Tall Buildings Council, Construction Industry Institute, FIATECH, National Association of State Facilities Administrators, and GSA—the largest single building owner in the nation.

The American Society of Landscape Architects, AIA, American Society of Civil Engineers, National Society of Fire Protection Engineers, Associated General Contractors, NAHB, and other associations likewise have had sessions on these subjects for their members. Even the codes and standards generating bodies and associations representing state and local building officials including ANSI, ICC, National Fire Protection Association, International Association of Plumbing and Mechanical Officials, the Association of Major City and County Building Officials (AMCBO), and National Conference of States on Building Codes and Standards have held meetings and conducted conference calls looking at the impact of these issues on their member's role as part of the construction team.

In nearly every one of these sessions, members of the construction team in discussing these forces have considered the issue of how to reasonably address these forces without raising unnecessarily the cost of new construction or renovation or of building operations and maintenance. In such discussions, two issues frequently emerge—the need to look at buildings in a holistic manner (not just as subcomponents or systems) and the need to consider the benefits of making those changes on the basis of a life-cycle cost point of view.

If the building is going to last 50 to 100 years, what are reasonable features to include in this building that will address the stresses under which it is likely to be placed during that lifetime?

In raising that question, the building team as it is currently comprised cannot necessarily answer it among themselves. Three other important players must be added to the table.

THE NEED TO WRITE THE CONSTRUCTION TEAM LARGER: INSURANCE INDUSTRY, BANKING COMMUNITY, AND ELECTED OFFICIALS

The speed with which the preceding forces are impacting the construction industry and the magnitude of the impact of a large-scale natural or future man-made disaster upon a region of our nation are making it imperative for more parties to come to the table and shoulder their share of the burden for the safety in our built environment.

These parties include the nation's insurance and banking industries and our elected officials. Ultimately, elected officials bear special responsibility for the future safety of their community for they either vote for and/or oversee the adoption, administration, and enforcement of the building codes and standards that provide for the basic levels of the public's safety, health, and security.

The Insurance Industry

As noted in Chapter 1, the insurance industry actually was among the first at the table—way back in the 1870s through the early 1900s this industry was the catalyst for the development and adoption of the nation's first comprehensive building and fire codes. More recently, however, the insurance industry as a whole has generally been absent from the building design, construction, inspection, operation, and maintenance discussions as to what features should be placed into structures to better protect them from man-made and natural hazards and the energy conservation and environmental and demographic forces described earlier in this chapter. Two industry-funded groups, the Insurance Services Organization, with it rating system for building departments and their enforcement programs, and the Institute for Business and Home Safety, with its aggressive program of supporting disaster mitigation and strong building codes, have been notable exceptions.

The magnitude of such events as Hurricanes Katrina and Rita and the threat of a major seismic event within several regions of the United States have some insurance firms deciding to cease writing policies for homeowner protection and increasing premiums for commercial structures. Likewise the industry has significantly raised premiums on the design and engineering and contractor community and created the environment noted in Chapter 1, where increasingly members of the construction team are becoming more concerned with limiting their liability than they are with functioning as an effective and cohesive team on a building project.

Insurance companies, both the individual firms and collectively as an industry, need to become more actively involved in discussions that are outlined in the next chapter as to future directions of our nation's construction industry and public safety in buildings.

The Banking Community

Where the insurance industry has a long history of involvement in building safety, with relatively few exceptions the banking community has been largely absent throughout the history of construction in the United States. Such events as Hurricane Katrina and even the World Trade Center disaster, where financial institutions have been not just knocked off line for a while but actually put out of business, should be a wake up call to this industry. The nation's banks need to be at the table understanding and playing a supportive role in the discussions as to what is an adequate level of safety in buildings, what measures should be taken to help assure business continuity, rapid recovery, and resilience from catastrophic events.

As will be noted later, the banking community also has a stake in the quality of construction, and adequate maintenance of buildings to assure that safety features that are built in remain fully functional. The banking community also has a role to play here wanting the codes enforcement programs that oversee building design and construction to be both effective and efficient. The costs of carrying loans while construction projects are delayed due to regulatory delays (true delays, not delays caused by the builder) should be of concern to banks. The faster that buildings get built, and built to meet or exceed the jurisdiction's code, the sooner the builder or building owner can receive rents or start on the next construction project in their region.

Last, our financial institutions need to be at the table helping the construction team deal with the forces described throughout this book for the basic reason cited earlier, as the health and even survival depend upon the nation's infrastructure being disaster resilient—able to "take the licking and keep on ticking."

The Elected Officials

Our elected public officials are the third additional party who need to be at the table. In community after community, state after state, and at the national level in the White House and U.S. Congress, elected officials hold hearings and issue reports whenever a disaster strikes. They are quick to demand much of their code enforcement personnel, but generally do not understand the importance of the codes and standards that are adopted (or not adopted) in their community and enforced (or not enforced).

Figure 7-22
Rhode Island
State Legislature

Elected officials understand jobs and economic viability and have been learning the hard way about disaster preparedness, mitigation, and response and recovery. They do not, however, have a holistic view as to how the buildings in their community interrelate with each other or how each segment of the critical infrastructure is dependent upon the other segments for disaster resilience.

It is easy for politicians to cut ribbons and make pronouncements about being "business friendly," but they need to look beyond those largely public relation events and sit down with the construction community, the building owners and managers, architects and engineers, contractors, product suppliers, and their building code enforcement personnel and map out a strategy that makes the community both disaster resilient and economically competitive within their region.

Partners in Disaster Resilience: Prevention, Response, Recovery

Given the broader definition of our national security and of resilience, and the forces described in this chapter, the adding to the construction team of the insurance and banking community and the elected officials forms the nexus of a group who all share varying degrees of responsibility (and liability) for the future of both the construction industry and the ongoing health, welfare, and life safety of the American public in our built environment.

WHERE DOES ALL OF THIS TAKE US BETWEEN NOW AND 2025?

So where does all of this take us? In Part II of this book we have looked at what current building codes, construction guidelines, and checklists can be followed to provide added levels of security in buildings, while changes are made to building codes and standards which mandate minimum levels of health, welfare, and life safety in construction to address safety concerns and lessons learned in the events of 9/11 and recent natural disasters. Thus far in Part III we have looked at forces that are impacting the future health, welfare, and life safety of our nation and the concepts of disaster resilience and expanding the composition of the construction team to include other responsible parties who are key stakeholders in the future of construction in this nation.

Most professionals who make a living looking into and writing about the future usually lay out three possible future scenarios: the first in which little changes from the current patters and trends of today; the second in which there is moderate change spurred on by further developments in technologies that are under consideration and development today; and the third that says everything will be different based either upon a dark scenario of some tragic event (an asteroid hitting the earth) or upon some very positive scientific breakthrough (cold fusion) that radically changes one of the major components of our existence.

In Chapter 8, "A World Transformed: A Vision of One Possible Future for the Construction Industry and Construction Team," we look at one possible scenario for our future. It will not be the radical change or dark or nirvana scenario that futurists love to ponder, but it will be one where all of the forces outlined in Chapter 7 come together to at least significantly transform the roles, relationships, and responsibilities of the construction team, the buildings they construct, and nature of the building codes and standards that they use.

8

A World Transformed: A Vision of One Possible Future for the Construction Industry and Construction Team

Using artificial reality tools, designers and their clients can enter the structures they are planning. They can have the simulated experience of walking round in the structures. They can examine the heft, textures, and look of materials, and consider engineering alternatives suggested by their computer design systems.

The growing practices of recording each structure's life history became a U.S. Law in 2013. Today, the electronic cornerstone of a structure contains a full record of its design, construction, and repair histories, use, energy consumption, ownership, and other particulars. Visual images, including full motion, are stored with other continuously updated data from sensors and monitoring devices. Any authorized user can query the record from the building, or remotely. The record is especially important to rescue workers, renovators, regulators, energy auditors, and owners."

—From Our Built World. *2025: Scenarios of US and Global Society Reshaped by Science and Technology*, by Joseph Coates, John Mahaffie and Andy Hines, Oakhill Press, Winchester, VA, 1997.

We see that construction has two choices: ignore all this in the belief that construction is so unique that there are no lessons to be learned; or seek improvements through re-engineering construction, learning as much as possible from those who have done it elsewhere.

—From Sir John Egan, Chairman, the British Government's 1999 Construction Task Force Report, "Rethinking Construction," following the Task Force's visit to Nissan, U.K.

The best way to predict the future is to design it.

—Buckminster Fuller

AT A CROSSROADS

This book has looked at the impact that the events of 9/11 and the large-scale natural disasters of 2005 had on the members of the construction team, described actions being taken to address lessons learned from those events, and noted the guidelines,

Figure 8-1

High-rise building in Seattle

codes, and standards that currently are available to the construction industry to enhance architectural security in buildings. Chapter 7 addressed a number of the forces that are at work causing the construction team to take a broader look at what is involved in homeland security and impacting the nature of their industry.

Many people believe it is hyperbole to speak of "a world transformed" in the aftermath of 9/11. High-rise structures are still built and renovated with little to no changes in existing codes. The construction team still is functioning in most parts of the nation in the same manner and with the same concerns as they did prior to the attack and the subsequent natural disasters.

Yet as noted in Chapter 2, the world has changed for the construction industry as indeed it has for the American people. It has changed in response to the American public's loss

Figure 8-2
Rockefeller Center,
New York City

of innocence and their consequential added safety concerns caused both by the war on terrorism coming to our shores and the large-scale devastation of Katrina. It also has changed due to the growing momentum of the other forces that were described in Chapter 7: demands for greater energy conservation, sustainable and environmentally responsible construction, changing demographics, and the impact of new transformational technologies and products.

The forces of technological innovation and the need for greater energy conservation, sustainability, and environmentally "friendly" construction have been with us for some time (at least from the 1970s). The involvement of the nation in what people are beginning to see will indeed be a long struggle with terrorism, coupled with what is now being acknowledged as climate change that in part is causing more devastating storms than we have experienced in the recent past, have shaken public confidence in many institutions, including the construction industry, which has an excellent overall safety record.

The next major natural disaster causing large losses of life and regional economic disruption—be it a hurricane or earthquake or the next major foreign or domestic terrorist attack—will further shake and erode public confidence, setting off a new wave of reports to determine who was at fault and what went wrong and calling for stricter regulations and another round of insurance policy premium increases or cancellations.

Yet, hardening of all of our buildings after each new attack until they resemble the fortresses of Medieval Europe, or the easily bypassed Maginot Line, will not measurably improve public safety. It will, however, divert future investments in education, health care, and research and development of innovative non-security-based technologies and reduce our overall economic productivity. Such a response will weaken the nation and make it even more vulnerable to future shocks not just from Mother Nature or terrorists but from our worsening position within the global economy. That is a future scenario of a path that no one but the terrorists want us to walk down.

We stand today then at a crossroads. We can continue to try and pretend that we can and must eliminate all potential risks in the built environment and start down the afore-mentioned path, or we can learn to live with acceptable risk and, with due deliberation,

Figure 8-3
Castle Tower,
Sluis, Netherlands

take the lessons that will be learned from these future events and where realistically prudent make changes in our codes and standards and construction techniques and practices, but not make every building a fortress, locking ourselves and our dynamic economy within walls of fear wondering: Where will they strike next? If a 150 ft setback is good now, maybe a 300 ft setback is better. If a high efficiency particulate air (HEPA) filter works now, maybe we should then install a ultra low particulate air (ULPA) filter.

No, instead, if we follow the wisdom of Buckminster Fuller's opening quote, then the expanded construction team (including elected officials and the banking and insurance industries) can design and play a meaningful role in helping our nation move into a brighter future—one with both disaster resilience and economic productivity. And the good news is that a number of the building blocks for that brighter scenario are already in place, and that the construction industry can meet and exceed the vision offered for it by the futurists, Coates, Mahaffie, and Hines in the opening of this chapter.

Figure 8-4
EPCOT and all of Walt Disney World stand out as examples of both innovative design and construction, and predicting the future by designing it. Walt Disney at map of EPCOT, Experimental Prototype City of Tomorrow, Walt Disney World Exhibit at MGM Studios

THE SCENARIO: ONE POSSIBLE VISION OF THE FUTURE

The Construction Industry in 2025

Based upon current trends and practices described in this book, here then, is one possible vision for the future. Nineteen years from now the nation's construction industry will do the following:

- Will look at each building in a holistic fashion and not as an aggregate of disassociated systems or parts.
- Uniformly use building information modeling (BIM) to reduce the cost and time involved in new construction and renovation and building commissioning and operation by linking together through all the members of the construction team at all stages during the life of that structure. This will enable the building owner to make use of that data to operate the building at maximum efficiency and facilitate the building's effective response to and recovery from stresses from both man-made and natural sources.
- Use BIM and new building materials and products to enable the building owner during the design stage to construct the building in a computer and test it against various different forces and stresses both man-made (terrorism and accidental) and natural, and determine what are the best design, construction, and operation and maintenance plans for that building to meet or exceed the risks set through risk analysis.
- Uniformly adopt and use new and innovative technologies, including nanotechnologies, polymers, low-power sensor networks, and other building sensors that reduce potential life-safety risks to the building occupants under potentially hazardous conditions and facilitate safe rescue and evacuation of occupants under catastrophic events.
- Uniformly reduce the numbers of deaths or injuries related to fires and indoor air-quality problems.
- Operate buildings using less energy and, in many cases, generating their own energy that can be relied upon during "emergency" situations and during normal operating conditions, which contributes energy to the power grid.
- Embrace and use green building design and technologies and green recycled building materials to reduce production of greenhouse gases and make buildings less intrusive or damaging to the natural environment.
- Enhance the effectiveness and efficiency of regulatory oversight of building design and construction by facilitating greater national code uniformity and by connecting the building regulatory system into the BIM process, from permit application through electronic review of three- and four-dimensional plans, field inspection, and issuance of certificate of occupancy.
- Remain largely a localized industry, constructing most buildings onsite with a number of national or regional large-sized firms that work in conjunction with local contractors and subcontractors. The workforce will be increasingly bilingual.
- Be able to rapidly provide affordable and relocatable mid- to long-term housing to areas struck by large natural and man-made disasters.

How Do We Get There? A Convergence

Convergence: the act, condition, quality of approaching the same point from different directions; tending toward a meeting or intersection.

—*Webster's New Collegiate Dictionary*, 11th ed., 2003

Over the past two decades, a diverse array of national initiatives have been launched by forward thinking individuals and organizations to help improve the effectiveness and efficiency of our nation's building design, construction, regulation, and operations processes. The tragic events of 2001 to 2006 are a catalyst; they have made it not only possible but critical to the future of the nation for these initiatives to converge, but to understand how that will occur it is important to look at their origins.

Growing Recognition of the Critical Role of Our Construction and Building Industry in a Time of National Need

Our nation's building construction and related industries are a $3 trillion per year domestic industry. Together the industry represents over 20% of our gross domestic product and provides the infrastructure within which most of our national wealth is either generated or housed and in which all Americans live, work, and play. Its health either stimulates or hinders economic growth; the economic competitiveness of our cities, states, regions, and nation in the global economy; and the health, welfare, and life safety of our citizens.

Because of their vital importance in the physical safety of our people and the economic vitality of our nation, our buildings are likely to remain one of the favored targets of terrorists. Despite the central role that our construction and building industry plays in our nation, it remains one of the most fragmented, least efficient, and poorly understood segments of our economy. In both residential and commercial construction, 80% of the construction is done by firms that only build on a local or regional basis; and the majority of these firms have 50 or fewer employees.

Adding to this fragmentation is the fact that construction is overseen by over 44,000 jurisdictions at the state and local government level, which regulate building design, construction, and renovation through a confusing, diverse, and, at times, conflicting array of codes, standards, rules, regulations, and procedures. For these reasons, economies of scale—reduced life-cycle costs and enhanced operating efficiencies achieved by other industries, such as automobiles and aircraft, through the effective application of information technology to the design, construction, and operation of such products—have not been achieved in the U. S. construction industry.

Diverse Approaches

Over the past two decades, however, different segments of the construction community, from federal agencies and research labs and state governments to alliances of building owners and construction firms, have undertaken initiatives to improve efficiency within their respective areas of concern in the building design, construction, regulation, and

Figure 8-5

Foundation work
for new residential
structures

Figure 8-6

New townhouse
construction,
Fairfax County,
Virginia

Figure 8-7
Multifamily housing under construction, Town Center in Reston, Virginia

operation processes. Within the private sector, numerous trade associations and professional societies pursued programs designed to improve regulatory or construction practices. The Building Roundtable in New York City and later the Construction Industry Institute (CII) and the Construction Users Round Table (CURT) have brought together some of the nation's largest firms to address the problem of construction inefficiencies, while codes and standards bodies have looked at ways to work with federal, state, and local governments to adopt and administer more uniform construction codes and standards.

In addition, in the 1990s the White House Office of Science and Technology Policy and the National Science and Technology Council's Committee on Technology and its Construction and Buildings Subcommittee began a concerted effort to better coordinate across the federal level of government construction and building research and development activities. They explored ways to partner with state and local governments to enhance the efficiency of the construction industry as well. During the 1990s, market forces were making elected officials at the state and local level more aware of the costs to them as purchasers and operators of buildings caused by countless regulatory and construction inefficiencies.

With federal support or funding and contributions from public and private sector organizations, a number of programs or initiatives by the late 1990s were launched to address segments of the construction inefficiency problem facing the nation. These included the following:

- The work of the National Institute of Building Sciences on greater use of information technology among federal construction agencies and in building operations
- The creation of FIATECH (Fully Integrated Automated TECHnology), a consortium of firms focused on fast-track development and deployment of technologies to substantially improve how capital projects are designed, built, and maintained

- The efforts of the Civil Engineering Research Foundation (CERF), now within the American Society of Civil Engineers (ASCE), to enhance greater efficiencies in construction practices
- The National Conference of States on Building Codes and Standards and its 55 national partners in the Streamlining the Nation's Building Regulatory Process initiative assembling and sharing best practices in government oversight of construction

The Mid To Late 1990s and Forces Accelerating Change: E-Governance and Challenges of Economic Competitiveness

In the late 1990s advances in the application and use of information technology to increase operating efficiencies across the private sector increased the pressure upon all levels of government, federal, state, and local to reassess their operations. In response to these challenges, some large firms successfully applied computer-assisted design operations and fully integrated design techniques to radically reduce the time it took them to design and build new facilities. At the same time, federal, state, and local governments hired chief information officers and initiated restructuring of their bureaucracies to streamline government, making it more effective and efficient and responsive to change.

Former Utah Governor and a past Chairman of the National Governors Association and now Secretary of Health and Human Services, Michael Leavitt, best summed up the challenge facing government efficiency by noting that his industries were telling him that in the global economy: "If we miss a single product cycle we are dead." Federal, state, and local governments now had to use information technology to improve the efficiency of their operations including regulatory oversight.

In response to these market forces, jurisdictions in Silicon Valley, California, and elsewhere in the nation began to reorganize themselves to effectively use information technology to streamline their building regulatory processes reducing regulatory overlap and duplication

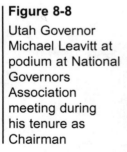

Figure 8-8

Utah Governor Michael Leavitt at podium at National Governors Association meeting during his tenure as Chairman

and unnecessary delays in the permitting, plans review, and inspection processes. Those efforts demonstrated the dramatic savings (up to 60% of previous regulatory costs) that regulatory reform could provide the construction industry.

By early 2001, over a half dozen national initiatives were underway in the public and private sector to apply information technology to the building design, construction, regulation, and operation processes to improve efficiency in the nation's construction and buildings industry. These included the following:

- The federal government was better coordinating both e-governance operations and federal construction activities through various programs and projects including those being shared within the White House Office of Management and Budget and the White House Office of Science and Technology Policy.
- FIATECH was moving forward with segments of the public and private sectors to develop a road map of the construction process that made greater use of information technology in capital projects (factories, refineries, etc.).
- The Partnership for Advancing Technology in Housing (PATH) initiative was sharing best practices with builders that enhance the use of innovative technologies including information technology in the design, construction, regulation, and use of housing in the United States.
- Civil Engineering Research Foundation, ASCE/Construction Industry Institute, and various associations of building owners were separately looking at greater efficiencies in the construction process involving their members through more uniform applications of information technology and various other streamlining initiatives.
- The Enterprise Integration Act was introduced and subsequently passed (2002) by the U.S. Congress authorizing the National Institute of Standards and Technology (NIST) to research and establish "standards and protocols to enable major manufacturing industries (including construction and housing) to electronically exchange product and standards related information."
- The National Institute of Building Sciences and International Alliance for Interoperability, NA (IAI) were looking at developing or supporting the adoption and use of interoperable standards for information technology hardware and software in the construction process.
- The Alliance for Building Regulatory Reform in the Digital Age had been established by the National Conference of States on Building Codes and Standards and 44 national associations and agencies representing the construction industry and federal, state, and local governments to enable the nation's construction industry to build "faster, better, safer, and at less cost" by streamlining the nation's building regulatory process through the greater use of information technology.

While the parties involved in these initiatives often overlapped and certainly were aware of each other's efforts, they all were progressing along relatively diverse paths, sometimes even competing for the same limited public and private sector resources of time, talent, and funding. Then terrorists struck the World Trade Center and the Pentagon and all of the transformations to the construction team's roles and relationships described earlier in this book began to occur.

9/11: PUBLIC SAFETY AND COMPETITIVENESS AS CATALYSTS FOR CONVERGENCE

As noted in previous chapters, the events of 9/11 resulted in our nation and the construction team taking numerous actions to better protect and mitigate the loss of life and property from future terrorist's attacks. In addition, many of the organizations that led the previously mentioned initiatives joined with their colleagues from other segments of government and the construction and academic communities in establishing The Infrastructure Security Partnership (TISP).

Toward a Common Vision for Enhanced Public Safety and Economic Competitiveness: Four Building Blocks That Already Are in Place

By 2005, the building industry had labored to address concerns of their members over the events of 9/11 and continued to support their earlier initiatives to improve the construction process, while working together within TISP. Elements of a common vision for enhancing public safety and improving economic competitiveness of the nation had begun to emerge among the associations and government agencies that represent the members of the core composition of the construction team (owners, architects, engineers, contractors, materials and product manufacturers and suppliers, codes and standards writing organizations, code enforcement personnel, and building maintenance personnel). While not yet centrally organized or focused, a convergence began to occur within many of the organizations and their members; as witnessed by the following trends:

1. Heightened attention to security in buildings and the need for risk analysis
2. An appreciation for the need for a disaster-resilience approach toward security rather than need to protect everything all the time
3. Recognition of the critical importance our infrastructure plays not only in national security but in economic competitiveness, as well as an awareness that our aging infrastructure is in dire need of repair (see Appendix for ASCE's 2005 Report Card on America's Infrastructure).
4. A greater commitment to work cooperatively with federal, state, and local governments to improve security and safety
5. A growing understanding of the importance to the nation for greater energy conservation and environmental responsibility
6. A growing understanding of the importance of life-cycle costs and the need to take a holistic view of buildings

Then Hurricane Katrina hit, the first truly region-wide disaster, and the interrelationships and interdependencies between the members of the construction team (the expanded construction team) began to focus attention on the fact that all of these earlier initiatives could be brought together to make the nation safer and more secure in the broadest sense of homeland security offered in this chapter.

With their origins in the 1980s, taken together the following four areas represent the building blocks for the positive vision of the future of our construction industry in 2025.

Figure 8-9

American Society of Civil Engineers, 2005 Report Card on America's Infrastructure

Area 1—Building Information Modeling and Three- and Four-Dimensional Systems

Building information modeling (BIM) technology, including the hardware, software and intermediate ware of such packages as NavisWorks and Buzzsaw, has been successfully applied and are now coming into wider use in the design, construction, commissioning, and operation of buildings. What was envisioned many years ago and pioneered by Stanford University's CIFE (Center for Integrated Facilities Engineering) and others is now embraced and promoted by the General Services Administration (GSA) and other federal agencies and is proving to be a cost-effective tool providing significant savings in both design and construction time and operating costs.

A solid building block for the future, what is needed to move this technology forward are:

• More forums such as those provided by the American Institute of Architects and the National Institute of Building Sciences (including IAI's buildingSmart project) at

Figure 8-10

Parsons Brinkerhoff Computer Assisted Virtual Environment (CAVE) display panel (Courtesy of Parsons Brinkerhoff)

which more building owners and architectural and engineering firms can learn how to make use of this technology in their future projects

- Software applications against which to run in three- and four-dimensional different disaster scenarios, which offer different levels of threat and risk and diverse attack scenarios to test its application in risk-threat assessment for buildings and help in deciding what enhanced safety features to include and what their maintenance cycles must be

- Greater and true interoperability of such systems, so data can be shared among the software packages from multiple vendors and multiple building functions from design and construction through operation, maintenance, remodeling, and ultimately through demolition.

- The ability of state and local building departments to issue permits, track and do plans check, and conduct field inspections tying directly into three- and four-dimensional BIM systems

Area 2—FIATECH Roadmap

The FIATECH Capital Projects Technology Roadmap is a cooperative effort of associations, consortia, government agencies, and industry to accelerate the deployment of emerging and new technologies that "revolutionize" the capabilities of the capital projects industry (industry that executes the planning, engineering, procurement, construction and operation of large-scale buildings, plants, and facilities and infrastructure).

As diagrammed in their roadmap shown in Figure 8-11, FIATECH's vision for the future for the capital projects industry is a highly automated project and facility management environment integrated across all phases of the facility's life cycle. Information is available upon demand, whenever and wherever it is needed by all stakeholders. This integrated environment enables all partners and project functions to instantly and securely "plug together" their operations and systems. Interconnected, automated systems, processes, and equipment drastically reduce time and cost of planning, design, and construction.

Scenario-based planning systems and modeling tools (such as those in the Vision of the Future) enable rapid, accurate evaluation of all options resulting in the selection of the best balance of capability and cost-effectiveness. Likewise new materials and methods reduce the time and cost of construction and greatly extend facility performance, functionality, aesthetics, affordability, and sustainability, as well as responsiveness to changing business demands or levels of security threat.

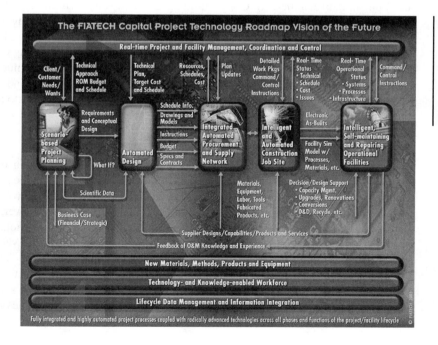

Figure 8-11

FIATECH Capital Projects Technology Roadmap (Courtesy of FIATECH)

The roadmap captures this vision. The map depicts a completely integrated structure composed of the following nine critical elements that FIATECH sees as a "virtual enterprise for the future."

1. Scenario-based project planning
2. Automated design
3. Integrated automated procurement and supply network
4. Intelligent, and automated construction job site
5. Intelligent self-maintaining and repairing operational facility
6. Real-time project and facility management, coordination, and control
7. New materials, methods, products, and equipment
8. Technology and knowledge-enabled workforce
9. Life-cycle data management and information integration

FIATECH has developed tactical plans for each of the nine areas and has obtained funding for portions of its implementation. The FIATECH Roadmap provides a model for the development of the future scenario provided in this chapter and can serve as a guide for other industries.

Area 3—Convergence of Energy and Environment

Federal, state, and local governments, as well as the LEED and Energy Star programs from the private sector, have firmly begun to move previously "good ideas" into the mainstream of building design, construction, and operation. For example, between January, 2005 and mid-August, 2006 twenty-nine bills were introduced in the U.S. Congress promoting energy efficiency and environmental quality in buildings. The joint development between the U.S. Green Building Council, American Society of Heating, Refrigerating and Air-Conditioning Engineers, and Illuminating Engineering Society of America has led to the new minimum standard for high-performance green buildings, which provides a tool that will migrate in many communities into a building code mandate further spreading the growth of this movement. As energy prices continue to climb and the environment continues to challenge the nation, this solid, holistic, and life-cycle view of design, construction, and operation of buildings will be absorbed into the mainstream of architectural design.

Area 4—Regulatory Streamlining

Recent efforts to improve the effectiveness and efficiency of the building regulatory process forms the fourth building block for the future. Given progress in the other three building blocks: BIM, the innovations proposed by FIATECH, the convergence of energy and environmental design, the building regulatory process, however, requires special focus in the immediate term or it risks becoming an even greater choke point in the construction process than it already is in far too many jurisdictions. Many of the associations representing members of the construction team, including associations representing state and local government, participated in the restructuring of the Alliance for Building Regulatory Reform in the Digital Age into a broader regulatory streamlining initiative that will include zoning and land use issues, along with issues related to building codes administration and enforcement.

Under the name, National Partnership to Streamline Government, participating national associations, government agencies, and colleges and universities are taking previously generated regulatory streamlining tools, including interoperable software, model procurement requirements, and the new guide from the Department of Housing and Human Development (see Chapter 7), and developing a project to gain their adoption and use by state and local governments across the nation. Documented cost and time savings to the public and private sector of 40 to 60% coupled with lessons learned from Hurricanes Katrina and Rita (and the Blue Cascades III exercise) have exposed the need for the following streamlining related initiatives which when implemented will further strengthen this critical building block for the positive future scenario for the construction industry and the nation as a whole:

- More building departments not only need to adopt the most current codes but also need to be adequately funded for qualified staff and an effective and efficient codes administration and enforcement system to assure compliance with those codes.

- Across the nation there needs to be concerted state and regional effort to identify and remove prior to any disaster those rules and regulations, processes, and procedures that overlap and are duplicative and likewise slow down the ability of the jurisdiction to rapidly recover through the issuance of building permits and through inspections.

- Greater uniformity in the codes and standards adopted and enforced within a region to reduce confusion and unnecessary costs and time delays during reconstruction that is caused by having a diverse array of building codes and product approval systems.

- Greater uniformity in the codes, standards, and administrative processes and procedures to facilitate access to qualified personnel from other building departments outside the disaster area to supplement their staff during the disaster damage assessment and recovery.

- Greater sharing of existing best practices that already are aiding in disaster preparedness and recovery, as well as reducing the regulatory cost of construction in some communities and helping the private sector reduce delays in the "speed to market" of their products and services.

- The ability for building departments to make greater use of information technology in their operations, including online permits, field inspections, and electronic plans review, helping to avoid becoming a major choke point in either the general construction or disaster recovery processes.

- Establishing mechanisms to set up measurements for jurisdictions to use in assessing their regulatory efficiency and effectiveness.

- Federal funding to support state and local jurisdictions in streamlining their building, zoning, and land use regulatory programs to better prepare for, respond to and recover from disasters and improve nation's economic competitiveness.

We Aren't Alone: Great Britain's "Rethinking Construction" and Disaster Resilience Efforts

As witnessed by Sir John Egan at the beginning of this chapter, the United States is not alone in recognizing the critical importance of the construction industry to its public safety and economic competitiveness and trying to determine what changes are necessary to increase the productivity of that industry. Under his leadership, the Construction Task Force in 1999 released a major study on barriers to increasing the productivity of

Great Britain's construction industry, which like that of the United States is fragmented, noncohesive, and comprised largely of small-sized firms. Their goal was to find and make recommended changes that annually reduce construction costs and times nationwide by 10% and reduce defects in construction projects by 20%. Among their recommendations are many that echo those addressed in the U.S. by diverse groups:

- Set up measures of progress
- Identify and support best practices
- Apply information technology to construction and oversight processes
- Partner in the supply chain
- Enjoy greater standardization of construction materials and products
- Observe national government demonstrating new technologies and processes
- Call upon national government to provide funding for demonstration projects.

ADDITIONAL BUILDING BLOCKS THAT NEED TO BE PUT IN PLACE

The convergence and mutual coordination between the preceding four existing building block programs, coupled with heightened public awareness caused by 9/11 and the natural disasters, form an ideal base upon which the members of the expanded construction team (insurance, banking industries, and elected officials) can come together to support the assembling of the following additional building blocks to make the positive future scenario offered in this chapter a reality. These remaining building blocks include the government and private sector embracing and incorporating into their day-to-day operations the following concepts:

- Life-cycle cost of all construction
- Acceptable risk for our buildings and other portions of our critical infrastructure
- Disaster resiliency of not just our buildings and our critical infrastructure but of our regional and national economy as a whole

Tort Reform

As noted in the opening chapter of this book, basic tort reform, relief from law suits that are frivolous or with awards that are not commensurate with the actual harm caused by an incident, are driving more and more good, competent construction firms, as well as doctors and other professionals, from their fields. That building owners are afraid to even conduct a basic threat analysis to even determine what improvements they may need to make in the building they are about to build or renovate benefits absolutely no one except those who would do harm to our nation.

Changes in some state laws that allow building owners and the members of their construction team to make corrections to defects found in their buildings prior to allowing a law suit over those defects certainly is a healthy move in the right direction. Another part of this building block that needs to be put in place is the simple amending of many of our state's existing "good Samaritan" laws to allow the construction industry to participate in disaster planning, training, drilling, response, and recovery programs.

Action on American Society of Civil Engineers's Infrastructure Report Card

The annual Report Card for America's Infrastructure issued by ASCE provides an ideal place to focus the implementation of many of the building blocks mentioned in this chapter. Being able to build, to borrow the phrase from an earlier streamlining initiative, "faster, better, safer, and at less cost," certainly can and should be demonstrated on our aging schools, roads, bridges, power generation facilities, and other physical structures that all are elements of our critical infrastructure.

Federal Government Becomes a Catalyst

While the private sector and state and local governments carry out their responsibilities in building toward this future, the federal government has a major role to play in the following areas:

Research and Development

As noted throughout this book, there are a number of areas in construction design, processes, technologies, and materials where the federal government through the National Laboratories, the Department of Homeland Security, and a number of colleges and universities is funding and supporting research and development on new technologies, processes, and procedures that make buildings more disaster resistant. That role needs to be expanded to focus on a number of projects including assisting the private sector in developing test methods and standards to apply to homeland security related products and materials.

Continued Support and Inclusion of BIM and New Technologies

The federal government through the GSA, Department of Defense, Department of State, Veterans Administration, and other agencies has served as a test bed for many of the enhancements in construction technology covered in this book. That role needs not only to be continued but more opportunities should be provided for these federal agencies to share the benefits they are seeing from their use of BIM, LEED, and other programs and technologies with their counterparts in the private sector-perhaps in a way reminiscent of the Department of Agriculture's earlier role with the farmers of this nation.

Grants Provision to Support Building Blocks and Implement Regulatory Streamlining

Seed money to assemble the building blocks noted in this section is badly needed. This is especially true of the diverse programs that already are in existence and which support their convergence into a cohesive national campaign, similar to the project that the British have undertaken in response to the Egan Report. In addition to such activities, state and local governments are in need of matching grants to implement streamlined administrative practices and procedures that have been proved successful elsewhere in the nation.

STEPS THAT CAN BE TAKEN BY THE CONSTRUCTION TEAM TO FULFILL THIS VISION

The fulfillment of this positive future vision for construction in this nation will not be accomplished by any one group. Nor is this vision anything that can be imposed from the top down. It will take instead a coming together of all of the members of the expanded construction team, including elected officials at all levels of government, to work simultaneously at both the national and the local level to strengthen all of the building blocks that already are in place and assemble the ones that have yet to be created.

Whether it is on an individual building, or as suggested here and in Chapter 7, on regional implementation of the TISP Regional Disaster Resilience Guide, or at the national level on the overall role of the construction industry within the nation's economy,

Figure 8-13

New commercial building under construction, suburban Chicago

every one of the following members of the expanded construction team must shed their pre 9-11 world view as individual actors in the construction process and begin to truly function as partners within a cohesive and coordinated team:

- Owners
- Architects
- Engineers
- Contractors
- Building materials and product manufacturers and suppliers
- Codes and standards bodies
- Code enforcement personnel
- Building managers and operators
- Insurance industry
- Banking industry
- Elected officials

TIME AND OPPORTUNITY TO ACT

We have in this book provided a description of those architectural security codes, guidelines, and best practices that are currently available to the construction team to consider using where needed as appropriate enhancements to buildings that are under construction or renovation. Within the next few years, additional guidelines and modified codes and standards will be available based upon the lessons learned from 9/11, the anthrax attacks, and the 2004 to 2005 hurricanes.

But as noted in Chapter 7, other forces and natural and man-made disasters will challenge the construction team and the nation for years to come. Some of those events will provide the nation with useful data to help us further strengthen some aspects of our codes and standards. Other events will make us consider falling into the trap of trying to protect everything and making changes that only weaken our economy and make us less resilient within the global economy.

The vision offered in this final chapter offers a path forward through those challenges. Based upon strong building blocks already in place, that path is well within our reach. It will, however, involve the nation's public and private sector working cooperatively together to embrace and support, both financially and in some cases politically, the adoption and use of both the existing tools, resources, and best practices that have been outlined here and those that have been suggested. The latter includes the need to embrace the concepts of acceptable risk, life-cycle cost, and disaster and economic resiliency; undertake meaningful tort reform; and address the need for upgrading our existing infrastructure, regulatory reform, and government funding and support for these endeavors.

A chain is only as strong as its weakest link. Our weakest link thus far has been that we have not appreciated the interconnectivity that exists between all of the members of the

Figure 8-14

Informal memorial at World Trade Center, Ground Zero, April 2006 (Photo Courtesy of Lisa Wible)

construction team and that team's connection with the health, safety, and economic vitality of our nation. Recognizing those roles and responsibilities and acting simultaneously at both the national and local levels will bring our nation far more architectural security than can ever be achieved through the design, construction, or operation of a system built in isolation, building by building or upgrading our codes and standards, disaster by disaster.

The appendix of this book offers the reader connections to the organizations, both public and private, that comprise the expanded construction team. It is your link, if you are a building owner, architect, engineer, contractor, other professional, or student to becoming involved in helping to design a more secure future for our nation and our built environment.

> Unable to actually imprison us, these terrorists want us to imprison ourselves. Sorry, but no way. It breaks my heart to think about the people who lost loved ones on September 11, but I will not let it break my spirit.
>
> —Thomas Friedman, *New York Times*, September 25, 2001

Appendix: Resources, Web sites, and Chapter Notes

OBJECTIVE

This appendix is designed to serve both as a resource guide and to offer clarifications and expansions on information sources cited in each of the chapters of this book. The purpose of the resource guide information is to enable the reader to access the most current information on the codes, standards, guidelines, and best practices that building owners, architects, engineers, and other members of the construction team can draw upon in considering the design of new or retrofit of existing buildings to enhance the safety and security of their occupants.

For ease of use, the appendix is divided into two sections: Part I: covering resources in the public and private sector, and Part II: containing chapter notes.

Part I provides a listing of all of the public, joint public–private, and private sector agencies, associations, or organizations that are listed within the book and provides e-mail addresses for those organizations.

Associations representing the public sector are listed in the public sector section. The trade associations and nongovernmental associations cited in this publication are included in the private sector listing. There are several entities that are joint public–private sector partnerships and they have been listed in a separate category of their own. Within these three categories agencies, associations, or organizations are listed alphabetically and the acronyms and Web sites for each entry are provided. The following section provides expanded information on or links to sources of documents covered in each chapter of the book.

PART I: RESOURCES: LIST OF AGENCIES AND ORGANIZATIONS

I. A. Public Sector Resources (Governments and Public Associations Representing the Public Sector)

Federal Government

Department of Defense, DoD: www.dod.gov

Defense Advanced Research Projects Agency, DARPA: www.darpa.mil

Department of Homeland Security, DHS: www.dhs.gov

Department of Housing and Urban Development, HUD: www.hud.gov

Department of Energy, DOE: www.doe.gov

Department of Justice, DoJ and National Institute of Justice: www.ojp.usdoj.gov/nij

Department of State, DoS: www.state.gov

Environmental Protection Agency, EPA: www.epa.gov

Federal Emergency Management Agency, FEMA (part of DHS): www.fema.gov

General Services Administration, GSA: www.gsa.gov

National Academy of Sciences, National Academy of Engineering, Federal Facilities Council, FFC: www7.nationalacademies.org/ffc/

National Institute of Standards and Technology, NIST: www.nist.gov

Technical Support Working Group, TSWG: www.tswg.gov

U.S. Architectural and Transportation Barriers Compliance Board, USATBCB: www.access-board.gov

U.S. Army Corps of Engineers, USACE: www.usace.army.mil

U.S. Department of Agriculture, DoA: www.usda.gov

U.S. Department of Commerce, DOC: www.doc.gov

United States Senate Committee on Homeland Security and Government Administration: http://hsgac.senate.gov

White House Office of Science and Technology Policy, OSTP: www.whitehouse.gov

State Government

Port Authority of New York and New Jersey: www.panynj.gov

State of California, Building Standards Commission: www.bsc.ca.gov

State of Florida, Department of Community Affairs: www.dca.state.fl.us

State of Louisiana, Office of the State Fire Marshal: www.dps.state.la.us

State of New York, Secretary of State: www.dos.state.ny.us

State of New Jersey, Department of Community Affairs: www.state.nj.us/dca/dcahome.htm

State of Oregon, Department of Consumer and Business Services: www.oregon.gov/DCBS/

State of Rhode Island, Department of Health: www.health.ri.gov

State of Washington, State Building Code Council: www.sbcc.wa.gov

Local Government (County/Municipal/Townships)

City of Chicago: www.CityofChicago.org

City of Los Angeles, Department of Building Safety, LADBS: www.ladbs.org

New York City Department of Buildings, NYCDB: www.nyc.gov/dob

Pittsburgh, PA: www.city.pittsburgh.pa.us

San Francisco, Department of Building Inspections, DBI: www.sfgov.org/dbi

Associations Representing Public Sector

Association of Major City and County Building Officials, AMCBO: www.ncsbcs.org

Council of State Governments, CSG: www.csg.org

Industrialized Buildings Commission, IBC: www.interstateibc.org

Institute for Building Technology & Safety, IBTS: www.ibts.org

National Association of Counties, NACo: www.naco.org

National Association of State Facilities Administrators, NASFA: www.nasfa.net

National Association of State Chief Information Officers, NASCIO: www.nascio.org

National Association of State Energy Officers, NASEO: www.naseo.org

National Conference of States on Building Codes and Standards, NCSBCS: www.ncsbcs.org

National Conference of State Legislators, NCSL: www.ncsl.org

National Emergency Management Association, NEMA: www.nemaweb.org

National Governors Association, NGA: www.nga.org

National League of Cities, NLC: www.nlc.org

U.S. Conference of Mayors, USCM: www.usmayors.org.

I. B. Joint Partnerships: Public and Private Sector

Alliance for Building Regulatory Reform in the Digital Age, and the National Partnership to Streamline Government: www.natlpartnerstreamline.org

I. C. Private Sector and Association Resources

American Institute of Architects, AIA: www.aia.org

American Management Association, AMA: www.amanet.org

American National Standards Institute, ANSI: www.ansi.org

American Planning Association, APA: www.apa.org

American Society of Civil Engineers, ASCE: www.asce.org

American Society of Heating Refrigerating and Air Conditioning Engineers, ASHRAE: www.ashrae.org

American Society for Industrial Security, ASIS: www.asis.org

American Society of Mechanical Engineers, ASME: www.asme.org

American Society for Testing and Materials, ASTM: www.astm.org

Applied Technology Council, ATC: www.atcouncil.org

Associated General Contractors of America, AGC: www.agc.org

Builders Hardware Manufacturers Association, BHMA: www.buildershardware.com

Building Diagnostics Research Institute, BDRI: www.builidingdiagnostics.org

Building Owners and Managers Association International, BOMA: www.boma.org

Center for Aging Services & Technologies, CAST: www.cast.org

Construction Industry Institute, CII: www.cii.org

Construction Specifications Institute, CSI: www.csinet.org

Construction Users Roundtable, CURT: www.curt.org

Design-Build Institute of America, DBI: www.dbia.org

Fully Integrated Automated TECHnology, FIATECH: www.fiatech.org

Illuminating Engineering Society of North America, IESNA: www.iesna.org

International Alliance for Interoperability, IAI: www.iai.org

International Code Council, ICC: www.iccsafe.org

(Successor organization to:

Building Officials and Code Administrators International: BOCA
Council of American Building Officials: CABO
International Conference of Building Officials: ICBO
Southern Building Code Congress International: SBCCI)

Insurance Services Organization, ISO: www.iso.org

Institute for Business and Home Safety, IBHS: www.ibhs.org

Lower Manhattan Development Corporation, LMDC: www.renewnyc.com

National Association of Home Builders, NAHB: www.nahb.org

National Fire Protection Association, NFPA: www.nfpa.org

National Center for Energy Management and Building Technology, NCEMBT: www.ncmbt.org

National Institute of Building Sciences, NIBS: www.nibs.org

Steel Door Institute, SDI: www.steeldoor.org

Sustainable Building Industry Council, SBIC: www.sbic.org

Tall Buildings and Urban Habitat Council, TBUHC, www.ctbuh.org

The Infrastructure Security Partnership, TISP: www.tisp.org

Underwriters Laboratory, UL: www.ul.com

U.S. Green Building Council, USGBC: www.usgbc.org

U.S. Fuel Cell Council, USFCC, www.usfcc.com

Virtual Builders Roundtable: www.virtualbuilders.org

PART II: CHAPTER NOTES

Chapter 1: Codes and Regulations and the Construction Team

Page 3: Source for size of construction industry data: U.S. Department of Commerce, Census Bureau Construction Industry Statistics, 2005; National Institute of Standards and Technology, and proceedings from the Alliance for Building Regulatory Reform in the Digital Age, Second Summit on Streamlining the Building Regulatory Process Through Interoperability, September 14, 2004, Fairfax County, VA.

Page 3: Number of buildings in New York City, NY; Los Angeles, CA; and Clarke County, NV, sources: building officials of these three jurisdictions and interviews held in the writing of this book during 2005 and 2006.

Page 8: Over 40,000 jurisdictions adopt and/or enforce building codes and standards; source: National Conference of States on Building Codes and Standards publications: "Introduction to Building Codes and Guide to Effective and Efficient Codes Administration," 2004 edition.

Page 8–9: The citations on law are drawn from:

Acret, J. C., "National Construction Law Manual," second edition, Thalen Reid & Priest LLP, BNI, *Building News*, 1998.

Acret J, C., "Simplified Guide to Construction Law," Thalen Reid & Priest LLP, BNi, *Building News*, 1997.

O'Leary, A.F., "A Guide to Successful Construction—Effective Contract Administration," FAIA, MRIAI, BNI, *Building News*, 1999.

Greenstreet, R., "The Design Professions and the Law," in *Design Professionals and the Built Environment: An Introduction*, Knox, P., and Ozolins, P., editors, New York: John Wiley & Sons, 2000.

Pressman, A., AIA. *Professional Practice, 101*, New York: John Wiley & Sons, 1997.

Nadel, B. A., FAIA, *Building Security: Handbook for Architectural Planning and Design*, New York: McGraw-Hill, 2004.

Demkin, J. A., AIA, editor, *Security Planning and Design, A Guide for Architects and Building Design Professionals*, New York: John Wiley & Sons, 2004.

Pages 13–19: States require licenses for contractors and subcontractors: National Conference of States on Building Codes and Standards, "Introduction to Building Codes and Guide to Effective and Efficient Codes Administration," 2004 edition.

Page 16: Op. cit., NCSBCS "Introduction to Building Codes," 2000 edition.

Time Table on Evolution of Building Codes in United States.

U.S. Building Codes and Standards Timeline

1600	First fire and building structure regulations brought to colonies
1783	Police power to states
1850	New York City adopts first city building code
1871	Chicago fire
1896	National Fire Protection Association (NFPA) founded
1905	National Board of Fire Underwriters publish model building construction regulations
1906	San Francisco earthquake and fire
1911	NFPA publishes first electrical code in United States
1914	State of Wisconsin adopts first statewide building code
1915	Building Officials and Code Administrators (BOCA) Association founded
1921	ASME publishes first elevator standards
1922	International Conference of Building Officials(ICBO) founded
1927	ICBO publishes first building code
1930	BOCA publishes first building code
1940–1941	Southern Building Code Congress (SBCC) founded and publishes first code
1943	Coconut Grove fire, Boston, MA
1950	First standards issued for heating, ventilating and air conditioning
1965–1975	28 states adopt statewide building codes
1982–1992	First model energy code produced
1992	Hurricane Andrew
1995	The Model Code Groups (BOCA, ICBO, and SBCC) merge into the International Code Council (ICC)
2000	First ICC codes released
2001	World Trade Center (WTC) disaster
2003	NFPA issues Model Building Code, NFPA 5000, with modifications for WTC disaster

Page 17: ICC Code Development Process

The following was excerpted from the 2004 NCSBCS report to the Nation's Governors. Additional information in the ICC Code Development Process can be obtained by visiting the ICC Web site at www.iccsafe.org.

The ICC *International Codes*

Safeguarding Public Health, Safety, and Welfare

Introduction The International Code Council, Inc. (ICC) is a private, nonprofit organization dedicated to developing a contemporary, comprehensive, and compatible regulatory system for the built environment through a single set of consistent *performance*-based regulations that are effective, efficient, and meet government, industry, and the public needs—the *International Codes*.

The objective of the ICC is to bring together, in a single forum, the many interests involved in the construction industry to work toward the common interest of the following:

* Safeguarding public health, safety, and welfare, including affordability, and preserving the nation's resources through *proven* building codes and standards

* Enhancing economic development through widespread adoption and consistent application of state-of-the-art technology without state, regional, or national limitations

* Streamlining the building regulatory system through a single family of codes that brings consistency and compatibility to multiple layers of requirements existing at the international, federal, state, and local levels

* Advancing innovation through performance-based provisions that require consistently high levels of building performance and safety

Through an open, inclusive, and balanced consensus process with built-in safeguards to prevent domination by any single interest, the ICC has accomplished these objectives.

Safeguarding the Public Interest - *Proven* Codes and Standards

The founding members of ICC, the Building Officials and Code Administrators International, Inc. (BOCA), International Conference of Building Officials (ICBO), and Southern Building Code Congress International, Inc. (SBCCI),have more than 150 years of collective experience in developing model building codes for the nation's cities, counties, states, and the federal government. Accordingly, a Federal Trade Commission report indicates that more than 90% of the nation's communities that enforce building codes use one or more of the code systems developed by ICC members as the basis for their construction regulations.

ICC, with the collective experience of its members, is the only organization of its kind that develops model building code regulations covering *all* aspects of the built environment. These comprehensive model regulations of the *International Codes* are also coordinated with each other, ensuring that no element of building hazard remain unchecked or is missed through haphazard, conflicting, or inconsistent requirements. Furthermore, the *International Codes* espouse affordability in all regard through an inclusive development process that takes into consideration the needs of all participating members of the public. These include the end-users such as building owners and managers, homeowners, members of the building materials industry including manufacturers, builders, architects and engineers, and public officials, to mention a few.

The *International Codes* are based wholly on the time-tested provisions of the regional model building codes, which have been adopted and put into use throughout the country. These provisions have endured the test of time and have incorporated emerging socioeconomic and public policies in the twentieth century, including the principles of smart growth and good planning now becoming more and more critical in preserving the nation's resources. The *International Codes* implement building concepts, technology, and practices proven effective, efficient, and affordable over time throughout the United States and the world.

Enhancing Economic Development Cutting Through Borders

Since the early part of the twentieth century, the ICC member organizations have developed the three independent sets of model building codes used regionally throughout the United States: the BOCA *National Codes,* ICBO *Uniform Codes,* and SBCCI *Standard Codes.* These regional code systems served the interests of the building community and the general public well over the years. However, as the international marketplace moved toward standardization in building performance and code requirements, a single set of codes was called for to be more responsive to an ever-changing and intensely competitive marketplace. The ICC member organizations combined their experience and expertise to develop the *International Codes* under the ICC umbrella in response to these changing marketplace and public needs.

Streamlining the Building Regulatory System: Consistency and Compatibility

The ICC published the premier edition of the ICC family of codes in the year 2000 This edition includes the *International Building Code, International Energy Conservation Code, International Fire Code, International Fuel Gas Code, International Mechanical Code, International Plumbing Code, International Private Sewage Disposal Code, International Property Maintenance Code, International Residential Code,* and the *International Zoning Code.* These codes are coordinated with each other to provide a complete and appropriate package for adoption and use by any governmental jurisdiction. The ICC family continues to grow and the *International Performance Code for Buildings and Facilities* and the *International Existing Building Code,* which were completed in 2001 and 2002, respectively.

The *International Codes* complete the regulatory system by coordinating within a single family of codes several hundred design and construction documents developed by other organizations and government entities. These documents, or "standards," include additional or more specific details as to how to accomplish the public policy objectives, or the scope, as defined by the codes. For example, the *International Building Code* and the *International Fire Code* reference more than 660 additional documents. With its partners in the building code development industry, ICC provides the single-most comprehensive and coordinated set of model building code regulations—the *International Codes.*

ICC has also established a consolidated National Certification Program to standardize credentialing requirements for building regulatory/code enforcement personnel throughout the United States. During the past 20 years, the programs offered by the three ICC members have been widely used by code enforcement professionals, evolving from voluntary participation to being mandatory for hiring, employment, advancement, or licensing at all levels of government.

These certification programs have had a significant and positive impact on professionalism in code enforcement. The knowledge level of code enforcement professionals has increased, as has the level of public protection they offer through higher-quality code enforcement.

Advancing Innovation Through Building Performance and Safety

Today, the *International Codes* set an acceptable level of safety to which all buildings must perform in order to ensure community safety. This concept of "building performance" is the basis of all *International Codes,* providing strict safety levels to which buildings must resist hazards, such as fires, earthquakes, tornadoes, hurricanes, and flooding, as well as other natural or man-made hazards. By setting required minimum levels of building performance and safety, rather than strict or highly prescriptive requirements, the ICC performance-based codes provide the necessary flexibility for incorporation of state-of-the-art technology, which today changes quite rapidly.

To further meet the needs of the rapidly-changing marketplace, the *International Codes* are revised every year. These revisions are published in the years between full editions of the codes as "supplements." The 2001 and 2002 supplements to the *International Codes* have been published. And the next complete edition was published in 2006. This annual revision process ensures the incorporation of the latest technology into the *International Codes* without dramatically modifying the base requirements.

In order to ensure that emerging building material, methods, and sciences are readily acceptable under the *International Codes,* the ICC members offer unmatched technical, educational, and informational products and services in support of the codes. Together, these member organizations have more than 250 highly qualified staff professionals at 14 offices throughout the United States. Additionally, the National Evaluation Service, Inc. (NES), supports and complements the *International Codes.* This program makes possible the use of new and innovative building products and methods of construction by confirming their conformance to the codes.

An Open, Inclusive, and Balanced Consensus Process

ICC's code development process is reflective of the organization's effort to enhance the continued development of the coordinated, comprehensive, and contemporary family of codes espousing the broad-based principles of building performance safeguarding public health, safety, and welfare. The ICC code development process incorporates balanced committees; gives groups and individuals unfettered ability to submit proposed code changes; supports free and open discussion of submitted code changes by any interested person; provides the ability to challenge code development committee recommendations; and supports voting by all members of the ICC member organizations.

The procedures for submitting code change proposals, proposal distribution, public hearings, and hearing reports provide ample opportunities for materially impacted interests to observe, participate, and voice their views on code development proposals. In fact, providing interested parties with two public hearings is unique to any open consensus process. It is also important that as many people as possible contribute to the code development process. Accordingly, any interested individual or group can submit a code change proposal and participate in an open debate where all proposals are considered All members of ICC member organizations in attendance at the initial code development public hearings are eligible to vote on floor motions during assembly consideration of code development committee actions.

The ICC also incorporates several safeguards within the code development process to ensure against domination or abuse of the system by any single interest. First and foremost, code officials and other government regulators, whose job is to ensure the public's safety, have final oversight responsibility on all code change proposals. Following consideration of all public comments, each proposal is individually balloted by eligible voters. Final action on all proposals is based on the aggregate count of all votes cast. This important process ensures that the *International Codes* reflect the latest technical advances and address the concerns of the industry in a fair and equitable manner without undue influence by any single interest.

The current ICC process meets or exceeds the requirements for a consensus process in several important regards:

- It ensures that a consensus of the construction community is achieved in the decision-making process.
- It allows both the ICC code development committees and eligible voting members at the code change hearings to participate in establishing the results of each proposal.
- It allows voting members to either ratify the committee's recommendation or make their own recommendation.
- It ensures the results of all votes are published in the report of the ICC code development hearings.

Conclusion

ICC promulgates the only set of *proven* comprehensive model codes for the built environment today. ICC is committed to a consistently open, balanced, and inclusive code development process. Combined with certification, training, and education programs, ICC and its member organizations provide depth of experience, breadth of services, and technical expertise unmatched by any other organization.

Code enforcement officials, architects, engineers, designers, homeowners, contractors, and others can now work with one consistent set of code requirements throughout the United States. Manufacturers can put their efforts into research, development, and promotion rather than designing to the specifications of multiple sets of standards. Coordinated education and certification programs can be used nationally. The single set of *International Codes* encourages states and localities that currently write their own codes to adopt the *International Codes* without local technical amendments. As such, adoption will lead to consistent code enforcement and higher quality construction, and, ultimately, to a safer built environment across all social and economic boundaries.

Page 17: NFPA Codes and Standards Development Process (Extracted from Report to Nation's Governors by NCSBCS, 2004). For additional information, visit NFPA Web site at www.nfpa.org.

The NFPA Codes and Standards Development Process

NFPA codes and standards, including those related to the built environment, are developed by more than 250 different technical committees, and these committees are the principle consensus-developing bodies within the NFPA codes and standards development process. NFPA membership is not required in order to participate on an NFPA Technical Committee, and appointment is based on such factors as technical expertise, professional standing, commitment to public safety, and the ability to bring to the table the point of view of an affected interest. Each technical committee consists of up to 30 volunteer voting members representing a variety of interests, including the fire services, code enforcement, business, industry, insurance, trade or professional associations, user groups, and federal, state, and local government officials. Each technical committee is constituted so as to contain a balance of affected interests, with no more than one-third of the committee from the same interest group. The committee must reach a consensus by at least a two-thirds vote of the voting members in order to take action.

To conduct their work, technical committees are organized into committee projects with an assigned scope of activities. Depending on its scope, a committee project may develop one code or standard or a group of related codes and standards, and the project may consist of a single technical committee or multiple committees coordinated by a technical correlating committee.

The NFPA process is unique in the level of public participation allowed in the development of its codes and standards. All NFPA codes and standards are revised and updated every three to five years, in revision cycles that generally take 104 weeks to complete. A revision cycle begins with publication of a call for public proposals to amend existing codes and standards or to shape the content of new codes and standards. This is followed by a 60-day period during which anyone may submit a proposal to a technical committee. The technical committee then meets and acts on each proposal. The public proposals, the technical committee's action on each proposal, as well as committee-generated proposals, are published for public review and comment in a document known as the "Report on Proposals," or "ROP." The ROP is free of charge and is distributed through a downloadable version on the Internet and through CD-Rom and print versions mailed to all submitters of public proposals as well as to anyone else on request. A 60-day period then begins during which anyone may submit a public comment on any aspect of the ROP. As with the proposals, the technical committee considers and acts on each comment and the result is then published in the "Report on Comments," or "ROC," which again is widely distributed, at no charge.

This two-stage period of public input is a uniquely valuable feature of NFPA's process because it allows a technical committee to receive public input and take initial action during the proposal stage and then to have that action reviewed and challenged through further public input during the comment stage. As a result, issues can be reconsidered and solutions refined.

The process of public input and discussion does not end with the publication of the ROP and ROC. Following the completion of the proposal and comment cycles, there is yet a further opportunity for public input and discussion through the technical sessions that take place twice yearly at NFPA membership meetings. NFPA membership is broad-based and open to anyone who shares the public safety mission of the NFPA.

The technical session is where the final technical committee report on each proposed new or revised code or standard is presented to the membership for a recommendation. The membership makes its recommendation through appropriate motions, debate, and voting. Anyone can attend the technical session to make or debate a motion, and anyone can vote who has joined the NFPA at least 180 days prior to the session. Through this process, the membership can recommend that a proposed new or revised code or standard be returned, in whole or in part, to the technical committee for further study. Motions can also be made, based on already published proposals and comments, to recommend amendments to the technical committee's work. These amendments are subsequently submitted to the vote of the technical committee and are frequently accepted by the committee.

Finally, for anyone who does not agree with the results reached by the process, an appeal is available to the NFPA Standards Council, a 13-member, impartial body that oversees the NFPA codes and standards development process and is responsible for issuing the completed NFPA codes and standards. Additional, more limited review is also available through a petition to the NFPA Board of Directors. This open, consensus development procedure (which is accredited under strict criteria for fairness and due process by ANSI) allows the full airing of all information and points of view and the "forging of true consensus."

The Consensus Codes Set for the Built Environment
The full *Consensus Codes Set* for the built environment became available in 2003. The *NFPA Building Code* was published in July of 2003. This set is now available for state and local adoption together or separately, or through reference in other model codes and standards. Here is a brief overview of the principle components of the *Set*.

1. Existing NFPA Codes and Standards The NFPA's existing codes and standards already affect virtually every building process, service, design, and installation in today's society. NFPA 70, the *National Electrical Code,* for example, has been adopted in some manner in every state in the nation and has been setting the standard for electrical safety for over 100 years. Other widely used NFPA codes include NFPA 1, *Fire Prevention Code;* NFPA 54, *National Fuel Gas Code;* and NFPA 101, *Life Safety Code.* These codes (supplemented by NFPA's extensive set of reference standards) will form an integral part of the *Consensus Code Set.*

2. Organizational Partnerships The *Consensus Codes Set* will not be the work of NFPA alone. In keeping with NFPA's commitment to consensus and to quality, the NFPA has formed partnerships with like-minded organizations with similar interests in public safety and with areas of expertise that complement those of the NFPA. For example, NFPA has entered into an agreement with the Western Fire Chiefs Association (WFCA).

Under this agreement, the WFCA, the developer of the *Uniform Fire Code,* will join forces with the NFPA, the developer of NFPA 1, *Fire Prevention Code,* to produce a single fire prevention code using NFPA's consensus code development process.

The International Association of Plumbing and Mechanical Officials (IAPMO) has agreed to develop the next editions of its plumbing and mechanical codes using a consensus process based on NFPA's own regulations. *The Uniform Plumbing Code* and the *Uniform Mechanical Code* will provide users with two more pieces of NFPA's set of fully integrated codes and standards. NFPA will also continue to collaborate on NFPA 54, *National Fuel Gas Code,* with the American Gas Association, with whom it has had a strong partnership for many years. Finally, ASHRAE has agreed to provide its highly respected and widely used energy codes, ASHRAE 90.1 and 90.2, for incorporation within the *Consensus Code Set.*

NFPA and its partner organizations all have established track records of working collaboratively with other codes and standards organizations. Together they will work to insure that the *Consensus Codes Set* will provide a coordinated, easy-to-use, state-of-the-art set of consensus codes and standards for the built environment.

Page 18: Sample of regulatory process for construction of a residential structure

Guide to More Effective Charts: Cindy Wants to Build a House

The following diagrams (Figures A-1 to A-6) were developed by the National Conference of States on Building Codes and Standards for its national Streamlining the Building Regulatory Process Project in 1999. The diagrams document all of the steps and regulatory programs that must be gone through from the conceptualization of building a house, through its construction to the issuance of its certificate of occupancy. The diagrams are generic and reflects the process generally found in most communities that have adopted zoning, land use, and construction codes and standards. The diagrams are reproduced as it appears in HUD, "Guide to More Effective and Efficient Building Regulatory Processes Through Information Technology."

Chapter 2: Challenges Facing the Construction Team: Revising Codes and Standards, Redefining Roles and Responsibilities

Page 24: "World Trade Center Building Performance Study: Data Collection, Preliminary Observations and Recommendations," Federal Emergency Management Agency, Federal Insurance and Mitigation Administration, FEMA Region II: New York, New York, with American Society of Civil Engineers and Greenhorne and O'Mara. FEMA Publication 403, May 2002.

Page 29: Data Source for Figure 2-6, American Geophysical Union (AGU), FEMA, U.S. Department of Commerce and State of Louisiana.

Figure A-1

Board 1: Cindy
wants to build
a house

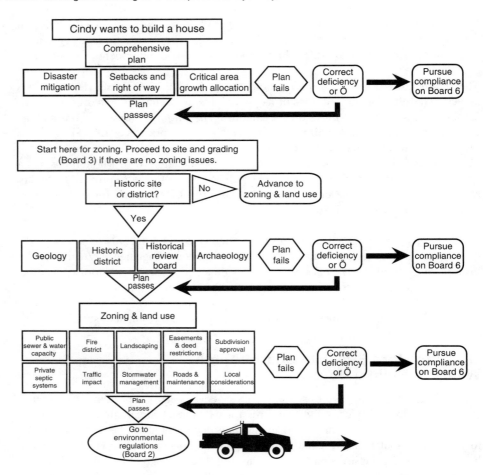

Page 31: ASHRAE's "President's Presidential Ad Hoc Committee for Building Health and Safety under Extraordinary Events," Committee members included: James E. Woods, Building Diagnostics Research Institute, Chairman; Dwight Berancek, U.S. Army Corps of Engineers; Harvey Brickman, Tishman Realty & Construction Company; H. E. Burroughs, Building Wellness Consultancy, Inc.; William J. Coad, Coad Engineering Consulting; D. Scott Fisher, State Farm Insurance Co.; George O. Glavis, U.S. Department of State; Ralph E. Goldman, Comfort Technology; Andrew K. Persily, National Institute of Standards and Technology; Lawrence. G. Speilvogel, Lawrence G. Spielvogel Inc.; Bob Thompson, U.S. Environmental Protection Agency; Ronald P. Vallort, Ron Vallort and Associates; and Martin Joseph Weiland, ASHARE.

Page 31: ASIS, "The General Security Risk Guideline," guideline approved November 13, 2002. Guideline Committee members from ASIS included: Sean Ahrens, CCP; Norman Bates; Chad Callaghan, CPP; Pamela Collins, EdD, CFE; Grant Crabtree, CPP; Michael Crane, CPP; Edward Flynn, CFE; Arthur Kingsbury, CPP; Michael Stack; Basil Steele, CPP; Don Walker, CPP; Timothy Walsh, CPP; and Timothy Williams, CPP.

Figure A-2

Board 2: Environmental Compliance

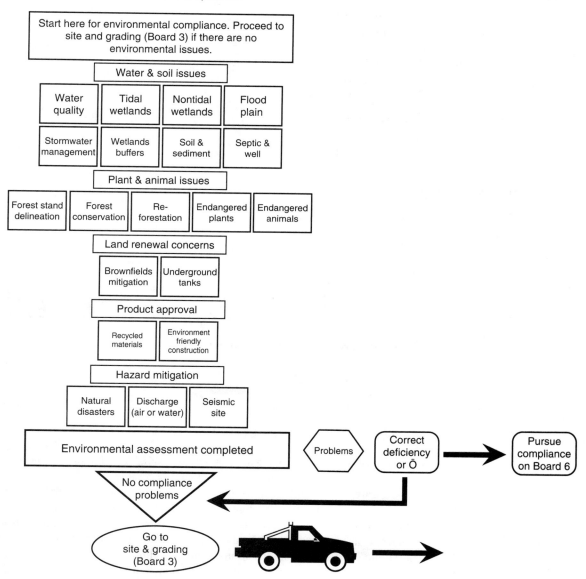

Page 31: "Best Practices for Project Security," NIST GCR-04-865, produced for the NIST's Building and Fire Research Laboratory Office of Applied Economics by Stephen R. Thomas, Jonathan R. Sylvie, Candace L. Macken, of the CII, July 2004. Available for downloading from NIST, BFRL Web site at www.bfrl.nist.gov.

Page 33: For complete listing of FEMA publications, visit FEMA Virtual Library and Electronic Reading at www.fema.gov/library/prepandprev.shtm.

(*continued on next page*)

Figure A-3

Board 3: Site and Grading

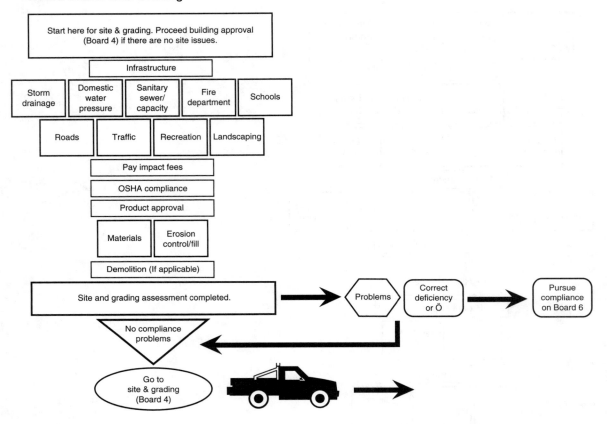

Page 33: ASCE Building Security Council: A service available to building owners that enables them to have their building evaluated and recommendations provided for enhancing security. Rated buildings are classified into four categories ranging from high risk to high profile (iconic) structures down to low-risk small office and residential structures. It recommends appropriate countermeasures to enhance security from site perimeter to inner core; uses a detailed "BSC Building Security Rating System Checklist Guide." For more information contact Walter T. Marlowe, PE, CAE, Executive Director at wmarlowe@buildingsecuritycouncil.org.

Page 33: "Facts for Steel Buildings Number 2: Blast and Progressive Collapse," Kirk A. Marchand and Farid Alfawakhiri, American Institute of Steel Construction, Inc., Copyright 2004, available online at www.aisc.org.

Page 34: "Minimum Design Loads for Buildings and Other Structures," ASCE/ SEI-7-02 and new edition 7-05 are available through ASCE through their website at www.asce.org.

Figure A-4

Board 4: Building Construction Approval Process

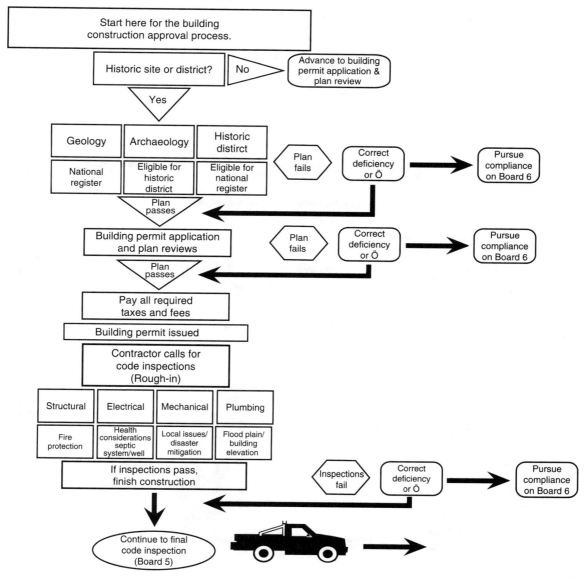

Page 34: Florida Building Code updated provisions are available on the Florida Department of Community Affairs website at www.floridabuilding.org.

Page 36: Members of the ICC Ad Hoc Committee on Terrorism Resistant Buildings (AHC-TRB) include William Connolly, AIA, Director and NJ Department of Community Affairs Division of Codes and Standards, Chairman; Edmund Goodfeld, Building Inspection Underwriters, Inc. PA; Derek Horn, Deputy Development Services Director,

(*continued on next page*)

Figure A-5

Board 5: Building Permit Application and Plan Review Process

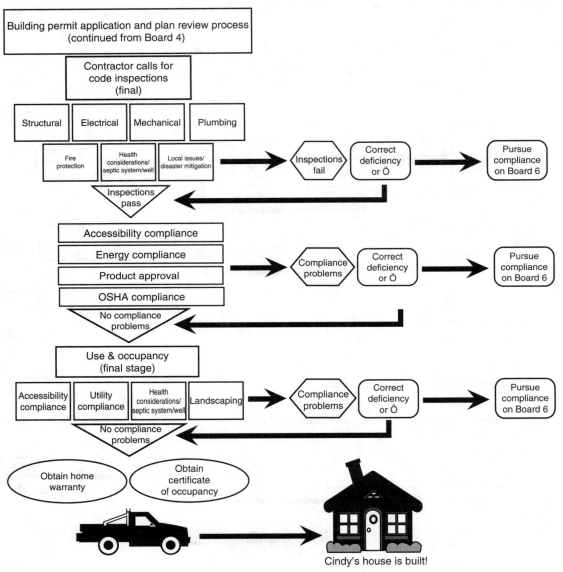

Cindy's house is built!

City of Phoenix; Development Services Department, Vice-Chairman; Gary C. Lewis, Chief Inspector, Summit, NJ; Lanny McMahill, Electrical Inspections Supervisor, Phoenix, AZ; Ray Moore, Professional Engineering Services, Salt Lake City, UT; Jim Schifilliti, President, Fire Safety Consultants, Inc.; Dam Smits, Calumet City Fire Department, Crete, IL; and Staff Liaison for ICC: John Battles, PE, CBO.

Minutes notices on committee work can be found by going to www.iccsafe.org.

Figure A-6

Board 6: Compliance Issue

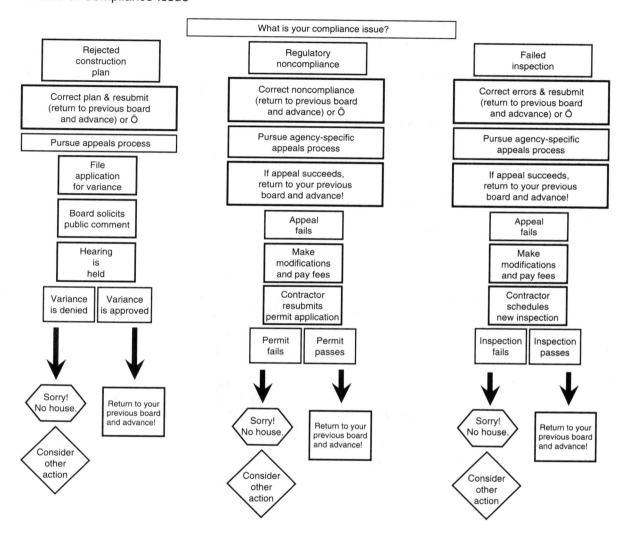

Page 37: NFPA is accepting names for membership on its High-Rise Building Safety Advisory Committee (HBSAC). For more information visit www.nfpa.org.

Members of the National Institute of Building Sciences Multihazard Mitigation Committee to Translate the NIST World Trade Center Investigation Recommendations for The Model Building Codes include Gerald Jones, PE Co-Chair; Herman W. Brice, Co-chair; Scott W. Adams; George Capko, Jr., PE; William M. Connolly, AIA; Carl Galioto, FAIA; Ronald O. Hamburger, PE, SE; Paul K. Heilstedt, PE, Hon AIA; John D. Hooper, SE; Stephanie A. King, PhD, PE; Marsha Maaz; Arturo Mendez; Dennis Mileti, PhD; Lawrence G. Perry, AIA; Timothy A. Reinhold, PhD, PE; Martin H. Reiss, PE; James T. Ryan, CBO; Jim W. Sealy, FAIA; and Robert Smilowitz, PhD, PE.

NIST Liaison Staff included the following: Richard W. Bukowski, PE; Stephen A. Cauffman; and S. Shyam Sunder, ScD.

NIBS/Multihazard Mitigation Council Staff included the following: David A. Harris, AIA, Executive Director, NIBS.

Page 39: TISP. Copies of the "Guide for an Action Plan to Develop Regional Disaster Resilience" can be downloaded by visiting the TISP Web site at www.tisp.org. The TISP Web site list of publications also is an excellent source for viewing the latest guides, guidelines, and other documents for design and construction of disaster resistant buildings.

Page 41: A copy of the National Construction Safety Team Act of 2002 and a copy of the full text of the NIST World Trade Center Collapse Report are available for downloading at the NIST Web site: www.nist.gov/public_affairs/factsheet/constructionact.htm.

Page 45: Copies of the presentations made at the September 13 to 15 NIST conference on the WTC report are available at www.nist.gov.

Chapter 3: Findings from the World Trade Center Towers Collapse and Other Post 9/11 Disasters

Page 53: Members of the National Construction Safety Team for the NIST World Trade Center Report included the following: S. Shyam Sunder, SC D, (NIST) Lead Investigator; Richard Gann, PhD, (NIST) Final Report Editor; William L. Grosshandler, PhD, (NIST) Associate Lead Investigator; H.S. Lew, PhD, PE, (NIST), Co-Project Leader, Project 1; Richard W. Bukowski, PE, (NIST), Co-Project leader, Project 1; Fahim Sadek, PhD, (NIST), Project Leader, Project 2; Frank W. Gayle, PhD, (NIST), Project Leader, Project 3; John L. Gross PhD, PE, (NIST) Co-Project Leader, Project 6; Therese P. McAllister, PhD, PE, (NIST) Co-Project Leader, Project 6; Jason D. Averill (NIST) Project Leader, Project 7; J Randall Lawson (NIST) Project Leader, Project 8; Harold E. Nelson, PE, Fire Protection Expert; and Stephen A. Cauffman (NIST), Project Manager.

Page 54: A complete copy of the NIST WTC report can be downloaded from NIST at: http://wtc.nist.gov

Page 68: Chapter 9 of the Final Report on the Collapse of the World Trade Center Towers (pages 201 to 230) contains all of the details of the of 30 NIST recommendations.

Page 69: NIST provides periodic updates to the progress of actions being taken in response to its 30 WTC Report recommendations. These can be viewed by going to: http://wtc.nist.gov/recommendations/recommendations.htm.

Page 77–79: Comments received by NIST in the summer early fall of 2005 to their draft recommendations in the WTC report can be viewed on the NIST Web site by going to http://wtc.nist.gov.

Page 81: More information on the United Kingdom's progressive collapse standard can be found by going to www.nist.gov.

Page 81: ASCE Pentagon report. To order a copy go to www.pubs.asce.org.

Page 84: HUD report documentation on how much better homes in Florida were built after 2002 than they were before changes in statewide code and through Partnership to Advance Technology in Housing (PATH) project has available information on Hurricane Retrofit Strategies. For the latter visit www.pathnet.org/sp.asp?id=16371.

Page 84: New statewide code for Louisiana. For more information go to www. dps.state.la.us. New state code for coastal counties of Mississippi go to www.namic.org/newsreleases06/060330nr2.asp.

Page 85: Copies of the NIST report on Hurricanes Katrina and Rita can be downloaded by going to: www.nist.gov.

Chapter 4: Beginning with the End in Mind: Assessing Risk, Threats, and Mitigation Strategies

Page 90: Survey on public and private sector changes in practices or regulations in aftermath of 9/11. A survey was conducted by the author of 80 of the nation's largest jurisdictions and 20 of the nation's largest architectural and engineering firms regarding what changes they had made since 9/11 in their practices or in their codes, standards, or regulations that they enforce in response to the terrorist attacks.

Of 10 private sector respondents to the survey two said that there had been no changes; eight said that they were spending more time with their clients conducting risk-threat analysis of the buildings they were designing; and seven said that they had either added to their firm or brought in outside consultants and experts on disaster mitigation design, construction, or materials.

Of the 80 of the nation's largest city and county jurisdictions surveyed, the 32 respondents noted that 12 said that there had been no changes; 20 said that they had made one or more of the following changes; 10 reviewed emergency egress provisions and made modifications to their existing requirements for high-rise, iconic, or large public structures; six adopted updated versions of either NFPA standards or ICC codes that include some provisions associated with the disaster; four developed and adopted changes to several parts of their building code including emergency egress, fire, and life safety provisions and structural design.

Page 92: The major modifications made by the Port Authority of New York and New Jersey in the aftermath of the 1993 Terrorist bombing involved parking structure access and emergency communications and egress requirements.

Page 98: Source: U.S. GSA: annual reports to Congress, 2002 and 2005 and July 27, 2005, statement of F. Joseph Moravec, Commissioner, and U.S. GSA before the U.S. House of Representatives Committee on Government Reform.

Page 99: GSA's 2002, "Protective Design and Security Implementation Guidelines," can be downloaded by going to www.gsa.gov.

Pages 106–110: FEMA Risk Assessment Guides can be downloaded by going to www.fema.gov or visiting the FEMA library at www.fema.gov.

Page 111: To download a copy of NIST, "Cost Effective Responses to Terrorist Risks in Constructed Facilities," go to— www.nist.gov.

Page 114: A copy of ASHRAE's "Risk Management Guidance for Health, Safety, and Environmental Security under Extraordinary Incidents" can be downloaded by going to www.ashrae.org.

Page 117: Information on how to obtain a copy of ASHRAE's "Guideline O-P, the Commissioning Process," visit the ASHRAE Web site at www.ashrae.org.

Page 117: ASHRAE will release its "Guideline for Risk Management of Public Health and Safety in Buildings" in late 2006. Visit the ASHRAE Web site at www.ashrae.org for information on its exact release date and ordering instructions.

Page 118: A copy of AMA's "The Facility Managers Emergency Preparedness Handbook" can be ordered from AMA by going to www.amanet.org/books/catalog/0814407188.htm.

Pages 111–114: NIST "Final Report on the Collapse of the World Trade Center Towers," describes the majority of these changes.

Chapter 5: Existing Construction Standards, Codes, Practices, and Guidelines That Promote Security and Disaster Resilience in New Construction

Page 132: *Building Security: Handbook for Architectural Planning and Design*, Barbara A. Nadel, FAIA, McGraw-Hill, 2004. *Security Planning and Design: A Guide for Architects and Building Design Professionals*, Joseph A. Demkin, AIA, editor, NY: John Wiley & Sons, 2004.

Page 133: For more information on "SafeScape," visit the American Planning Association Web site at www.apa.org, and the APA book, *SafeScape: Creating Safer, More Livable Communities Through Planning and Design*, by Al Zelinka and Dean Brennan, Chicago, IL: APA, 2001. SafeScape also is referenced within the American Planning Association's Policy Guide on Security, adopted by APA's Chapter Delegate Assembly March 19, 2005.

Page 135: Source: U.S. GSA.

Page 139: A copy of NIST's "Best Practices in Project Security" can be downloaded by going to www.bfrl.nist.gov.

Page 161: To access these software programs—WINGARD, WINLAC, SAFEVUE—go to www.gsa.gov.

Page 167: To access the Centers for Disease Control/National Institute for Occupational Safety and Health May 2002 document, "Guidance for Protecting Building Environments from Airborne, Chemical, Biological or Radiological Attacks," and a series of 17 other terrorist- or disaster-related events go to www.cdc.gov.

Page 172: A copy of the U.S. Department of Education Office of Special Education and Rehabilitative Services and the National Institute on Disability and Rehabilitation Research report on their conference on "Emergency Evacuation of People with Disabilities from Buildings" can be obtained by going to www.edu.gov-National Institute on Rehabilitation Research and clicking on publications.

Pages 175: Additional information on the National Earthquake Hazards Reduction Program (NEHRP) and Applied Technology Council (ATC) is available by going to the following sites: NEHRP at www.nehrp.gov and ATC at www.atcouncil.org.

Pages 181: To access information on New York City's code amendments visit the New York City Department of Buildings portion of the city Web site at www.nyc.gov/html/dob/html/reference/code_update.shtml. To access information on the city of Chicago's 2002 evacuation ordinance, visit the city of Chicago Web site at http://library2.municode.com/mcc/DocView/13322/1/639 and click on ordinances. Page 118–119: A copy of "Emergency Evacuation Procedures for Disabled Individuals" used by the Los Angeles City Fire Department can be downloaded by going to www.lafd.org.

Page 181: A copy of Pittsburgh's "All Hazard Plan" can be downloaded by going to www.city.pittsburgh.pa.us/BBI/html/important_codes.html. Once there, click on the second bullet in upper left-hand corner of page on "Ordinances." Once on Ordinances site, click on Title 8.

Chapter 6: Existing Buildings: Inspections And Retrofitting

Page 187: To access copies of the presentations made during the February 15–17, 2006, TISP, "Critical Infrastructure Resilience, Infrastructure Security for the Built Environment Conference" visit the TISP Web site at www.tisp.org.

Page 187: Source for data on the number of nonresidential buildings and percentage of existing buildings still in use in 2020 is the U.S. Department of Commerce in numerous documents including speeches of former commerce secretary Evans.

Page 189: Information on the California Unreinforced Masonry Building Law is available from the California Seismic Safety Commission at www.seismic.ca.gov.

Page 191: For a copy of the White House Report, "The National Strategy for Physical Protection of Critical Infrastructure and Key Assets," visit www.whitehouse.gov/pcipb/physical.html.

Page 201: For more information on HUD's "Nationally Applicable Recommended Rehabilitation Provisions," visit the HUD Web site at www.huduser.org. The site includes access to a report prepared for HUD by Building Technology Inc. in August 2001 entitled, "Smart Codes in Your Community: A Guide to Building Rehabilitation Codes," which can be downloaded.

Page 202: A copy of the Council on Tall Buildings and Urban Habitat Task Force Meeting report can be downloaded from the Council's Web site at www.ctbuh.org

Page 217: For more information on Fuel Cell technology visit the DOE Web site at: www.eere.energy.gov/hydrogenandfuelcells or the U.S. Fuel Cell Council Web site at: www.usfcc.com

Page 224: The Rhode Island "HVAC Building Vulnerability Assessment Tool" can be downloaded from the Rhode Island Department of Health Web site at www.health.ri.gov.

Page 230: A copy of "Managing Risk in Earthquake Country" can be downloaded by going to www.1906eqconf.org.

Page 231: Building code agencies for California, Washington, and Oregon can be accessed by going to the following sites: California Building Standards Commission at www.bsc.ca.gov; Oregon Department of Consumer and Business Services, Building Codes Division, at www.oregonbcd.org; and Washington State Building Code Council at www.sbcc.wa.gov.

Page 233: A copy of the San Francisco Department of Building Inspection publication, "What You Should Know about Unreinforced Masonry Buildings" can be downloaded by going to that agency's Web site at www.sfgov.org/dbi.

Chapter 7: Homeland Security and the Issues of Energy, Sustainability, Environment, Accessibility, and New Products, Materials, and Techniques

Page 241: Source of data on size of China's economy: study by Economist Intelligence Unit (EIU), for more information visit hhtp://newsroom.cisco.com/dlls/2006/prod_033006.html.

Page 243: To view or download a copy of the Katrina reports, go to the following Web sites: White House report, "The Federal Response to Hurricane Katrina: Lessons Learned," February 2006, at www.firstgov.gov; and Senate report, Senate Committee on Homeland Security and Governmental Affairs, "Hurricane Katrina: A Nation Still Unprepared," May 2006 at http://hsga.senate.gov.

Page 244: List of Presidential Homeland Security Directives issued by the George W. Bush Administration: HSPD 1, "Organization and Operation of Homeland Security Council," October 29, 2001; HSPD 2, "Combating Terrorism Through Immigration Policies," October 29, 2001; HSPD 3, "Homeland Security Advisory System," March 11, 2002; HSPD 4, "National Strategy to Combat Weapons of Mass Destruction" Classified, December 11, 2002; HSPD 5, "Management of Domestic Incidents" (Initial National Response Plan), February 28, 2003; HSPD 6, "Integration and Use of Screening Information," September 16, 2003; HSPD 7, "Critical Infrastructure Identification, Prioritization and Protection," December 17, 2003; HSPD 8, "National Preparedness," December 17, 2003; HSPD 9, "Defense of United States Agriculture and Food," January 30, 2004; HSPD 10, "Biodefense for the 21st Century," April 28, 2004; HSPD 11, "Comprehensive Terrorist-Related Screening Procedures," August 27, 2004; HSPD 12, "Policy for a Common Identification Standard for Federal Employees and Contractors," August 27, 2004; HSPD 13, "Maritime Security Policy," December 21, 2004; HSPD 14, "Domestic Nuclear Detection," April 15, 2005; and HSPD 15, "War on Terror," March 8, 2006.

Page 246: For more information on the Target Capabilities List and the Universal Task Lists visit www.ojp.usdoj.gov/odp/assessments/hspd8.htm.

"Jurisdictions will be required to meet the FY 2006 NIMS implementation requirements as a condition of receiving federal preparedness funding assistance in FY 2007," page 2 of the letter from DHS Secretary Michael Chertoff to governors of each state (and territory) issued in January 2006.

Implementation requirements for 2006 include: adoption of NIMS within state by executive order or proclamation; develop baseline assessment of NIMS requirements that state already meets and develop a strategy for full compliance; follow Federal Incident Command System laid out in NIMS; promote intrastate and interagency mutual aid agreements; and key "personnel take" and complete online NIMS certification courses.

Page 248: Table 1-7 "Overview of U.S. Petroleum Trade."

Pages 250–252: Visit the PacificNorthwest Economic Region Web site at www.pnwer.org for more information on Blue Cascades III exercise. In addition, a copy of the National Partnership to Streamline Government report on the Blue Cascades III exercise is available at www.natlpartnerstreamline.org.

Page 252: Disaster resilience definition is found on page 8 of the TISP, "Guide for an Action Plan to Develop Regional Disaster Resilience."

Page 253: Source of data on aging American population: U.S. Department of Health and Human Services, Administration on Aging publication, "A Statistical Profile of Older Americans Aged 65+" last updated March 1, 2006.

Page 255: For more information on DOE energy efficiency and renewable energy programs visit www.eere.energy.gov/buildings/building_america/; for PATH, visit www.pathnet.org; and for NASEO, visit www.naseo.org.

Page 256: Source of data on American dependence on foreign sources of oil, "Energy Information Administration Monthly Energy Review," April 2006.

Page 257: National Center for Energy Management and Building Technologies, NCEM-BT, can be visited by going to www.ncembt.org.

Page 259: For more information on EPA Energy Star program visit www.energystar.gov.

Page 259: Additional information on the LEED program can be obtained by visiting www.usgbc.org.

Page 261: For more information on NAHB Model Green Home Program visit www.nahb.org.

Page 264: For more information on the issue of "Visitability," go to www.cast.org.

Page 265: Due out from HUD in late October of 2006, the guide can be downloaded by going to www.huduser.org.

Page 266: A copy of Preston Haskell's article can be downloaded by either searching for it on the Internet or going to www.thehaskellcompany.org.

Page 267: Copies of presentations given during the December 12, 2005, meeting of the Virtual Builders Roundtable can be downloaded by going to www.virtualbuilders.org.

Page 271: For more information on the National Partnership to Streamline Government and its predecessor organization, the Alliance for Building Regulatory Reform in the Digital Age, see "Viewpoints" in the *Engineering News Record* , May 8, 2006, or visit www.natlpartnerstreamline.org. The following is a list of Alliance Partners:

Members and affiliate partners of the Alliance for Building Regulatory Reform in the Digital Age:

American Institute of Architects

Associated General Contractors of America

Association of Major City/County Building Officials

Building Owners & Managers Association International

Civil Engineering Research Foundation (CERF)

Commonwealth of Pennsylvania

Commonwealth of Virginia

Council of State Community Development Agencies

*Design Build Institute of America

Fannie Mae

*Federal Emergency Management Agency

Industrialized Buildings Commission

Institute for Building Technology and Safety

International Alliance for Interoperability

International Code Council

National Association of Counties

National Association of Home Builders

National Conference of States on Building Codes and Standards

National Fire Protection Association

National Governors Association

National Institute of Building Sciences

National Institute of Standards and Technology (NIST)

U. S. Conference of Mayors

U. S. Department of Agriculture

U. S. Department of Energy

U. S. Department of Housing and Urban Development (HUD) & Partnership for Advancing Technology in Housing (PATH) & *America's Affordable Communities Initiative - Bringing Homes Within Reach Through Regulatory Reform*

U. S. General Services Administration

*Commitment pending

Alliance Affiliate Partners:

American Subcontractors Association

Arizona State University Del E Webb School of Construction's

Housing Research Institute

Carnegie Mellon University

City of Milpitas, California

City of San Jose, California

ComCARE Alliance

Council for Excellence in Government

Council of State Governments

Fairfax County, Virginia

FIATECH

*Harvard University's Joint Center for Housing Studies

Massachusetts Institute of Technology

National Association of State Chief Information Officers

National Association of State Facilities Administrators

*National Science Foundation

New York City

Stanford University Center for Integrated Facility Engineering

State of California

      State of Maryland

      State of Oregon

      State of Washington

      Virginia Tech Center for Housing Research

*Commitment pending

Page 272: To view the "100 Influences That Have Shaped the Buildings Market" go to http://buildings.printhis.clickabilty.com/pt/cpt?action=cpt&title=100+Influences+That+H.

Pages 272–276: Sources for this section included: MIT Enterprise Technology Review, January, 2003; Virtual Builders Roundtable; NIST conference call with state and local building regulatory officials, April 25, 2005, NCSBCS and AMCBO; *Government Technology News* (issues in 2005 to 2006); *RFID Journal*, 2005 and 2006; *Engineering News Record*, issues in 2005 and 2006; U.S. National Nanotechnology Initiative, Purdue University.

Page 278: For more information on ISO, visit their Web site at www.isomitigation.com and for the IBHS, visit www.ibhs.org.

Chapter 8: A World Transformed: A Vision of One Possible Future for the Construction Industry and Construction Team

Page 281: Futurists Joseph F. Coates, John B. Mahaffie and Andy Hines in 1996 undertook a project to review their previous future predictions for advances in science and technology that they made in 1970 through the mid-1980s. Looking at trends in the mid-1990s, they extrapolated where science and technology might take the United States by the year 2025. The result of their effort was the 1997 publication from which the opening quote for Chapter 8 is extracted: "2025: Scenarios of U.S. and Global Society Reshaped by Science and Technology."

In their work, they look at three distinct segments of the world. The United States, Japan and Europe are looked at in one group (called World 1), the second group, which makes up the majority of the world's population includes developing nations (World 2), and the third and final group is comprised of those impoverished nations that are not able to benefit from the global economy and are destitute (World 3).

Issues related to the built infrastructure are covered in Chapter 10 (pages 271 to 301) of their work, "Our Built World." Now, nearly 10 years after their book was released, a number of their predictions, including those quoted at the opening of the last chapter of this book, appear to be closer to becoming a reality than by 2025.

Page 284: Named after France's Minister of War in the early 1920s, André Maginot, the Maginot Line was built between 1930 and 1936 by the French government to block any repeat of the World War I lightning strike invasion of northeastern France by Germany. The German Blitzkreig of the spring of 1940 merely bypassed this expensive defense network by sweeping through the lightly defended (and presumed impenetrable by tanks) Ardennes Forest. The Maginot Line was later captured by German paratroopers and heavy artillery that leisurely hammered all of the fortifications within the line's extensive underground network of tunnels and gun emplacements, which stretched from Luxemburg to the Swiss boarder.

Page 288: Source on size of construction firms included NAHB, Associated General Contractors, U.S. Department of Commerce.

Page 289: See e-mail addresses for the building roundtable, CII, and Construction Users Roundtable at the opening of the Appendix.

Page 289: NIBS, working together with several federal agencies and the private sector, assisted promoting greater use of information technology in construction through the NIBS Facility Information Council. Visit the NIBS Web site for more information on that council.

Page 289: Visit the FIATECH Web site at www.fiatech.org for additional information on that organization, its members and programs, including the Capital Projects Roadmap Initiative.

Page 290: The ASCE in 2005 incorporated CERF as one of its operational units: see www.asce.org.

Page 290: The Streamlining the Nation's Building Regulatory Process project originated by the National Conference of States on Building Codes and Standards, Inc., operated between 1995 and early 2001. In the summer of 2001 that initiative was superceded by a new initiative, the Alliance for Building Regulatory Reform in the Digital Age. Old work products from the Streamlining the Nation's Building Regulatory Process project, including model streamlining processes, are available on the NCSBCS Web site at www.ncsbcs.org by clicking on the bar at the top of the homepage that says "Technology" and then clicking on the word "Streamlining" on the subsequent page.

State Chief Information Officers are represented today by NASCIO, which is headquartered in Lexington, Kentucky. More information on NASCIO can be obtained by visiting their Web site at www.nascio.org. (NASCIO is one of the founding members of the National Partnership to Streamline Government.)

Governor Michael Leavitt at the National Governors Association Winter Meeting in Washington, D.C., February 1999.

Page 291: Enterprise Integration Act, 2002, can be viewed by going to http://thomas.loc.gov.

Page 292: Report Card for America's Infrastructure was begun in 2001 by ASCE by bringing together a panel of 22 of the nation's leading civil engineers to review "hundreds of studies, reports and other sources and interview over 2,000 engineers," to ascertain and rate the state of the nation's infrastructure in 12 areas: aviation, bridges, dams, drinking water, energy, hazardous waste, navigable waterways, roads, schools, solid waste, transit, and wastewater. In 2005, when ASCE issued their latest report card three additional categories were added: public parks and recreation, rail, and infrastructure security.

The grades assigned to these 15 areas in 2005 averaged out as a D with only solid waste (a C+) and bridges (a C) scoring above a C– level. A copy of the report card for 2005 can be viewed at the ASCE Web site: www.asce.org. ASCE estimates in their 2005 report that a national investment of $1.6 trillion is needed to make improvements to the nation's infrastructure.

Page 295: A major initiative undertaken by NIBS to develop the nation's first standard for three-dimensional modeling by the end of 2006 will significantly facilitate the growth of this technology and its use by the construction industry. Information on the NIBS, "National BIM Standards Project," can be found on the NIBS Web site: www.nibs.org/BIMcommittee.html.

Page 297: For more information on the National Partnership to Streamline Government, visit their Web site at www.natlpartnerstreamline.org.

Page 299: The "good Samaritan laws" in this nation can be visited at www.aia.org/adv_st_goodsamaritan.

Page 302: Associations and organizations representing members of the expanded construction team are included in the listings in Part I of the Appendix.

Index